Napoleon's Campaigns
in Poland 1806-7

Napoleon's Campaigns in Poland 1806-7

Robert Wilson

LEONAUR

Napoleon's Campaigns in Poland 1806-7
by Robert Wilson

Originaly published in 1810 under the title:
*Brief Remarks on the Character and Composition
of the Russian Army and a Sketch of the
Campaigns in Poland in the Years 1806 and 1807*

Published by Leonaur Ltd

ISBN: 978-1-84677-416-4 (hardcover)
ISBN: 978-1-84677-415-7 (softcover)

http://www.leonaur.com

Publisher's Notes

The views expressed in this book are not necessarily
those of the publisher.

Contents

To Field-Marshal
His Royal Highness the Duke of York

under whose administration the british army has
recovered its consideration abroad, and been
established on a basis commensurate with the
power and dignity of the British empire, this work
is respectfully dedicated by the author

Preface

A few weeks only have elapsed since I commenced the arrangement of the present publication. Until that time I never thought of submitting what is here contained to the public, although the materials have been at my command, dispersed in private correspondence with my family during the period that I served with the Russian army, and to which I was attached with the Honourable Mr. Hutchinson, by Lord Hutchinson, then Minister Extraordinary to the Court of Prussia. The mission of Lord Hutchinson consisted of his brother, Lieutenant-Colonel Eustace, Captain Harvey, and myself. It was afterwards joined by Lieutenant-Colonel Bathurst. Colonel Sontag was attached to the Prussian army. Colonel Froberg Montjoie was on his way to join from Koenigsberg, but being overtaken by the enemy, refused to surrender, and died after a desperate resistance. His brother, in the Bavarian service, was one of the first persons who recognized his body.

I could have wished that the details of the Russian campaign had engaged the labours of a more able writer, so as to have assured the narrative all the interest it merits from the statesman, the soldier, and the world in general.

The constant expectation of active employment since my return to England diverted my attention to other objects, or tendered me fearful of undertaking a work that I might have to abandon in its progress; for unfortunately my manuscript being almost as difficult to decipher as hieroglyphics, I have experienced that my personal superintendence was daily necessary.

The perusal, however, of a French extra-official narrative of the campaigns of 1806 and 1807, and a late British publication on the character, customs, and manners of Russia, with a review of that work, awakened my feeling, and induced me to attempt the vindication of a brave people, notwithstanding the friendly relations between the Russian and British governments are unhappily interrupted.

I determined to expose the false and exaggerated statement of our common enemy, by contrasting it with an important historical narrative of facts, so that the future historian may be able to discriminate between truth and fallacy, and to mitigate the evils which a work written at a gloomy period in Russian history was calculated to occasion, when better times and a more enlightened government have succeeded.

The interests of Russia and England are inseparably connected; and whilst we experience regret at the adoption of a policy at variance with such a principle, it is injudicious to alienate the affections of a great nation by remarks characterized at least by asperity, and particularly when the military portion of that empire has established such high claims to grateful admiration for the gallantry with which it profusely shed its blood to maintain the interests of the common cause.

These are the motives that have influenced me to this undertaking, and these motives will, I trust, find numerous advocates to espouse the cause in which I have engaged, and assure the triumph of truth.

Lord Hutchinson is indisputably high authority; and although I have had no communication with him relative to this publication, I dare to affirm, that he will corroborate all that I have stated respecting the Emperor and his government, and the courage, conduct, and merits of the Russian army; and that he will express his concurring sentiments in more impressive language than I have used, whenever suitable opportunity offers.

I am also confident that he will hold up to admiration the loyal feelings, the patriotic ardour, and the social virtues which characterize the Russians; that he will unite with me in lamenting any depreciation of a people amongst whom so many eminent qualities at present exist, whose moral and physical state is so rapidly ameliorating, and that he will still more regret that some temporary causes should have induced a gentleman of high endowments, and a writer of considerable merit, to delineate the general features of such a people so unfavourably and harshly.

Lord Hutchinson will deny, in common with every British nobleman or gentleman who has visited Russia, or resided in the country, that "Russian hospitality and social generosity are but the indulgence of a vain ostentation." The charge of *ostentation* is indeed untenable, and bears in its own construction palpable refutation. It is alleged, that "during the time of Paul's reign, when there was *great danger in associating* with Englishmen, yet the nobles of Moscow would receive them *gladly at any risk,* and sometimes *close their gates* upon them to *conceal* from the police the kind of hospitality that was going on within. But the principle of all this being state and show, and the exhibition of the master's superiority and vanity, it is needless to add that no kind of refinement and delicacy is shown in the manner of entertaining the guests"—Surely those who encountered great personal perils to render attention to the proscribed deserve more charity. But what principle of state or show could influence to this deportment? What exhibition of vanity could be indulged in an act that, by its own nature, prohibited publicity? It could not be an action of vanity; or, if it were, in the language of Junius, "the gratification was limited to a narrow circle, and the vain were depositories of their own secret"

But the British merchant, the masters of ships, the common mariners, will emulously vindicate the Russians from this aspersion, and repeat their attestations, that during the march towards Siberia, in Paul's reign, (at the very period to which the previous remarks allude,) the high and low, the rich and poor, were indiscriminately experiencing, and especially at Moscow, from all classes of Russians, the most disinterested, generous, and affectionate aids, notwithstanding such benevolence and expression of amity exposed the Russians to severe punishment; and the gentlemen of the British factory will not only confirm this statement, but add that the most cordial service, the most liberal arrangements, the most scrupulous good faith, have to this very hour continued to diminish the evils of political hostility.

"Such are these barbarians;" (for so they have been described by the unfortunate misconception of writers whose abilities render

11

their opinions greatly authoritative with the public,) "such the debased and grovelling character of this whole people" whose institutions and establishments the same writers thus pursue with animadversion.

"The phenomenon of a city populous and civilized, in the heart of Siberia, 1,500 miles from St. Petersburg, is as monstrous and unnatural a thing as the parent from whence it sprang—the tyranny which reigns at Petersburg itself—the boundless tyranny which outrages nature by planting that city in the marshes of the Neva."

Has the Almighty then formed a part of the globe which civilized men must not endeavour to cultivate? Is the attempt to extend civilization 1,500 miles from Petersburg a crime abhorrent to nature, as violating her boundaries for savage life? Have the *Russian despots* deserved the execration of humanity for having permitted the cultivation of the desert, and *making it to smile*, for those who are doomed to tenant it? Have they mercilessly abused the attributes of majesty by encouraging the exile to diminish the rudeness of his sufferance, when the object of punishment or precaution was attained by the removal of the offending party to this remote region?

Is Peter the Great to be recorded as an enemy to the human race, for having selected the banks of one of the noblest rivers in the world, and a sea-port, as the site of one of its most magnificent capitals, which, annually aggrandizing in majesty and importance,—diffuses wealth and incitement to industry through all parts of an immense empire?

Thousands in this metropolis can disprove the charge, that "nature is still more profaned in stunting the shoots of human happiness in this capital;" thousands will declare, that so far from any aspect of misery, Petersburg presents a spectacle of astonishing grandeur and growing prosperity; and that scarcely one beggar is to be seen in streets containing nearly two hundred thousand inhabitants.

The public documents will authenticate the assertion, that so far from any existing desire to impose the shackles of slavery, extraordinary encouragements are given to the progress of freedom; and that the total abolition of slavery is the principle of the Russian government, which indefatigably pursues this difficult but noble object, and *for which purpose a Committee is at this very time sitting,* under the superintendence of the Emperor.

There is another writer who charges Russia with religious persecutions in Poland, and who introduces an erroneous note on the subject to correct a supposed error, thus making the blind to lead the blind; for of all countries in the world there is not one where toleration is so systematically established,—where religious worship is exercised with such perfect freedom.

Instead of waging war upon the Poles on account of their toleration, the intolerance of the Polish Catholics, and the persecution of the *dissidents,* were the avowed causes of the interference of Russia, which interference was justified by the violation of the treaty of Moscow, in the year 1686, wherein the free exercise of religion was guaranteed to the members of the Greek church.

In 1766, the Empress Catherine, in consequence of these persecutions, thus declares to the King and the confederated Republic of Poland—"That she sees with grief the state of the citizens called *dissidents.* That they have always been considered and treated as members of the State. That their rights attacked in different times have been confirmed to them by treaties and conventions of the most sacred character amongst men. That Russia, having guaranteed the execution of these treaties, her Imperial Majesty demands of the Diet, that the *dissidents* may be re-established in the use of their churches, and in the free exercise of all the ceremonies, of their religion. That they may be permitted to build new churches in places where there are none. That the tax granted to the Catholic priests upon the marriages, baptism, and interments of the *dissidents, should be abolished, as contrary to the liberty of religion, which is a law of Nature.* That the Greek *Dissidents,* as well as others, shall enjoy all their rights. That their priests be only submitted to secular jurisdictions. That intermarriages between persons of different religions be permitted; and that the children of both sexes, who are the offspring of such marriages, may be educated in the religion of their respective parents. That the equality of the nobles is the foundation of their liberty; and the exclusion of the Dissidents the *error of one party of the* State, who seek to establish a *precarious fortune on the ruins of the other,* and who prefer the advantage of a moment to the durable good of a solid society. That the Empress requires that all the nobles (Catholic and Dissidents) treat and negotiate together, and determine according to the laws of the State, what share each ought to have in the administration of the Republic; *and finally, that a constant refusal to listen to the dissidents, and render them justice, will violate the contract which unites them to the rest of the nation, and will restore to them the full possession, the natural liberty to appeal to the rest of the human race, and to choose amongst their neighbours, judges, allies, and protectors.*

The dissidents represented,—"How can we acknowledge as the legislative power the assembly of a part of the nobility, the will of a faction? *From whence have they a right to judge us, to condemn us, to deprive us of the prerogatives of citizens? To take away from us that authority which ought to be common to every member of the State. It is not an arbitrary and tyrannical tolerance that we wish of our fellow-citizens. We will not have either domination or slavery, but the equality of condition which we have merited, in rendering to the country equal services;—this equality that we hold from nature, from reason and policy, which the laws have guaranteed us, and which have protected us in various times against the attempts of our adversaries,"* &c. &c.

Their enemies only answered by employing the obscure pretext, of religion to animate against them a people of slaves, in whom the passions are strong, the judgement almost null, and the understanding too weak, to discern truth and falsehood confounded together in subtle questions. This necessitous class, *deteriorated by its chains, was influenced by the thirst of rapine concealed under the terms of the defence of the ancient religion—of the prevailing religion—of the religion of their fathers against heretics and men odious to the Godhead itself;—by all these artifices and appearances of a celestial interest employed in the aforesaid quarrels of religion to conceal the baseness and iniquity of a temporal interest.*

The Empress finally again addressed the King and the Diet urging the same arguments, and "declaring *that she did not seek a preference for any religion; but she invited the Polish nation to reflect upon the consequences of measures which cut off from the Republic the affections of a sixth part of its members;* and that she hoped and expected that the whole nation would adopt the principles of concord and humanity which she placed under their eyes, and that they would not force her to take measures repugnant to her feelings."

Persecution continued, and Poland was partitioned, so as to render her a less formidable agitator to the neighbouring powers.

The erasure of Poland from the list of States has ever been deemed an atrocious outrage, but certainly Poland had abused her independence. For nine hundred years this fine country (with very little intermission) had been the prey of factions and disorder, which had kept the bordering States in continual inquietude, whilst they desolated and degraded the people. A king without authority, a turbulent and avaricious nobility, and a people greatly favoured by nature, overwhelmed with oppression and poverty, were the characteristics of this nation.

Its habits of violence and anarchy were at variance with the good order of society, and its constitution was not analogous to the general spirit and political system of Europe.

The principle of the Elective Monarchy, so plausible in theory, was in practice found to be the source of innumerable evils, which destroyed the country, were injurious to the repose of Europe, and only gratified the sordid or ambitious views of the nobility of Poland, whilst the people, "always enslaved, always indifferent to the choice of a master, experienced neither joy nor regret in the election." Blackstone, in his Commentaries, after stating the plausible advantages of Elective Monarchy, and the inconvenience of its practice, concludes:

> An hereditary succession is therefore now established to prevent that periodical bloodshed and misery which the history of ancient Imperial Rome, and the more modern experience of Poland and Germany, may show us are the consequences of Elective Kingdoms.

With respect to the present temper of the Poles, and their preference for Russian government, I feel authorized to appeal to Lord Walpole, who is thoroughly acquainted with that country.

If the government of Poland had not been vicious—if the state of society had not been depraved—twelve millions of people would have found means to preserve their independence, when the inclination to remain a nation was so strong and prevalent; nor would ambition have projected the subjugation, or could Catherine have been enabled before the last partition to reply to a prelate of Poland, who was endeavouring to convince her that the monarchical Republic of his country was a Sovereign State, independent of all other earthly power, and that there was an injustice in her Majesty's proceeding towards it—"Reverend Father, If Poland was an inde-

15

pendent State, you would not have been here to intercede for it; as it is, you can give me no security that your country will not fall under the dominion of those who may one day attempt to disturb the happiness of my people. To care for the present, and provide for the future safety of this empire, the Almighty has imposed on me the heavy duty of a sovereign; and you know, Reverend Father, that to the accomplishment of our divine mission all earthly considerations must give way."

But it is not within the limits of this work to discuss the merits or demerits of the Russian administration of government; nor will I controvert that the social organization and political institutions of Russia are incomplete, or deny that the Russian armies, in the progress of their conquests, desolate and destroy. Yet as I have asserted in the body of the work that the Russian system of government is wise, benevolent, and singularly liberal, when conquest has incorporated new possessions in the Russian empire, I am anxious to prove, that although Russia may not repair the wrongs and injuries of the contest by immediate indemnifications, still she subdues the spirit of revenge, and conciliates the affections of the conquered, by the mild administration of her rule and respect for national customs and laws, on which she only gradually innovates, when innovation is evidently necessary for the general service of the empire.

In addition to arguments urged in the body of this publication, and the testimony of Vancouver, I hope to add a statement by the Honourable Mr. Hutchinson; who, when with the Russian army, was no less conspicuous for his courage and military talent, than he is in his own country for his patriotism and philanthropy; and who, animated by those feelings that have prompted me to this undertaking, has promised me to record his observations and opinions, and combat those accusations and charges which have been made against the government and nation of Russia.

If it were necessary still farther to establish the general fact of the conciliating character of the Russian government, I would adduce in evidence the conduct of the conquered provinces during the time of the distress of Russia, when her armed force was advanced to the frontier, and opportunity was presented to a numerous population for successful rebellion, if the Russian yoke had been oppressive. But where did the insurgents rise? Where did traitors co-operate with the invading enemy? Where was there even a symptom of disaffection?

The Livonians, the Fins, the Courlanders, the Poles, the Tartars,[1] &c. were un-awed by military control, and yet they conspired not against the Muscovite power, nor even advanced a pretension for an amelioration of their condition. Was this the conduct of a people who were victims of unparalleled cruelties, and unceasing insults and wrongs, "whose only refuge was death, and whose asylum was the grave?"—Had such been their state and feelings, the iron rule of Bonaparte would have been welcome, and the wretched would have sought the consolation of revenge, notwithstanding the assured ultimate augmentation of their own griefs; for the passions of nations, as well as of individuals, are seldom or ever under the control of interests.

These and various other incontrovertible facts justify me to reply in the name of Alexander, and in the language of the Macedonian monarch, to the charge—

"*Auferre, rapere, trucidare, falsis nominibus, imperium, atque quando solitudinem faciunt, pacem appellant.*"[2]

"*Veni enim non ut fitnditits everterem gentes, non ut dimicliam partem terrarum solitudinem facercm, sed ut illæ quoque quos bello subegissem victoria: meæ non pæniteret.*"[3]

I confess that I do feel a great, an inalienable attachment to the Russian nation. As this sentiment, however, was gradually impressed by an impartial examination of the Russian character, and the validity of its pretensions to esteem, such a bias, formed by the conviction of experience, will surely be allowed to augment rather than impair the force of arguments which have been adduced for the purpose of establishing amongst my own countrymen an equal and just regard for a nation so worthy of their cordial amity; a nation which is so strongly predisposed, from admiration of British character, as well as from sense of reciprocal interest, to renew and perpetuate the connexion.

---

1. In the whole Crimea there were not 1,500 Russians, and they were employed to guard the arsenals and sea-ports. Amongst 60,000 Tartars there was not a single Russian soldier.
2. Under false pretexts they rob, despoil, and desolate the empire, and when they have rendered it a desert, they call its solitude—peace.
3. "I came not to extirpate nations, not to make a desert of one half of the globe; but that even those whom my arms subdue should not deplore my victory."

Yet I have traced the imperfections of the Russians without extenuation, not only injustice to the public, but with an hope that so faithful a delineation may produce an impression in Russia to justify increased commendation of friends, and to disarm the powers of future malevolence.

There may be some persons fearful that the suggested aggrandizement of Russia might destroy that balance of power which can alone restore repose, or at least a respite, to the world. But force should be opposed to force; and France, aspiring at universal dominion, must be repelled and confined within the necessary limits by her bordering States applying themselves on a continental power of great and consolidated strength.

England, least of all nations, has cause to be jealous of Russian acquisitions on the shores of the Baltic. It is not from that Bay or the Euxine that the British trident can ever be disputed. Indeed it is the real interest of England to encourage those establishments that must render maritime objects and intercourse of more essential importance to the prosperity of Russia.

There is already a great disposition in Russia to reduce her own naval power, and appropriate the sums hitherto annually expended on her navy to other branches of the public service; I know a Russian admiral of considerable character and influence, who has more than once advised the disposal of the Baltic fleet, as being an unnecessary burthen on the revenue of the empire in the present circumstances of Europe, and rather a check to the political independence of the government, than an instrument to maintain its consideration.

Physical obstacles present insuperable impediments to the naval importance of Russia, so long as her coast dominion is bounded on one quarter by seas, which for six months every year are motionless by ice, and whose waters on the other quarter for nearly two-thirds of the year are rendered unnavigable, from the want of sea room to contend with the hurricane wildness of the elements.

If England has cause for any apprehension from the northern nations, it is not to an inland power, *but to the port-teeming coast, the natural arsenals, and the maritime population of Norway that she should direct her vigilance and cares.*

Should Russia, presuming on her forces, hereafter project schemes of territorial ambition incompatible with the independence or interests of nations that we are bound, by a general policy or particular relation of amity, to protect, various checks may be applied to control her immoderate pretensions. But the present great, nay, only object of Europe, ought to be the diminution of Bonaparte's extravagant power and influence, and all measures inducing that effect should supersede a minor policy which would retard its progress.

Nor is the hope of that success vain. France has not acquired real strength by her late usurpations. The war with Russia proved to Bonaparte that universal dominion was not to be achieved by force of arms. The battle of Asperne, and the military confidence acquired by Austria, still further reduced his military preponderance. The conduct of the Tyrolese, the augmentation of the British forces, the military organization of Portugal,[4] and the resistance of Spain, of glorious Spain, whose energies have been proved unconquerable, which nation, on declaring war against the usurper, founded the most rational hopes of victory, by the resolve of perseverance, and who only requires a *regular military organization of a portion of her powers* to achieve immediate independence, has impaired his offensive means to such a degree, that Europe, daily augmenting in hatred of the tyrant, and detestation of French oppression, invigorating by the illustrious and successful example of the contending nations, can assure her own deliverance whenever she resolves on bursting the bonds which have so long shamefully fettered her superior force.

The inordinate power of Bonaparte is rapidly retrograding. He scarcely now maintains equality with his *declared* enemies; and the force of opinion, stimulated by his never-ceasing tyranny, is arraying hourly against him an host of enemies, who will ere long gird France with an impenetrable belt, of independent nations.

---

4. That organization *commenced in August* 1807, with the Loyal Lusitanian Legion, which was expressly raised under the auspices of Lord Castlereagh, the Chevalier de Souza, arid the Bishop of Oporto, *to ascertain the military powers* of the Portuguese under proper superintendence. *The success of the Legion* determined his Majesty's Ministers to extend the system; *and in March* 1808, General Beresford was sent with various British officers to reform the Portuguese army. It is true that this measure proved fatal to the *parent establishment;* but Spain, Portugal, and *the enemy* have recorded the memory of its existence, and the reputation of its services will survive the *fiat of its dissolution.*

The proposed attitude of Russia must accelerate that moment, and under her aegis advanced to the southern frontier of Sarmatia, the enslaved nations north of the Rhine could successfully elevate the standard of revolt, and a line of banners wave in unison from the Alps to the Pyrenees.

The name of Bonaparte being mentioned, I must here take occasion (in consequence of some allusions expressed by an Honourable Gentleman in the House of Commons, and for whom, in common with my country, I entertain the highest respect,) to renew those charges which I alleged against him in my narrative of the expedition to Egypt; positive that time will establish the validity of my accusations, and certify the guilt of Bonaparte in those transactions.

Respect for the lives and families of several persons not less eminent for virtue than science, obliges me still to withhold the evidence on which I frame those charges; and there exist other momentous considerations to restrain me from a voluntary display of that authority, which would assure the sacrifice of persons who are entitled to protection instead of injury; but I repeat again, that although the *onus probandi ultimately lies with me,* this was a. case where the accused should have insisted upon trial, so as to have forced the proofs, and not have directed his ambassador to have made a clandestine remonstrance for the punishment of the accuser, and the suppression of the charges.

Upon; the military conduct of Bonaparte in the Russian campaigns I have animadverted without any feeling of prejudice. The facts on which these opinions are formed are submitted to the public; and if I have drawn unwarrantable conclusions, errors of argument may convict me of presumption or ignorance, but not of a breach of veracity, with the design to mislead friends and calumniate foes.

Military misrepresentations can enjoy but a short triumph: They are assured an inevitable exposition. The independent spirit of truth sooner or later scrutinizes those narratives that are traded by partiality or enmity, and ultimately consigns their records to oblivion or disgrace.

I have therefore endeavoured to write on the minutest circumstance with the greatest attention to accuracy, so that inquiry may assure my statements general and unequivocal confirmation.

I have been ambitious that the public should not class me in the list of those pernicious historians of whom Tacitus says, *Adeo maxima quaeque ambigua sunt, dum alii quoque modo audita pro compertis habent, alii vera in contrarium vertunt et gliscit utrumque posteritate.* I have not commented so fully as might have been done on the Russian conduct of the campaign. Various considerations of imperative force obliged me to leave my readers to form their own opinion on that subject. But I have mentioned a strong fact respecting the battle of Eylau, feeling confident that General Bennigsen would rather be charged with the responsibility of justifying his decision for the retreat, (in opposition to that of every other general officer) than that the enemy, by its concealment, should enjoy the advantage of declaring un-contradicted to the world, that the victory on their part was so decisive, that the propriety of maintaining or relinquishing the field was never a subject for Russian discussion.

The situation of confidence in which I was placed, and the opportunity afforded me, from peculiar circumstances, to acquire knowledge of the political views and transactions of that period, and which always influence, in a greater or lesser degree, military operations, has imposed upon me the obligation of silence, as far as those political incidents were not of a nature to be made public without a breach of duty or honour. I have therefore anxiously avoided any trespass on information which it was my duty to acquire, either by direct official communications, or which I obtained by virtue of the relations of intercourse that my employment originally enabled me to hold with persons *in* authority. And I trust none of the respective governments will have cause to reproach my want of attention to a principle which ought to guide all officers employed on similar services.

There is yet much that would interest undeveloped, but other pens in other times must complete what I have left unfinished.

Different feelings have obliged me to use great caution where I would have wished to eulogize. It would have been indeed unpardonable in me to have been ignorant, even at an earlier date, that the *odia in longum jaciens quæ reconderet auctaque promeret,* was the characteristic of Bonaparte; but I should have had no plea of extenuation, *after the conferences at Tilsitz,* for committing, by an indiscretion, any person deserving of British admiration or gratitude, to the resentment of an inhuman spirit, which declared on that occasion that "it loved vengeance—that it was a passion, a sentiment congenial to its heart."

As I did not propose to write for emolument, or with the vain hope of acquiring literary distinction, I thought it better to express my ideas and sentiments in my own language, and therefore I have not submitted this work to any revision.

The occasional counsel of a younger brother, and the unremitting attention and superintendence of my printer, have alone amended some of its imperfections. I know that Reviewers will examine the work itself, and not pay any attention to the apology for its crude state and defects; but if I cannot influence that dread tribunal, (and truly I have not adopted the principle, laudare Athenienses, laudari Atheniensibus,) I may perhaps disarm the hostility of contemporary writers by the modesty of my literary pretensions, and obtain some mercy from an indulgent public on account of the motives which have again induced me to present my works to their notice.

I have annexed the French Bulletins, not from any respect that I bear towards them, but for the sake of impartiality; and when I do cite them in the course of my narrative, it is only to points where their admission confirms, and where they would not misrepresent to their own disadvantage. For how can any one value, as authentic documents, Bulletins of which the subjoined is but a weak specimen of their general falsehood?[5] Bulletins in one of which (that of Friedland) Bonaparte declares that he has killed, wounded, and taken twenty thousand more Russians than were in the field of battle.

The following letter, which I have received, will account for the disappointment of those hopes that I had entertained of sub-

---

5. *Extract of Massena's Dispatch:* The English were *never* engaged in so brisk an affair! We took 2 pieces of cannon, 1 stand of colours. Killed the colonel of the 43rd, the colonel of the 16th dragoons, Major Brown, 52nd regiment. 60 officers killed, 24 buried on the ground. 400 sergeants and privates killed, 700 wounded. 400 prisoners. Total 1560 killed, wounded, and prisoners. *General Craufurd's official Return, from the Returns signed by the Commanding Officers of Regiments.* Officers killed (one of which was a field-officer) 4, sergeants 3, soldiers 29. Officers wounded 22, sergeants 10, soldiers 104. Officers prisoner 1, sergeants 1, drummers 1, privates 80. Total 255. Massena's account 1560. Difference between truth and falsehood 1305.

joining a statement from the pen of Mr. Hutchinson; but even this letter proves the nature of his testimony, and the result of his experience, after a very intimate acquaintance with the Russians, and a much more extensive tour through the Russian country than was made by those whose unfavourable observations have been submitted to the public.

Whenever Mr. Hutchinson transmits the memoir which he warrants me to expect, I will hasten to give it as a part of *my* present work, as I do think with Mr. Hutchinson, that it is a great national object to prove that the *"Veritas pluribus modis infracta, obtrectatio et livor, non in Anglia pronis auribus accipiuntur."*

London
November 24, 1810
My dear Wilson,
I have received your note, and am rejoiced to learn that you are about to vindicate our most kind and gallant friends, the Russians, from the aspersions cast upon them by some late publications in this country. It will afford me infinite satisfaction to give you what assistance I can in this your very laudable undertaking; and I shall lose no time in furnishing you with such remarks upon the state of Russia, the condition of her people, their habits and manners, as my own observations during a late extensive tour have enabled me to make. Short and desultory as these must necessarily be, from my never having had the most distant idea of being required to. lay them upon an author's desk, I shall still, I fear, not be able to let you have them in time for your publication, being at this moment much occupied in other pursuits, to which I am under the necessity of attending; but I hope soon to have it in my power to furnish you with them.

I can assure you with great truth, that I feel most indignant at the shameless calumnies and unfounded accusations which have been made against this people, and that too in the most illiberal manner. We are not justified in libelling and defaming the court, the nobles, the army, and the peasantry of Russia, because we are unfortunately at war with her.—Justice is due even to an enemy. To describe an entire people as vicious and barbarous, and with whom no intercourse should be held, is in itself practising that which we arraign and condemn. There

23

is nothing moral, wise, or polished, in labouring to perpetuate dissensions between States; nothing more arrogant, more
injurious, and discreditable to our country, than to be profuse
in our censures of other nations—to be ever ready to credit
and publish their faults and defects, and to attribute to millions
those vices which we may have observed in the conduct of individuals. There are certain great imperious duties, incumbent
on nations towards each other, which ought not to be violated
under any varying circumstances of peace or war.

Believe me to remain,

My dear Wilson,

Your very sincere and faithful

Christopher Hely Hutchinson

Sketch of the Campaigns

When General Bennigsen arrived on the borders of the Vistula with his corps, he fixed his headquarters at Pultusk, and sent forward, into the environs of Warsaw, Sedmorasky's division. One part remained at Prague; the rest, composed of chasseurs, a regiment of hussars, and some squadrons of Cossacks and cavalry, passed the Vistula, and an advanced guard proceeded to the river Bsura; but on the approach of the enemy, on the 26th of October, 1806, it retired, after some inconsiderable affairs; reached the Vistula, and burnt the bridge of Warsaw. The enemy, having occupied Warsaw, constructed several heavy batteries, which obliged General Sedmorasky to retire behind the Bug, where he took position at Zsegz and Dembè, whilst the division of Galoun defended the tract between the confluence of the Narew and the Bug, and the Austrian frontier near the village of Areickow. The division of Count Ostreman was at Makow; that of Zachen between Ostrolenka and Pultusk. General Bennigsen proposed to remain on the defensive, until the junction of General Buxhowden's corps with his own was effected.

The enemy, having passed the Vistula, advanced to the Bug, the passage of which river was long disputed; but, finally, Marshal Ney threw over a bridge, near Nowidwoe, at the confluence of the Wkra, the Bug, and the Vistula; but the first detachments which passed were cut off by the Russians,[1] and General Bennigsen, finding that the corps of Buxhowden was delayed, resolved, with his own corps, to attack the enemy at Modlin.

---

1. The forty-first French Bulletin states the Russian loss as considerable, and that they lost only 20 killed and wounded.

As Davoust's corps of the French had strongly fortified an height that commanded the left bank, of the Wkra near Pomechowe, and as a column, from the badness of the roads, could not arrive at the appointed time, this plan was abandoned, and the position of Nowemiasto, Sochoczyn, and Czarnowo, was occupied for the defence of the Wkra. In the mean time Marshal Soult passed the Vistula at Wyszogrod, Marshal Augereau with his corps between Zakroczyn and Utrata a little below the embouchure of the Bug into the Vistula, and the corps of Marshals Ney, Bessières, and Lasnes, passed the Vistula at Thorn—an open city, 37 leagues to the north of Warsaw, 34 south-east of Dantzic.

General Lestocq having been ordered to retire by General Bennigsen, obeyed after several remonstrances, when Marshal Ney marched against the corps of Lestocq, and Lasnes, and Augereau upon Plonsk. The former joined Davoust at Modlin; the latter appeared before Nowemiasto on the right bank of the river Wkra. The river Vistula is 400 toises broad, and forms a considerable barrier in the summer; but at, this time of the year it was rapidly freezing, and its line being irregular, and deeply reentrant towards the Oder in several parts, the troops posted near Thorn would have been greatly exposed to be cut off by an enemy passing above or below; and although General Lestocq, naturally anxious to save as much of the remnant of Prussia as possible, wished to remain on the Vistula, nevertheless, General Bennigsen might have been right in his order, as being charged with a more general responsibility.

General Bennigsen finding that he could not resume the offensive with his single corps, resolved to fall back upon Pultusk, where there was a reserve of the army, his heavy artillery, favourable ground, and to which the enemy could only advance, from the state of the roads, with light guns. The arrival of General Kaminskoy occasioned the dereliction of this project, as the General imagined that he could force the enemy behind the Wkra, and made his dispositions accordingly; but Bonaparte having arrived on the Wkra on the 23rd, did not give him time to execute his movement; for he ordered his army to attack the Russians on the same evening, and, on the 24th, at the three points of Czarnowo, Sochoczyn, and Nowemiasto.

For 14 hours, Count Ostreman, with a part of his division, resisted the corps of Davoust, Lasnes, and the guards, but at length they succeeded in forcing the Wkra, when the Count retired upon Nasielsk, without any serious loss,[2] and afterwards to Strzegooin, where the divisions of Zachen, Barclay de Tolloy, and Sedmorasky having united, the whole marched to Pultusk. During this time, Prince Gallitzin, with several regiments of cavalry and infantry, had marched to the succour of the post at Nowemiasto, but did not advance farther than Lopaczin, on the river Sonna, when he was attacked by Marshal Augereau's corps, and a considerable number of cavalry which had passed the river Wkra at Kursomb, not far from Nowemiasto, and by whom he was compelled to retire on the road of Pultusk, but on which he fell in with a part of Zachen's division which was on march to rejoin its corps. Obliged to halt at Golymin, the Prince was there attacked by the corps of Augereau, and the cavalry under Murat, upon the same day on which the combat of Pultusk took place.

The troops which had assembled at Strzegooin, (composing 60 battalions and 55 squadrons, without including the Cossacks,) arrived in the environs of Pultusk on the 24th and 25th of December, and took up a position with the left applied on the town, and the right thrown forward into a wood, commencing in front of the right between 200 and 300 paces, and extending along the front of the whole line, but towards the centre retiring above 2000 paces. The right was the strongest part of the position—There General Barclay de Tolloy commanded—The centre was under the orders of General Zachen—The left was commanded by Count Ostreman—The reserve by General Sedmorasky. General Baggavout, with two regiments of the line and a regiment of chasseurs, composing part of the advanced guard, was posted 400 paces in front of Count Ostreman, and near some houses on an elevation which formed part of the site of the town;—the cavalry was placed between 1500 and 2000 paces in front of the line; and in their front some corps of chasseurs were pushed by General Barclay into the forest.

The 45th Bulletin states, in the following remarkable terms, the condition of the Russian army at this time, and presents a striking

---

2. The 45th Bulletin gives the Russians credit for a vigorous resistance; but states their loss to be some prisoners and 6 guns, and several generals wounded. On the part of the French one general wounded, a few men killed, and 200 wounded.

instance of French presumption and falsehood, which were properly punished even when the manuscript was tracing:

> All the Russian columns are cut off, and are wandering at hazard in a disorder difficult to imagine; The Russian general committed the fault of cantoning his army with the French army on its flanks, separated, it is true, by the Narew, but with a bridge on the river. If the weather was fine, one might predict that the Russian army would not be able to retreat, and, without even a battle, would be lost; but in a season where night sets in at 4 o'clock in the evening, and where it is only daybreak at 8 in the morning, the pursued enemy has all chances to save himself, particularly in a difficult country, and one intersected with woods. Besides, the roads are covered with five feet of mud, and the thaw continues; artillery cannot advance above two leagues a day. It is then to be foreseen, that the enemy will retire from the dangerous position in which he is placed, but he will lose *all* his artillery, *all* his carriages, *all* his baggage.

The position of the French army on the 25th in the evening was as follows: The left, composed of the corps of Marshal Prince of Ponte Corvo, and of Marshals Ney and Bessières, on march from Biézun on the route of Grodno. Marshal Soult on march to Ciechanow. Marshal Augereau on march to Golymin. Marshal Davoust between Golymin and Pultusk. Marshal Lasnes at Pultusk.

The position, between Pultusk and the wood, was apparently one large plain, but was intersected in front with small defilés. Behind the plain extended deep ; but towards the right was divided by the river Narew, and on the left by the forest in part occupied by General Barclay.

In the evening of the 25th, the corps of Davoust approached and made a reconnaissance.—On the 26th, at ten o'clock in the morning, the enemy, consisting of the corps of Davoust and Lasnes, with the French guards, commenced the action by a cannonade from the centre neither brisk nor well sustained, as he had not been enabled to advance his cannon.

Towards mid-day, however, the attack was more vigorous on the left of the position, and the Russian fire of musketry was considerable. The Russian cavalry had also several opportunities to charge, which they did with complete success. The enemy making no impression on the left, notwithstanding repeated efforts, directed some attacks against the centre, but there also being foiled, he concentrated and threw nearly his whole force upon the right, and by an overbearing and unexpected weight of fire obliged the Russians to retire, (but not in any disorder,) upon their successive reserves, and artillery. The enemy elated, and confident, from this retrograde movement, continued, notwithstanding heavy loss, to advance upon the Russian batteries in the wood, some of which, being gallantly maintained to cover the retreat, they carried by assault.

General Bennigsen, however, having resolved on battle, was determined to sustain it—to oppose force to force, and manoeuvre to manoeuvre; he therefore directed General Barclay to recede, and throwing back the right of his line, and retiring the cavalry from his front, opened a well directed fire of artillery from one hundred and twenty pieces, which so astounded and destroyed the enemy, that they almost immediately gave way, and several regiments being sent to the support of General Barclay, he vigorously advanced, and the original ground was altogether recovered,[3] a great number of the enemy killed, and the darkness of night alone preserved the remainder, for they fled in great confusion and consternation, augmented by the attack of the Russians on their right, and which was already forced when the day closed.

When General Kaminskoy had found his position behind the Wkra forced by the enemy, he resolved to retire the Russian army behind the Niemen river, and gave directions accordingly to the corps of Buxhowden and Bennigsen; but his orders were given under such circumstances, that General Bennigsen considered himself as authorised to use his own discretion, and therefore preferred to give battle at Pultusk, hoping that General Buxhowden or General d'Anrep would support him; by some unfortunate misapprehension or disagreement, probably originating in the want of acknowledged superior direction and authority, neither of these officers had advanced to his assistance; he therefore thought it more prudent to retire during the night, notwithstanding his success, as Soult was on march for Ostrolenka, and as he feared to be surrounded by the

---

3. The French admit that no troops on a parade could have executed manoeuvres with more steadiness and accuracy than the Russians through the whole of this battle.— The day began at this season about eight in the morning, and closed at four p.m.

whole French army, reuniting to revenge its partial disgrace, if he remained on the position of Pultusk; and this determination was indeed almost indispensable, since he had not any provisions in his camp or in the neighbourhood.

The French force which had opposed him was so severely beaten, that their flight continued during the night, and they abandoned many guns, Bonaparte's equipage, &c. nor could the Cossack's, who patrolled two German miles in front of Pultusk, on the 27th, find even a rearguard of the enemy. The French did not re-advance until the second day, and General Corbineau did not enter Ostrowiec until the 1st of January, 1807.

The loss of the Russians was less than 5000 men, and the French, at the most moderate computation, had 8000 killed and wounded, amongst whom were five generals, including Marshal Lasnes, and other distinguished officers.

Had Buxhowden, who was distant but eight English miles during the action, or d'Anrep, with his division, but co-operated,[12] the action at Pultusk might have decided the campaign; for the entire annihilation of the enemy opposed would have been then certain.

But the result of this affair made a very favourable impression for the character of General Bennigsen, and on the Russians. It was the first check that Bonaparte, who was present at the battle, although he does not avow it in any of his Bulletins, had experienced on the Continent, a charm was broken, and the French army foresaw that their future combats would be no longer chases of pleasure.

The Russian Generals resumed confidence. The stain of Austrelitz was effaced from their escutcheons, and the soldiers recognized themselves as not unworthy of the companions of Suwarrow. It was in vain that Bonaparte denied the victory. It was in vain that he boasted the trophy of some cannon which the Russians had abandoned in consequence of the state of the roads, on their subsequent march. He could not deceive the army. He was not able even to rally his interrupted operations so as to pursue the offensive until he had possessed himself of what yet remained of Prussia; and thus, if he could not render the battle equivocal in history, diminish the mischievous consequences of its loss. It was in vain that he announced the entire destruction of the Russian army, and his consequent return to Warsaw, there to repose until he chose to renew the campaign. His march had been arrested, all his enterprises discomfited, and he had scarcely proclaimed that he had repelled the Russians eighty leagues, when the same Russians re-appeared in the field to assure him with terrible evidence of their existence. The affair of Golymin on the same day contributed to animate the Russian courage and *amour propre*. Prince Gallitzin, with 15 battalions and 20 squadrons, having found himself obliged to take post there, whilst Count Pahlin, with the regiment of hussars of Somskoy, and General Laptow, with a regiment of chasseurs, effected their retreat upon him, was vigorously attacked by the whole corps of Augereau and the cavalry under the orders of Murat, but maintained his ground; and, towards evening, being reinforced by the division of General Dockturof, and a part of the division of General Tutchikow, he advanced, and drove back the enemy, from every point. The enemy admitted two generals wounded in this affair, and Augereau had a horse killed under him, he states his general loss to be 800 killed and 2000 wounded. Nevertheless, in consequence of General Kaminskoy's order for a retreat, and the uncertainty of the issue of the combat sustained by General Bennigsen, it became necessary for him to retire upon Ostrolenka, which he did in most perfect order, and there joined the corps of General Bennigsen, who, on the 27th, had marched to Rozan, and on the 28th to Ostrolenka. From thence he retired to Novogorod, with the united divisions of Generals Essen and d'Anrep; and General Buxhowden, with his corps, marched to Kolno. The intention was to repass the Narew,. but the state of the ice preventing the construction of a bridge, the army was obliged to fall back as far as Tykoczyn to cross the river.

The enemy, aware of General Kaminskoy's order for the Russian army to retrograde, and unwilling, after the battle of Pultusk, to re-advance it by any active operations, made their disposition of winter quarters. Marshal Bernadotte went to Elbing, Ney to Güttstadt, Augereau to Thorn, Davoust to Przasznic, Lasnes to Markow, Soult to Pultusk, and Bonaparte with his guards to Warsaw.

General Buxhowden, at Tykoczyn, was removed from the army, and General Bennigsen received the supreme command. Desirous to profit of his success at Pultusk, and the confidence there acquired by his troops, he determined to continue the plan proposed by General Buxhowden, who had promised the King of Prussia to save Koenigsberg still menaced by the gradual approach of the corps of Marshals Ney and Bernadotte.

The army, 70,000 strong, with 500 cannon,[4] having passed the Narew, marched to the Bobra river, and crossed at Gonionetz and Innowa, except the corps of General Sedmorasky, 12,000 strong, which remained at Gonionetz.

The route of march was directed upon Bialla, where the headquarters were established on the 15th of January. On the 16th they were transferred to Arys; on the 18th to Rhein, where the divisions of Generals Dockturof and Tutchikow, which had been detached, joined General Bennigsen's army, and on the 19th the advanced guard fell upon several of the detachments of the enemy in their cantonments.—From Rhein the troops marched to Heilige Linde, and then to Bischoffstein.

Unfortunately, General Bennigsen was not acquainted with the full security in which General Ney confided, or by directing the march upon Wirtemberg, instead of Bischoffstein, the whole of the Marshal's corps would, probably, have been obliged to capitulate; but, nevertheless, many prisoners were daily made.

The General being informed that Marshal Bernadotte was retiring with precipitation from Elbing, by Preuss Holland to Mohrungen, resolved to press him, and on the 24th marched to Arensdorf, and on the 25th to Liebstadt; but on the same day the advanced guard, under General Markow, commenced an attack near the village of Georgenthal, two English miles in front of Mohrungen, on a very formidable position occupied by the whole corps of the enemy, and finally supported by General Dupont's division. General Markow was repulsed, but towards evening, General d'Anrep arriving with a part of the cavalry, drove back the enemy, who were pressing, the advanced guard, and recovered the original ground. After the action was over, while the General was fixing his posts for the night, he was

---

4. Bonaparte states the Russian army that opened the campaign as 150,000 strong. It was, at no moment, from the commencement to the termination of the campaign, of that force. It would have been well for Europe if it had. Previous to the passage of the Vistula, its force was only 90,000, and the reinforcements from Moldavia, &c. did not augment it to above 100,000. Between that and 80,000 was the extreme amount, for the reinforcements could not gain more upon the loss.

unfortunately killed by a rifle shot. His death excited very great regret, as he was a brave and able officer, and an estimable man.

This partial combat was prejudicial; for had notice been given of the position of the enemy at Mohrungen, to General Zachen, who, was at Elditten, and Count Ostreman at Heiligental, the corps of Bernadotte could have been surrounded; but, during the action, Prince Michael Dolgorucky entered the town of Mohrungen by the rear with two squadrons of Courland dragoons, and some Cossack's, surprised the enemy's guards, took the whole baggage of Marshal Bernadotte, and several hundred prisoners,[18]and the Marshal with difficulty escaped.

In General Bernadotte's baggage, the money levied on the town of Elbing for his own private use, 10,000 ducats, exclusive of 2,500 for his staff, was recovered; and there were found, to a great amount; various-pieces of plate, candlesticks, &c. bearing the arms of almost all the states of Germany. The Marshal's servant was so ashamed of this plunder, that he would not claim it when purposely desired to point out his master's property; but as the articles were taken in the Marshal's own quarter, and in his trunks, and were in such quantity, they must have been there with his knowledge.

There was likewise found an order for the reception of Bonaparte at Warsaw, directing where he was to be hailed with shouts of Vive l'Empereur, together with official accounts of actions prepared for publication, and private duplicates, with the real facts stated, for Bonaparte's own perusal. General Bennigsen has the papers.

A circumstance well worthy record occurred during the conflict in front of Mohrungen. The regiment of Moscow Grenadiers, posted on an elevation, were sitting down, when a light brigade of the enemy advanced to charge. The grenadiers seeing so many *Crapauds,* as the French helmeted battalions were called, approaching with fixed bayonets, burst out into a loud laugh, which so disconcerted the enemy, that they instantly fled, pursued by volleys of shot.

No troops could evince more courage than the Russians, who fought undaunted by the superiority of numbers. Their loss was 2000, but the enemy's was not less, although they state it at only 100 killed and 400 wounded;-and the two eagles taken, remained in possession of the Russians, notwithstanding Bernadotte asserts the recovery in his report.

General Markow fell back at dusk upon Liebstadt, but the enemy retiring upon Deutsch Eylau during the night, Prince Michael Gallitzin with the cavalry pursued them, and made many prisoners. Bonaparte, to cover the retreat and inspire a belief that the Russians were severely checked, states their entrance into Mohrungen only on the 27th.

The grand army then advanced to Mohrungen, which it reached the next day, the 26th, and Prince Bragration having the command given to him of the advanced guard, pressed the enemy from Deutsch Eylau, daily making prisoners, capturing baggage, &c. and nearly destroying the whole of the rearguard of the enemy, who fled towards Thorn, raising the blockade of Graudenz, &c. to which place the Prussian corps, under General Lestocq, was directed with a considerable convoy, of which it was greatly in want, and which enabled its governor to maintain that most important fortress—The very key of the Vistula, against all the efforts of the enemy during the succeeding campaign.

Such were the important consequences of this hardy and active movement—in which the detour of the marches was also very considerable, from partial thaws which made the small rivers impassable—undertaken at a season of the year when the climate opposed the most desolating impediments—in a country where necessary supplies were scarcely to be found—where no hope of spoil encouraged—and no prospect of diminishing labours cheered the toiling soldier.

Such were the operations of those "cut-off columns wandering in the hope of saving themselves behind their frontier, defeated, disgraced, and fugitives, without artillery, means of transport, or baggage, and the loss of 30,000 men."[5] Bonaparte, indeed, pretended that he finally encouraged the advance of the Russians; but the relief of Graudenz was an event that he never could have proposed in his calculations, even if he did consent to have his winter quarters insulted—To defer the rich prize of Koenigsberg, and expose Marshals Bernadotte's and Ney's corps to the losses they sustained in a rapid retreat; and the most credulous of his partisans could

---

5. To this time the Russian army had but lost from their original numbers, when the campaign commenced, 23,000 men, killed, wounded, prisoners, and sick.

never have believed that such events could have occurred within one month after "his *victory at* Pultusk, and the repulse of the Russians *eighty* leagues."

At Mohrungen on the 31st of January, General Bennigsen was deliberating on what farther operations he should undertake, and several plans were under discussion, when a French officer, on his way to Marshal Bernadotte, was taken, and on him an order was found, acquainting the Marshal "that Bonaparte had resolved to resume the offensive; that the French army was to assemble at Willenberg, where the Emperor would be on the 31st, but that the Marshal with his corps was to act against the right of the allied army, vigorously, yet with that judgement which Bonaparte had a right to presume upon, from the Marshal's long experience of war:" and the instructions concluded with the remark, "You will see that the *Emperor proposes to cut off the Russian army from their frontiers.*"

This intelligence, which ought not to have been unexpected, created some surprise; but General Bennigsen observed, that although he had not sought, yet he was not in a condition to shrink from a general battle: and therefore instead of gaining a march upon the enemy, by falling back from Mohrungen, he ordered his army to make a flank march to the left, and assemble at Yunkowo, and the head-quarters were transferred there on the 1st of February. On the 3rd the Russian army drew out in order of battle, and awaited the enemy's attack until mid-day, in a position extremely unfavourable, being surrounded by woods that commanded the open space, and which shelved in the centre into an hollow where the village was situated, when the General being convinced, after a very accurate reconnaissance, that he must fight, in his then position, with great disadvantage, changed his intentions, and became desirous to regain the Aller, which would give him a liberty of action, and option of operations; he therefore determined to force with his advanced guard the posts in front of his position and the town of Allenstein, whilst with his main army he crossed the Aller at the villages of Kattflies and Rudikimen, and he hoped by an immediate advance to anticipate the enemy in the occupation of Allenstein with any considerable force: but no sooner did the advanced guard appear in march, than the French army deployed, and commenced a sharp fire of musketry from a line of woods which ran in front of the Russian position; and soon, afterwards the left of the Russians was engaged in a very brisk affair, as the enemy attempted to carry, with two divisions, the bridge of Bergfried, which was thrown over the Aller, long frozen, but impassable on account of the deep snow that rested on its bed. This bridge was taken and retaken three times, and finally remained in possession of the Russians, but their loss had exceeded 600 men, when night terminated the action.

Bonaparte pretends, in the 56th bulletin, that he remained master of the bridge, but the fact is contradicted by the very importance which he attaches to its possession.

The Emperor went himself to the village of Getkendorf, and arrayed in battle the corps of Marshal Ney on the left, the corps of Marshal Augereau in the centre, and of Marshal Soult on the right, and the Imperial Guards in reserve. He ordered Marshal Soult to march on the road of Guttstadt, and to carry the bridge of Bergfried, that he might debouch in rear of the enemy with the whole corps of his army, a *manoeuvre which gave to this battle a decisive character:—Conquered, the enemy was lost without resource.*

After stating the imaginary capture of 1,600 Russians at Guttstadt, and the valour of the divisions of Laval and Lagrand, he proceeds:

The two regiments, the 24th, and the 4th, and a battalion of the 28th in reserve, were sufficient to dislodge the enemy from the wood: they passed the bridge *au pas de charge, pierced the twelve Russian battalions,* took four pieces of cannon, and covered the field of battle with killed and wounded.

The 40th and 46th, who formed the second brigade were behind, impatient to deploy; but. already the enemy was in flight, and frightened, abandoned all his fine positions.

Again the Russian army is destroyed and disgraced! This bridge, which is to give the battle a decisive character, which leaves the Russians no escape, is in the hands of the French!!! *Sed forsan miseros meliora sequentur.*

The General now understood that the French army had actually assembled in front of Allenstein, and proposed to attack him the next day, and that the corps of Ney was manoeuvring to turn the right of the Russians and throw the Prussians between that corps and Bernadotte's.[6]

He saw the impossibility of continuing at Yunkowo, and regretted his movement from Mohrungen, since he now had to retire in presence of an enemy, and General Lestocq's corps was exposed to imminent hazard.[7] Fortunately the capture of the courier had retarded Marshal Bernadotte's operations two days, and to this propitious circumstance much of the future fortune of the Russians, by a diminution of their difficulties, may justly be ascribed.

The Russian army commenced its retreat at eleven o'clock at night upon Wolsdorf, but having to defile through the village of Yunkowo, considerable confusion prevailed, from the darkness of the night, the severity of the weather, and the clashing columns, uncertain of the snow tracts they were to follow, and the carriages, &c. which choked up the passage.

The rearguards, under the command of the Generals Prince Bragration, Barclay de Tolloy, and Baggavoute, instead of leaving the ground before day-dawn, as was proposed, had been obliged to continue upon it, but in possession of Bergfried until nine o'clock, when the overpowering numbers of the enemy pressed them back into the village with some disorder. Here, however, the Russians rallied behind barricades, formed with wagons, tumbrils, &c. and disputed the enemy's advance until the order of march was re-established, when they gradually retired, contesting desperately every inch of ground, in order to protect the army, whose columns

---

6. The French army had re-assembled on the 31st of January at their several rendezvous: the 5th corps at Brok, the 3rd corps at Mysiniez, the 4th corps at Willenberg, the 6th corps at Gilginburg, the 7th corps at Neidenburg, the cavalry under Murat at Willenberg. Marshal Bernadotte and his corps at Strasburg, on which he had fallen back. Marshal Lefebre and the 10th corps at Thorn, for its defence, and the left bank of the Vistula. Total, 7 corps, exclusive of the guards and cavalry, of which 5 corps, the guards and the cavalry, marched against Bennigsen and Lestocq.
7. When General Bennigsen marched from Mohrungen, Lestocq's corps was at Freystadt, and its advance at Bischoffswerder covering the relief of Graudentz, but it was then ordered to Deutsch Eylau, where it received further directions to proceed, on the 2rd of February, to Osterode, on the 3rd to Mohrungen, and on the 4th to Liebstadt. Its previous route of march, on the advance, had been from Friedland, where it had been driven, to Domnau, Landsberg, Schlodien, Preuss Holland, Shierstein, Reisenburg, Rosenburg, Freystadt.

moved on but very slowly; for instead of three columns of march, as had been directed, the state of the country had obliged the dereliction of one road, and the formation but of two columns; the heavy cannon had also experienced such impediments that it was necessitated to break from its prescribed tract, upon one of the roads destined for the troops.

Bonaparte was himself all day with the advanced guard of his army, which suffered very heavy loss—not less than 1500 men, and of which there were many prisoners. The French adventured, as they had been used to do after other armies, and paid for their presumption severely. The Russians did not lose more, as they had the advantage, from the character of the country (alternately small plains and fir woods) of defending the entrances into the woods, whilst the enemy in his unsheltered movements to gain them was exposed for a considerable time to the Russian fire.

About six o'clock in the evening, the rear-guard, after a march of six leagues, was enabled to take post, and night closed the action.

On the 4th at night the Russian army again moved upon Frauendorf. The enemy had then occupied Guttstadt, and possessed themselves of some regimental baggage of little value. This news reached the General upon the road, when he detached 3,000 men to secure his left at Heilsberg.

The French advanced guard daily relieved, did not press the unchanged rear-guard of the Russians much on the 5th, and the prisoners said that the cause of this comparative forbearance was the severe loss sustained on the preceding day, which probably influenced more caution; and perhaps an additional reason may be found in the detachment of Marshal Ney with his corps, and two divisions of cavalry, who were ordered to attack the Prussian corps, reinforced by two Russian regiments, and which Bonaparte considered as hopelessly cut off.

The aspect of affairs was certainly not encouraging. General Bennigsen was sensible that the interests of Russia required a protracted warfare; not only that Russia might prepare her further means of offence and defence, but as she entertained speculative hopes of Austria's co-operation, and was authorized to expect British aid when the Baltic opened; whereas, if he hazarded battle, he was depriving her of these contingencies, and committing, under very inauspicious circumstances, the empire to the fortune of a single action. On the other hand, the strongest representations were made by his officers against any further retreat, more prejudicial by actual loss, as they stated, than a severe conflict. The general feeling of the army was not only in unison with such representations, but its expression and general state somewhat alarmingly coincided with these opinions; for indeed a Russian force was never by character of composition or system calculated to retreat, and the severe and inclement night-marches, after the day's fatigues, with the aggravating anxieties about food, would have been sufficient to conquer the discipline of troops far better regulated.

The soldiers had to prowl and dig for the buried food of the peasantry—so that between search of provision and duty they had scarce time to lay down, and when they did, they had no other bed than the snow, no shelter but the heavens, and no covering but their rags.

General Bennigsen himself indeed wished to save Koenigsberg, in as much as its preservation was the cherished object of the King, and the General gratefully remembered that the King of Prussia had been to him a benefactor, whose interests he was bound to protect, when not compromising those of his own sovereign.

The map was therefore examined, and Preuss Eylau was selected as the field of battle: the heavy and reserve cannon were sent by a wide route to that ground, and the Prussian column was ordered there.

On the 5th, at night, the grand army moved to Landsberg, and the troops from Heilsberg were ordered to rejoin the army, which they did, although they had been attacked at Heilsberg by Marshal Davoust, who had marched expressly to prevent their junction, and who obliged them to retire before him, but with a steadiness that effected their safety, notwithstanding the enormous superiority of the enemy.

The army reached the position in front of Landsberg early in the day, as the march did not exceed ten English miles, and the rear-guard took post two miles in front of the position, about three o'clock in the afternoon, where it was soon afterwards seriously engaged with the corps of Marshals Soult and Augereau, and the cavalry under Murat.

The main army had been incautiously bivouacked directly in front of the town through which the whole had to defile, and woods, bordering and closing upon each flank, extended deep to the rear.

About four o'clock the enemy having brought up three corps of their army, menaced a very earnest attack, and manoeuvred so as to turn the rear-guard, at the moment the advanced guard, which brought the lines of the Russian army under fire, and occasioned great confusion in the streets of the town, which were crowded with wagons, guns, &c. as usual.

But Prince Bragration contested his ground so gallantly that he never receded one foot, notwithstanding heavy losses, which were chiefly occasioned by a Russian regiment of horse charging, failing, and rushing back upon the Russian infantry pursued by the enemy—two battalions[8] were in consequence entirely trampled on or cut down.

The general moved forward several regiments to support the advanced guard, and the action was maintained with obstinacy until night terminated the carnage, and relieved the apprehensions of those who had military experience enough to know the danger of the position.

The Russian loss amounted to near 3000 men, and two stand of colours. Prince Gallitzin, who had joined at Mohrungen, was killed, to the great regret of the army, as he was a young man of excellent disposition and promise.

General Bennigsen being anxious to remove as soon as possible from his unfavourable ground, had ordered the army to march at dusk, and most happily so early, for one column having been directed to pass by a tract on the right of the town, was obliged to return and fall in behind the other column, moving through Landsberg, as the snow was impracticably deep in the rivulet which ran on the right in their direction of march.

By twelve o'clock on the 7th the army had gained its position in rear of Preuss Eylau, but a division was left in the town to support the advanced guard, and to maintain the town after the advanced guard had retired into the line as was proposed.

Two miles in front of Preuss Eylau the enemy pressed Prince Bragration, when the regiment of Petersburg dragoons, emulous to retrieve the misfortune of the previous day, charged a column of the enemy, cut to pieces the two battalions composing it, and captured two eagles. At the same time the Russian infantry charged

---

8. The French bulletins state two regiments.

two other columns advancing to storm the height, and put to death so considerable a number, that an elevation, which the fugitives had attempted to gain, was for three weeks afterwards, actually cased with their dead. The enemy's cavalry then attempted to turn the right wing, but four Russian regiments of infantry, and as many of cavalry, sustained and repelled these efforts with sanguinary execution on the assailants. This severe check daunted the enemy so that the rear-guard retired without further molestation into Preuss Eylau; but no sooner had it passed through, than the division which was stationed to defend the town, by a mistake of the order, commenced its march also upon the position, the centre of which was not more than 300 yards from the interior houses.

The General instantly ordered other troops to replace them, but the vigilant and active enemy had already taken possession. They were, however, dislodged by a vigorous attack, but Bonaparte threw in another division, and as an encouragement promised the sacking of the town, whilst at the same time he made a movement with his left to lodge some infantry in a village, and avenue of trees, from whence he could incommode the Russian right, and open a communication with Marshal Ney, then momentarily expected by the route of Schloditten.

As the heavy artillery had arrived the same afternoon by that village, General Bennigsen was willing to abandon the contest for the town, and had directed a division, which was advancing to support the Russians again retiring from the suburbs, also to fall back; but the ardour was so vehement that the columns continued to move on with drums beating, and when they entered the streets charged the enemy with the bayonet, and killed many of them in the attack, and afterwards in the houses, where they were committing the most infuriated excesses under the authority of Bonaparte's order.

The greatest uneasiness had prevailed for the safety of this artillery, and the arrival of it is a reproach to the French; indeed there never was a superior pursuing force which did so little where so much might have been effected. The numerous and deep woods; the long and steep *defilés,* through which the Russians had to pass, were all neglected by the enemy, who only attacked as a carpenter would drive his nail. But, on the other hand, the conduct of the retreat does infinite honour to the Prince Bragration and his rearguard, to the generals commanding the detached columns, and General Lestocq. It was a splendid military lesson, confirming what Xenophon, what the Duke of Parma, and what Moreau had practised, that *retreats* in presence of a *superior force* are not necessarily *races, and that conduct, and not speed,* can alone *prevent* inglorious disasters,' more ruinous and fatal than the enemy's fire. At the same time the uniform courage and the daring resolution of the Russians, which had inflicted heavy loss, inspired a respect that materially influenced the operations of the succeeding day. General Bertram afterwards, at Koenigsberg, told General Bennigsen that Bonaparte had confessed "the Russian retrograde movements to have been most ably conducted, and that they were full of instruction."

As the hillocks however on the French side closed up to the houses, the enemy still hung under their cover and fired into the streets. General Barclay de Tolloy, who commanded in the town, was severely wounded in the arm, by one of their random shots, after it was dark, which deprived the army of the services of a most valuable officer at an important crisis.

When General Bennigsen had taken up his position on the morning of the 7th, he had chosen for the alignment of his army, an open space of uneven ground of about two miles from right to left and a mile deep. This ground was bounded by fir woods, except in rear of his right and in a continuation of his left where the open country extended. The town of Preuss Eylau, which had no species of work for its protection, lay in a hollow about three hundred yards in front of the right of the Russian centre, which rose above it so as to overtop the roofs of the houses; in front of the Russian left was the village of Serpallen. On this ground General Bennigsen had formed his army, nearly 60,000 strong, which had concentrated, with the exception of Lestocq's corps, on the evening of the 7th, notwithstanding the efforts of the French marshals and Bonaparte's bulletins.

Four divisions of infantry in small columns, and one division in a single column, formed the first and second lines, and two divisions the reserve. The right wing was commanded by Lieutenant. General Toutschkoff, the centre by Lieutenant General Zachen, the left wing by Lieutenant General Count Ostreman, the cavalry by

Lieutenant General Prince Gallitzin, and the artillery by General Korfe. The whole advanced guards by Prince Bragration.

The cavalry protected both flanks, and was partially distributed in the second alignment.

The rearguard had orders to act according to circumstances; and having suffered so heavily, it was proposed finally to relieve it and draw it into the position, for which purpose the division had originally been sent into the town of Preuss Eylau-to cover its retreat.

The enemy, on their arrival in front of Preuss Eylau, had taken up a position nearly parallel, but on ground that domineered the Russian position completely, so as to expose the minutest object to their fire, whilst the intervals between the elevations afforded shelter to their troops and a concealment of their movements and force. There Bonaparte posted the corps of Soult on the right, Augereau on the left, and the guards and the cavalry under Murat, whilst Davoust manoeuvred on his right to turn the Russian left, and Ney on his arrival was to form on Augereau's left: the total force, exclusive of Bernadotte's, which did not arrive until two days afterwards, certainly could not be less than 90,000 men.

The unoccupied space between the armies was open and flat, intersected by lakes, passable on the frozen surface, in every direction.

About ten o'clock, the firing being diminished, and almost confined to the sentries, General Bennigsen withdrew to a house situated about three quarters of a mile in rear of his position, where he had directed the general officers to assemble for their orders; but he had not arrived half an hour when the wounded General Barclay de Tolloy was brought in, and almost immediately afterwards an officer arrived with the intelligence that the Russian division stationed in the town of Preuss Eylau had also withdrawn when their commander had been removed, and that the enemy, having possession of the town, had thrown out their sentries within half musket shot of the Russian batteries. The general immediately directed that division, reinforced by one regiment, to take post between the town and his position, to cover his alignment from surprise or insult; and apprehending that an attempt might be made at day-break to pierce his centre from Preuss Eylau, directed, in a very perspicuous order, two divisions to be formed in columns of reserve behind his centre, and a third behind his left wing, and a brigade from the right to fill up the interval winch was occasioned in the line by withdrawing one of the divisions for a division of reserve. The Prussians, momentarily expected, were directed to occupy the ground on the right, which the Russians by this movement weakened.. But notwithstanding the active superintendence of the general himself, this change could not be completed, on account of the darkness of the night, before day break; and after that the fire of cannon and musketry had commenced from the Russian batteries and the French and Russian tirailleurs in front of Preuss Eylau, and large vacancies continued in the alignment even until an hour after light.

Perhaps no night was ever more awful, no occasion ever excited an higher interest. The approximation—The contact of the adverse armies—The importance of their character and objects—The fortunes that awaited their achievements—The events that depended on them—The presence of 150,000 men undaunted at the aspect of battle's terrific preparations, but impatient for mutual slaughter—The wintry wildness of the scene, faintly cheered by the partial fires, on whose blaze the darkness of the storm rested, and whose flames, chilled by impenetrable icy beds, but exposed to view the shivering groups extended around—Knowledge of the Russian sufferance—Commiseration of their helpless distress—Admiration of their heroism—Anxiety for, their fate, kept unclosed the wearied eye, and oppressed the mind with variety and weight of thought: but at earliest dawn, when the firing of small arms commenced, universal joyous confidence dispelled all other cares but that of rendering the contest most destructive to the enemy.

Soon after day-break the Russian cannon opened, and played very heavily, but rather at hazard, as the French, columns were principally concealed by the favouring swells of their ground and the town and suburbs of Preuss Eylau. The French cannon quickly replied with vigor and effect, as every man of the Russian army was exposed from head to heel.

About half an hour after the cannonade began, the French made an advanced movement with their left in column, supported by a strong body of cavalry, to turn the Russian right, and another strong column passed out of the town of Preuss Eylau by the church, with the intention of storming the centre, whilst 150 pieces of cannon covered their approach, and 40 pieces of the Imperial Guard played upon the centre Russian lottery. These troops had not advanced above three hundred yards, repelling the Russian tirailleurs, when the Russian cannon shot, admirably directed, ploughed through the mass, and so shattered their order, that after a minute's pause they inclined for shelter behind a detached house, but, being still exposed, they rushed back in the wildest disorder to the town; whilst the other columns and the cavalry, also oppressed with bullets and grape, broke and fled, pursued by the Russian cavalry and light infantry, who again dislodged the enemy from the village and avenue of trees which they had sought to occupy the preceding evening.

The French, repulsed in their first assaults, maintained a very heavy fire of artillery from their heights and the salient points of the town, and as the whole Russian army was still exposed to their observation and fire, with much effect, as to the destruction of men.

Some time afterwards, several French columns attempted to carry the village of Serpallen in front of the Russian left, and in advance of which village there had been, from day-break, a, sharp fire of musketry; but General Baggavoute, who was stationed there, having received a reinforcement of two regiments of cavalry, attacked the enemy and drove them with great loss back upon the wood which bordered the right of the French position. Animated by this success, and further reinforced by the cavalry, the Russians charged various detached columns of communication with the completest success, and took several eagles, so that the enemy was obliged to reassemble his forces towards his own centre. The village of Serpallen had however been set in flames during the contest.

Heavy snow storms obscuring the atmosphere, and driving with great violence in the faces of the Russians, had hitherto favoured the approaches of the enemy, and a very heavy storm falling about mid-day, presented an occasion which the enemy did not omit to use, or the Russians to prepare against. When the darkness was clearing, six columns of the enemy, including the French guards, and supported by the cavalry and a numerous artillery, were discovered close upon the first line of the Russians. At that instant General Bennigsen galloped forward with his staff, directed the reserves to advance, and marched down to meet the enemy, whilst his exulting troops shouted acclaiming peals of victory.

The brave Russians, (it is difficult to refrain from enthusiastic expressions of praise when their conduct at this awful moment is recollected) inclining inwards, eagerly pressed on, indifferent to the shower of balls that plunged through their ranks, and uniting with the first line, the whole charged home upon the enemy, who, panic-struck by this unexpected attack, instantly gave way, abandoning their cannon and several eagles, and pursued, when the army ceased to advance, by the musketry lire of one of the deploying columns, and the artillery of all the butteries.

The efforts of the French cavalry had been equally unsuccessful; the Russian cavalry overwhelmed them, pursued them to the French batteries, took two eagles and twenty cannon from the fugitive infantry rallying upon their heights, and extended the almost unparalleled carnage to their very reserves.

A regiment of French cuirassiers had, during the storm, gained an interval in the Russian line between their centre and left wing; but the Cossacks and some hussars, immediately as they were perceived, bore down upon them. The cuirassiers, apparently like men stupefied by the magnitude of their own enterprise, and unprepared for success, rushed with a considerable detour, through the rear of the camp, and then turned towards the right of the Russian right wing, but their bodies successively tracked the course, and only eighteen escaped alive.

The Russian army, which had now advanced several hundred paces, was, if possible, more than ever exposed; but the columns remained as a rampart to be battered down, thus proving the superiority of their active and passive courage over an enemy who only advanced with a faltering step to be destroyed, or retired behind the cover that his position offered for shelter.

The enemy's attack having been thus completely baffled, measures were taking to secure the victory on General Lestocq's arrival, who was momentarily expected to appear, as officers had come from him, and orders had been sent for, him to expedite his march, when a French corps was observed advancing from a wood to turn the Russian left; and almost immediately a very severe fire was directed upon the Russians, who endeavoured to maintain Serpallen, but notwithstanding their gallantry and perseverance, were obliged to abandon it. Two regiments were then sent to extend the Russian left to Sausgarten, but the French advanced with such impetuosity that they rapidly gained ground towards the rear of the Russian army, and as another body of the enemy, Davoust's, was seen advancing upon the right of the corps which was hitherto turning their position, the left wing and the greater part of the centre was thrown back almost at right angles with the right wing. In the circumstances under which this movement was executed, disorder could scarcely be avoided, and the enemy reached the farmhouse behind the centre of the position, which had been General Bennigsen's head-quarters on the previous evening, whilst their artillery, posted on favourable eminences, played with great execution throughout the field.

Never was a change more sudden. The victors were yielding the field to the vanquished, and surprise and alarm were rapidly displacing confidence and paralysing exertion.

But whilst anxiety was at its height, and a supporting movement of the enemy from Preuss Eylau was apprehended, as one division alone remained in the Russian right wing,—at that critical moment, General Lestocq, (whose approach had been so long announced, and whose arrival had been so long earnestly expected, but who had to perform his march pressed by Marshal Ney's corps) entered the field by the village of Althoff, where a battalion of grenadiers and some Cossacks were left to check the progress of Marshal Ney—proceeded uninterrupted by the left of the enemy's army, to which his right flank was exposed—passed the Russian right—rapidly moved, in three columns, along the open tract in its rear, and advanced upon the village of Kutschitten, already occupied by the enemy.

After an able disposition for the attack of the village and the prevention of succour, the two columns destined for the assault, and supported by a battalion of grenadiers, impetuously rushed forwards, and were met by the enemy at the extremity of the village, but the greater part of the French were instantaneously put to death with the bayonet, and the fugitives in vain endeavoured to rally on reserves in the street—every impediment was forced, and, as a last resource, they fired the village for the purpose of sheltering their flight. The precautions of General Lestocq had however environed them with destruction; the troops, directed to intercept their retreat on Lampasch, or the wood between that village and Anklappen, charged as they sallied out, and not one man of the whole 800 who had originally defended Kutschitten escaped: one eagle was taken; and the three Russian guns abandoned in the retreat of the Russian left wing, were recovered by the Russian regiment of Wyburg. This service being achieved, General Lestocq formed his corps in two lines, the cavalry forming the second line; and one regiment extended the left of the infantry, to keep in check the enemy's right; he then advanced in the direction of the wood between Anklappen and Lampasch, with his rear towards the captured village of Kutschitten, upon the enemy, whose advanced line had been cannonaded during the storm of Kutschitten, and driven back to the entrance of the forest. The corps of General Lestocq never fired a shot until within a few paces of the enemy, when a furious action with artillery and musketry commenced. The Prussian guns, having an advantageous position, overwhelmed the fire of the French cannon, and, at the same time, occasioned their troops an unremitting heavy loss; and the Prussian infantry being at length less exposed than the enemy, in consequence of some broken ground, their fire occasioned such a carnage, that, notwithstanding the treble superiority, at least, of the French, the enemy were compelled, after half an hour's combat, to yield the ground, and abandon between 3000 and 4000 killed or wounded. The Prussians, who had, till that moment, remained in the most regular alignment, now advanced forwards to close upon the enemy, and chased them through the forest towards Sausgarten, until night arrested their victorious career. Thus was Marshal Bernadotte beaten by 5580 men, and the battle decided by that corps which the 65th Bulletin had already announced as entirely ruined.

The Russian left had also rallied, under the protection of the flying artillery judiciously posted, and the columns being formed, re-advanced, drove the enemy back as rapidly as he had proceeded, recovered the farm house, expelled him from the wood, and by a bold attack of cavalry, which destroyed an entire column, dispersed them in the greatest disorder.

Night had now closed in darkly, and only an occasional shot or shell was fired from the heights above Eylau; but as Marshal Ney had driven the Prussian battalion and the Cossacks from Althoff, (from whence they had retired with the most gallant and skilful conduct, so as to unite with the Russian right) and had occupied Schloditten, which post menaced the communication with Koenigsberg, General Bennigsen ordered a division under General Kaminskoy to storm it, which order was executed about ten at night, with irresistible ardour, and the huzzas of the charging troops being heard at Preuss Eylau, the enemy supposed that a general attack would be renewed, for which Bonaparte found his army so little prepared, that he sent off his heavy artillery, baggage, &c. to Landsberg, ordered Davoust to join him, and withdrew his troops back upon the heights immediately in front of the woods, where he with difficulty reassembled the wreck of his shattered and dispirited army, and awaited information of the Russian movements.[9]

About eleven o'clock, the Russian generals assembled (still on horseback) when General Bennigsen informed the circle that he had determined, notwithstanding his success, to fall back upon Koenigsberg, for he had no bread to give the troops, and their ammunition was expended; but by a position in the neighbourhood of such a city his army would be certain of every necessary supply and be assured the means of re-equipping itself so as to appear again in the field before the enemy could repair his losses.

All the Russian generals entreated General Bennigsen to keep the field, and not render nugatory a victory so dearly bought. They assured him that the enemy was in retreat; that his own army was ready to advance at the moment; and General Knoring and General Tolstoy (the quarter master general, and second in command) offered to move forward and attack whatever troops Bonaparte might have rallied, and thus complete the victory; and at all events they pledged their lives that if he but remained on his ground, the enemy would retire altogether. General Lestocq also urged the same arguments; but General Bennigsen thought it his duty not to incur the hazard of a reinforcement of fresh troops enabling the enemy to cut off his communications with Koenigsberg. He found the privations of his army now pressing heavy on their physical powers. He knew his own loss was not less than 20,000 men, and

---

9. Bonaparte asserts that he repelled the Russian attack on Schloditten; but Schloditten was nevertheless acquired, as stated above, and the Russians afterwards retreated through it.

he was not then aware of the full extent of the enemy's disorganization and loss, which was afterwards proved to exceed 40,000 men, including 10,000 who had quitted their colours under the pretence of escorting wounded, &c. and who did not return for many days; he therefore persevered in his original determination, directed the order of march, and after, thirty-six hours passed on horseback, without any food, and being almost exhausted, placed himself in a house filled with several hundreds of dead and dying, to obtain an hour's repose amidst the groans and shrieks of the wretched sufferers.

During the suspension of movements, a few moments were afforded to contemplate the field of battle, and never did a more terrible spectacle present itself. Fifty thousand brave men since sunrise killed and wounded, and a great part, being struck by cannon shot, exposed still on the ground without the means, without the hopes, of succour. Near fifty thousand heroes, still gallant in spirit, but worn out by fatigue and exhausted by hunger,[10] unable to keep the field which their valour had won, and about to abandon their mangled comrades, who were imploring their assistance and protection.

About midnight the army commenced its movements. The division of Count Ostreman, from some error respecting his order to retreat, did not move from his ground until nine o'clock in the morning, when he quietly traversed the field of battle immediately in front of Eylau, from right to left of the enemy's position, without being fired upon by a single musket, and continued his march uninterrupted. The Russian head quarters were fixed three leagues in front of Koenigsberg, where they continued until the third day, when General Bennigsen transferred them into the city, and withdrew his army from Mullhausen to Altenburg, whilst General Lestocq had direction to cover the Pregel and Aller at Friedland, to which he passed by the wood of Domnau, through Lampasch, without any interruption from the enemy.

On the 10th of February the French reconnoitred the Russian advanced posts with twelve regiments of cavalry under Murat;

---

10. The Prussians had provisions; but the Russians had no other sustenance than the frozen snow. Their wants had induced numbers during the battle to search for food in the adjoining villages, and the plain was covered by foraging parties passing and repassing.

but the Russian cavalry opposed them, and they fell back and took post in the neighbourhood. The Cossacks, being reinforced, resumed the offensive, commencing by an attack on the seventh regiment of chasseurs a, cheval, of which they killed 200 and made 3 officers and 50 privates prisoners. On the 14th of February, being supported by some hussars, they attacked six regiments under General Milhaud at Buckersdorff, killed 400 and brought in 288 prisoners. On the 15th, General Llambert fell upon the enemy's cavalry at Mahnsfield and Wormsdof, and completely dispersed it with the loss of two eagles, several hundred killed, and 400 prisoners. Of one regiment, the 17th chasseurs, not a man escaped except the colonel. Elated with these successes, the Cossacks and hussars allowed the enemy no repose by night or day; and between the 10th and 18th deposited in the prisons and hospitals of Koenigsberg a great number of officers, and 1500 of the French cavalry, mostly wounded by pikes; and certainly the slain could not be less; for there was so little disposition to make prisoners, that the Emperor afterwards directed a ducat to be issued for every captive. On the 13th, General Bertram had appeared at the Russian advanced posts, with a request for permission to go to the King at Memel, which, after some hesitation, was granted, and soon afterwards a proposition came from the French general in command of the advanced guard for an armistice, which was peremptorily refused.[11] General Bertram, on the 18th, after an unsuccessful mission, returned through Koenigsberg, and in passing entreated General Bennigsen to make some arrangement for mutual repose after so rude a campaign.

Bonaparte, finding that his cavalry was unable to cover his army, and that its daily loss was most serious; apprehensive of more daring enterprises, as the Russian army was reinforcing; baffled in his expectation that General Bennigsen would withdraw behind the Pregel, which he so presumptuously declared and unblushingly asserted in his 59th bulletin, dated the 14th of February, and again in

---

11. In General Bennigsen's letter to the King of Prussia, in which he announced the arrival of General Bertram, he wrote—"I will presume to observe, Sir, that it is not a moment to listen to an armistice, and the proposition alone serving as a proof of the state of weakness to which the enemy's army is reduced, is a sufficient reason in itself to decline it." Koenigsberg, 15th February.

the 60th, dated the 17th; unable even to obtain an armistice, and repulsed in his offer of peace,[12] finally resolved, notwithstanding he had been joined by Marshal Bernadotte's corps, to retire upon the Vistula; and on the 19th Preuss Eylau was evacuated by his troops, but the houses remained filled with French and Russian wounded, and above 200 French tumbrels and carriages tracked the enemy's route to Landsberg.[50] In Landsberg were also abandoned 760 French, and a number of French officers, whilst above twenty pieces of cannon were found, under the direction of the peasants, in the lakes about Eylau, which the enemy, from the want of horses to remove, had forced through the ice to conceal. Although the soldiery and peasantry had, since the battle, been continually employed in burying the dead, the ground was still covered with human carcases, and parts of the roads towards Landsberg were literally paved with frozen and encrusted bodies, which the returning cannon wheels had rather splintered than lacerated.

The French left 650 of their own wounded, and 150 Russians, under the care of two surgeons, but without instruments or means of dressing, without provisions, and with dead bodies intermingled in almost every room. In a wretched chamber, full of wounded officers, lay in one corner a French captain who had lost his leg; his countenance, although pallid, still retained an animated expression, as the vivacity of his mind was not subdued by pain, by want, or by the prospect around him. He remarked as a philosopher, jested as a wit, and was polite as a courtier. His courage was the admiration and support of his companions; his spirits their consolation and delight. On seeing some strangers, he said a mouthful of bread and a glass of wine would save his life; the surgeon, who was present, answered, *vous ne creverez jamais, vous avez trop de coeur:*—You will never die, you have too much heart. This brave man had been struck by a cannon shot in the battle of Eylau, and borne off the field by two men of his company. When he was put in the wagon be ordered the soldiers to return to their post and not accompany him.

12. General Bertram proposed a separate peace with Prussia, and offered, in such case, the restitution of all conquests as far as the Elbe; and on this being rejected, he signified that Bonaparte would, from regard to the King, perhaps reinstate him in full possession, if he would separate from Russia, but the King refused to treat except for a general peace.

When the surgeon came, he himself, with a pair of scissors, cut off the leg that was still connected by some flesh to his body, and then remarked, "now this embarrassment is removed, see, my friend, if what remains merits your care, or only wastes your attention." Not one expression of regret, on his own account, escaped him; he only lamented the disaster that had befallen the French army.

The burgomaster of Landsberg declared that 10,000 wounded had passed through his town; that General Desjeardines had been buried there, and that the night of the battle, the heavy artillery and baggage returned with numbers of men with and without arms, and had marched two leagues on the road towards Warsaw when the order on the 9th recalled it. At Güttstadt, Heilsburg, Liebstadt, and indeed every town and village, the French left great numbers of their unburied dead and wounded. Of the 14th regiment of the line, in Augereau's corps, 60 Officers, and 1500 men, had been killed or wounded.

Such had been the head quarters of Bonaparte for ten days; such the achievement of the victorious army!—whilst the *defeated* Russian general, at the distance of a few miles, was stationed in the *open* but important city of Koenigsberg, and his wretched and conquered troops were banqueting and invigorating with redundancy in the circumjacent villages. Such was the fate of the Russians, which Bonaparte, in his orders to his army, thus solemnly announced: "In, two days the enemy will cease to exist, and then your fatigues will be recompensed by a luxurious and honourable repose."

To appreciate justly the battle of Preuss Eylau, and ascertain its importance and influence on the objects of the campaign, some reference must be made to the preceding situation of both armies.

Bonaparte, after the affair at Pultusk, had withdrawn his army into winter quarters, but anxious from political, military, and financial objects, to possess Koenigsberg, and not entertaining a belief that the Russian army could make a movement to check his operations, he gradually approached two corps and forced back the small Prussian corps opposed. General Bennigsen, however, having by a rapid and vigorous march disconcerted these designs, and driven back Marshals Bernadotte and Ney with considerable loss and some discredit, Bonaparte found himself obliged to break up his winter quarters and take the field. Assembling with great activity his very superior army, he marched against the Russians to *cut them off from their frontier* arid press them upon the Vistula, on which river they had no establishment but Graudenz, which was about to surrender for want of provisions, and where there was no bridge over the Vistula, whilst a corps manoeuvred on the Prussian right to envelop them with fire and distract the movements of the Russians. Accident prevented the execution of that part of his plan; but by the occupation of Heilsberg, and his incessant pressure on the Russian rearguard, Bennigsen was compelled to give battle, *without any connection with the Russian frontier, with d French corps actually between him and the Aller,* and on which river, if he was defeated, he could not throw himself, nor could he gain the Russian frontier since the enemy would have reached Wehlau before him.

Thus far Bonaparte attained his object. The Russian retreat was arrested, and victory would have assured Bonaparte the complete destruction of the Russian army, and, at least, the possession of all the country to the Memel. He fights (he gains the victory, according to his own account); but what are the results of this most sanguinary battle?—what are the advantages that he obtains? and no one will deny his ingenuity and address to profit of every propitious incident.——The maintenance of his position in the field of battle, and the occupation, on the succeeding day, of the Russian ground—A State of inaction for eight days, except with his cavalry, which is disgraced and defeated with heavy loss in every rencontre—The retreat of his army on the tenth day, after having endured the greatest distress from famine and pestilence, and the abandonment of a great part of his wounded, tumbrils, &c. Can any one believe that Bonaparte proposed to fight a bloody battle without any consequent fruits to emblazon his fame and reward his soldiery? That he, who had been accustomed to destroy whole armies in the conflict of a few hours, and possess himself of empires with the rapidity of a victor in the race, should be satisfied with retracing his steps, to leave his enemy undisturbed, and in the possession of an interesting and wealthy city, without ramparts, without any other defence than the arms which he pretended to have subdued? Will any one imagine that he had anticipated the ability of a defeated enemy to check his career, or that he would not have expelled the Russians from Koenigsberg if he had the means still at his command? The Russians fell back upon no fortress, upon no succours. Their strength was not augmented, but their position was even more exposed than at Eylau. Why did he advance his cavalry? Why keep his army ten days in their miserable camp, if his object had been achieved on the 8th of February—if he had no wish to displace the Russians?—He may indeed be correct in the subsequent statement that he did not purpose to force the Russians in this position, but the forbearance was not surely the consequence of triumph and power, any more than the demand of an armistice, or the proposals of peace offered by General Bertram exemplified his humanity and moderation as a conqueror.

On the contrary, the Russian army,—instead of being harassed by a pursuing enemy; instead of those terrible toils and privations; those desolating marches by day and night; those revolting retrograde movements which rendered security scarcely desirable,—reposed and refreshed: and the King of Prussia, instead of seeing Koenigsberg in possession of Marshals Bernadotte and Ney, found himself recognized by Bonaparte as sovereign of the conquered provinces, solicited to make peace, and his family treated with *extraordinary circumstances of respect and atonement!* General Bennigsen certainly ceded the field of battle, but it was by his own option, and contrary to the opinion of his generals. The Russian army was not driven from its ground. The chief's judgement, not the enemy's force, or new combinations, compelled that measure, and when carried into execution, no enemy molested or even insulted his march. The dead and wounded were left; but the possession of the dead and wounded is not the prize of victory in these times;[13] and if it was, Bonaparte in his retreat restored the trophies which Russian valour had merited in the field, and which it was ready to maintain. The world at large can only judge of victory or defeat by the evidence of those actually

---

13. Bonaparte would not agree to that arbitration, for he claims the victory at the battle of Asperne. He has had painted a picture of both, and they are lodged in the Imperial library, with the inscription, "Gained by the great Napoleon." Would to God that be was only to win such battles in future! The French generals said "it was not even a battle but a massacre," and Bonaparte's Mamelukes observed, "that there never were such headstrong people as the Russians: there was no moving them without knocking them down like beasts, but that they gave strong *contre coups* even with their heels as well as horns."

present, and by subsequent facts. Those facts are decisively in favour of the Russians, whose situation was improved by the battle, whereas the enemy's was in every respect, morally, politically, and militarily, deteriorated; and against these facts Bonaparte alone records his later declarations "founded on a love of simplicity and truth," and which declarations are in direct contradiction to his previous orders and proclamations.

The French had no sooner moved from Preuss Eylau, and thus evaded an attack that was preparing against them on the arrival of General Sedmorasky with 10,000 men from the army left to cover Grodno, and a reinforcement of Cossacks, than the Russian light troops pressed upon them, and, in the route of Landsberg and Liebstadt, made many hundred prisoners, captured some cannon and much booty, &c. General Sedmorasky, rapidly advancing on the route of Bartenstein and Landsberg, destroyed above 1000 men; but at Peterswalde, near Güttstadt, where there were 4000 French, a Russian general (who had arrived three days from Petersburg) having taken post with a regiment of chasseurs and lodged himself in one of the most distant houses, his piquets were surprised, and he himself taken prisoner with forty men, and the prize secured before the battalion could form. This circumstance is noted as a lesson against too much confidence: had Cossacks been at the piquet this misfortune would not have occurred.

About the same time, a more serious affair occurred to 3000 Prussians stationed at Braunsberg. General Dupont with his division, marching in two columns, forced them, after a sharp resistance, drove them from their position in front of the town, entered it, and took eight pieces of cannon, and obliged the Prussians to retire upon Heiligenbeil with the loss of 600 men; but General Lestocq, who had been at Friedland, where he had been reinforced by 2000 horse, having orders to traverse the Russian front and gain his original position on the Russian right, arrived and checked the enemy's further operations.

To counteract these partial disadvantages, General Platow pursued his successes; and intelligence arrived that General Kozen had fallen upon an enemy's escort near Willenberg and released 1500 Russians and 1200 Prussians. At the same time official accounts were received of the action at Ostrolenka, by which it appeared that

General Essen, at the head of 15,000 men, having been directed to engage the enemy's attention so as to prevent Bonaparte from drawing towards him reinforcements, marched upon Ostrolenka—20 leagues to the south-east of Liebstadt, on the left of the Narew—by both banks of the river Narew to attack the 5th corps of the French army, which had been left under the command of Generals Savary, Suchet and Campagna, and reinforced with Oudinot's division. The Russians stormed the entrenchments, killed General Campagna and 800 grenadiers; but on the advance of Generals Oudinot and Suchet, with the remainder of the corps, the Russians fell back upon the sand-hills behind the town, and each army kept up a mutual destructive cannonade, by which the Russians lost 1000 men. At night the Russians fell back, and the French remained in possession of the town three days, and then retired.

On February 22nd, an account was received of the massacre of 26 Russians and several Prussians, because their wounds prevented them from marching with the escort, and which offence the Cossacks retaliated on capturing the party; but amidst these ferocious traits, occasionally a more grateful incident mitigated the barbarity of such a war, and the following afforded universal admiration.

A Russian officer, being stationed on the banks of a river, where his party and the enemy kept firing at each other, went into a house which was close upon the river, but a French officer advancing, reproached the Russians with the cowardice of their commanding officer, who instantly left the house on hearing the insult, and approaching the French officer, requested him to stop the firing of his people, that they might decide by the sword, in the presence of both parties, who was the most courageous. The French officer assented, and was in the act of commanding his men to cease firing when a Russian's ball pierced him to the heart. The Russian officer instantly rushed forward, and cried out to the French soldiers, "My life shall make reparation for this accident; let three marksmen fire at me as I stand here;" and then turning to his own soldiers, he ordered them "to cease firing upon the French, whatever might be his fate, unless they attempted to cross the river." Already a Frenchman had levelled his piece, when the French subaltern struck it down with his sword, and running to the Russian, took him by the hand, declaring that no man worthy the name of a Frenchman would be executioner of so brave a soldier. The French soldiers felt the justice of the sentiment, and confirmed the feeling by a general acclamation.

On the 29th of February, the head-quarters of the Russian army had reached Heilsberg, from whence the enemy, having been driven with loss, had fallen back upon the Parsarge.

Marshal Bernadotte was cantoned at Holland and Braunsberg. Marshal Soult at Liebstadt and Mohrungen. Marshal Ney in advance of the Parsarge. Marshal Davoust at Allenstein, Hohenstein and Deppen.

The main body of the cavalry in the country about Elbing, and the head-quarters at Osterode.

The Poles were at Neidenburg, and the 5th corps, which Massena now commanded, was cantoned upon the Omulew. The corps of Marshal Lefebre was before Dantzic.

A Bavarian division at Warsaw, and the 8th corps in Swedish Pomerania.

These corps were extremely weak[14] and, in addition to casualties of the field, sickness was so prevalent, that in Warsaw alone there were 25,000 men in the French hospitals, and the French cavalry were entirely unfit for active service.

To repair these losses Bonaparte raised the siege of Colberg, nearly evacuated Silesia—Jerome Bonaparte remained in Silesia with merely a sufficient force for the garrisons; ordered under the severest penalties a new levy in Switzerland; marched troops from Dalmatia, Calabria, Italy, and the very invalids of Paris to recruit his army in Poland; and, in a message to the Senate, dated Osterode, the 10th of March, demanded a new conscription,[15] of the year 1808, which, of course, was granted—he then determined to

---

14. Bernadotte's corps was not at Eylau, and Ney's corps had not suffered much in that action, but they were greatly reduced by the previous operations.
15. Although he had admitted 1900 killed, and 5100 wounded, in the battle of Eylau, General Clarke, in his report to the Emperor, on which the proposal to the Senate was founded, states, "The consumption of sickness in an army so considerable; the losses in the field of battle at Sehlieg; at Saalfeld; on the Day of Jena; at the combats of Prenzlow, Lubeck; at the affairs of Pultusk and Golymin; at the combats of Bergfried and Hoff, at the battle of Eylau; the brave men who are dead in consequence of their wounds, or who are returned to the depots to be invalided; have caused a diminution of 14,000 men to the French armies."

check, by daring countenance, and partial aggressions, the advance of the Russians, and to recover the moral of his army by the active character of his operations.

By this time he had also discovered that he had advanced from the Vistula with too great temerity, and that the port and fortress of Dantzic offered to his enemies a *débouchure* on his rear, which might, under a vigorous direction, separate him from France, or oblige a retrograde movement to preserve his bridges[16] and a passage over the Vistula, which would be ruinous to his army, if not as fatal to himself. This reasoning was suggested during the siege of Dantzic, when small detachments were sending there, and if General Bennigsen had carried 60,000 men to Dantzic, he would instantly have removed the war to the left bank of the Vistula; for Bonaparte would not have ventured to proceed against Russia, and he had not force to resist the combined Russian and Prussian armies, which would have been 80,000 strong, and keep in check the 50,000 Russians and Prussians which would have been left on the right bank of the Vistula. He had but a choice of evils, but evil must have followed either decision. There was no risk in the execution of such an operation, and it must be recollected that boldness in war is almost always prudence.

He therefore gradually approached Dantzic with his Polish, Saxon, and Baden levies, and after several affairs, drove the Prussians into the city, which was defended by 16,000 men and two Russian garrison battalions under Prince Tcherbatoff with some Cossacks.

Consonant with this plan, he directed his Marshals to make strong reconnaissances to distract the Russian general and recall his parties, who had already reached Allenstein, Ortelsburg, Willenberg, and Passenheim, and on the 3rd of February the French reoccupied Allenstein and Güttstadt, and a considerable corps from Wormditt attempted to carry a Russian post between Wormsdof and Arensdorf, but here the enemy were foiled with great loss, as a masked battery suffered them to approach close, and then poured rapid discharges of grape.

This movement occasioned a general concentration of the

16. He was then building two additional bridges at Marienwerder and Dirschau, but no strong town covered these or any of his former bridges at Prague, Sierock, Modlin, or Thorn.

Russian army[17] and the renewal of the campaign was expected; especially on the following morning, when an heavy cannonade commenced at Zechern, two leagues in front of Heilsberg, occasioned by the advance of a French corps who had pushed across the plain from the village, and lodged themselves in a deep wood, from whence they had annoyed the Russian advanced posts.

Fire attracted fire, and a serious action appeared probable, although not premeditated by either army. At length the Russians opened their guns, which were answered from the heights of Zechern, but the Russian cannon soon silenced that battery. Still the enemy's infantry hung in the wood, and already 500 Russians were wounded. General Zachen, who commanded, determined towards evening to finish this fretting contest, and ordered two regiments to charge into the wood, and two regiments of Cossacks, headed by their Attaman, were directed to co-operate. Upon the signal being given, the Cossacks rushed forward with their war yell, echoing terror, and killed or made prisoners in a few seconds above 160 men, with the loss of only 10 killed, and 14 wounded. The remaining French escaped by some rugged ground, and as the Russians menaced the storm of Zechern, the three French regiments, and a regiment of cavalry that had sustained this affair, marched off rapidly on Güttstadt.

Accurate intelligence was obtained from the prisoners, which exposed the enemy's views, and a particular, *but private,* incident, further gave General Bennigsen every information that he sought. Whether or not the enemy were suspicious of this incident, is not known; but, on the 6th, the French expecting to be attacked, drew out their forces along their line, and by this demonstration of vigilance, preserved themselves from an attack that was projected for the following day.

On the 7th, in the evening, the Cossacks sent in an adjutant of Marshal Ney, taken with a letter to the Emperor, in which the Marshal stated his loss at Zechern as 400 men, and added that he should wait at Guttstadt an order to retreat altogether, or an assurance of reinforcements; one alternative being necessary.

---

17. General Lestocq was brought to Muhlsack.—Although he had been opposed in his cantonments near Braunsberg to 24,000 men, and had been separated 60 miles from the Russian right, the enemy was never able to gain any advantage over his able dispositions and activity.

On the 8th the Cossacks sent in two officers and 64 privates, taken near Peterswalde, and from Ortelsburg 200 more prisoners, with advice that they had recovered from a French patrol two Russian quarter-masters and twenty men, who had, by mistake, gone into Allenstein, which belonged to the enemy's cantonments. On the same day, General Bertram came to the advanced posts and demanded to meet a General Officer, which was refused. Another officer came on the 9th to General Platow, and demanded an armistice between the advanced posts, and permission to bury the dead which remained on the plain of Zechern. General Platow answered, that the "weather being cold, there was no danger of any inconvenience from their want of interment, and that he should give himself no thought, about their obsequies, but he warned off, in future, all such frivolous messengers, unless they wished to increase the number of the unburied."

The Russian reinforcements had now began to arrive; amongst them was a superb regiment of Cuirassiers, the Catherina Slaber, (Catherina's Glory) commanded by General Kratow, and two Cossack regiments, whose sumptuous wildness was novel and interesting; and General Bennigsen having abandoned his plan of attack, removed his head-quarters to Bartenstein for the convenience of his arrangements.

To cover his cantonments from insult, Bonaparte threw forward, on the side of Willenberg, 15,000 Poles, and placed them under the orders of Massena; these, being new levies, did not add greatly to his real force, or inspire much respect among the Russians; but General Platow was directed to proceed on that side with three thousand Cossacks, and act against them.

In the mean time, the siege of Dantzic continued, and the enemy being lodged on the Nehrung, all communication by the coast-road, between Pillau and Dantzic, was cut off; but an attempt was made to surprise and force the enemy's posts stationed there, which failed. The attacking corps was therefore obliged to return to Pillau, with some trifling loss to the Prussian advanced guard.

On the 12th, Murat was checked in his advance with seven regiments of cavalry, on Bischoffstein, and General Zachen, in the neighbourhood of Wormditt, killed 100 dragoons, and sent in 200, of whom the greater part were severely wounded.

On the 18th General Platow broke in upon the enemy's line of posts between Passenheim and Willenberg, made 300 Polish cavalry, with seven officers, prisoners, after a great slaughter of their corps; and, having induced the 10th and 22nd Trench regiments of cavalry to charge in pursuit through a wood where he had ambuscaded half his Cossacks, he put to death, or captured the whole. In one regiment the colonel, who was a relative of Bonaparte, was killed; and a nephew of Josephine died the next day of his wounds. In the other, Marbeuf, a son of the governor of Corsica, and a *protégé* of Bonaparte, was taken.

On the 24th, the enterprising and active Platowagain marched from Passenheim to attack the confederates at Kutzen, Malga, and Omilow.The column directed on Kutzen being wilfully misled, the guide was executed and the two guides of the other columns were afterwards executed by the French. The second column advanced at dawn against three squadrons posted in the village of Malga, and drove them upon six supporting squadrons, when the whole fell back upon the woods of Wallendorf where the Polish infantry was stationed.The Cossacks then feigned to fly. The Polish cavalry pursued over the plain : when sufficiently forward; the Cossacks turned, charged, killed 300, and made the colonel, lieutenant-colonel, and 200 privates, prisoners.—At Omilow the Polish infantry lined the woods and kept the Cossacks in check, but a distinguished Cossack colonel (Karpow) thought that an opportunity presented itself for the attack of some infantry in a more open space. As he was advancing, the infantry formed a hollow square—his Cossacks hesitated: he, however, alone rushed forward, pierced, passed through, and was returning, cheering on his Cossacks, when a musket-ball struck him dead. Platow reproached his party at the funeral for not having revenged his death and devoted themselves to sacrifice the enemy; and when he kissed the forehead, (according to custom,) previous to the lid of the coffin being closed, he could not refrain from tears: wiping them away, he observed, "that he did not weep for the lot of mortality, but that friends could not go together out of the world."

It appears that General Zyoncheck, the commander of the Poles, had proposed to attack the Cossacks at Passenheim with 3000 infantry, 8 pieces of cannon, and 15 squadrons of cavalry, and that they were actually on march for that purpose when the fortuitous enterprise of the Attaman discomfited their design; but, on the 26th, the 300 Cossacks stationed at Ortelsburg, were driven out of that town. As that post was of great importance, being in the line of communication between General Essen's right wing at Ostrolenka and General Bennigsen; General Tchapliz, with his regiment of hussars, six guns, and 300 Cossacks, immediately advanced upon it, and, by a most able disposition and gallant bearing, compelled 2000 Polish infantry, with four guns, 800 French cavalry, and 300 Polish cavalry, to retire, with the loss of 50 killed, and some prisoners, which the peasants murdered in revenge for outrages committed by the corps during the night.

On the 29th the French again presented themselves in front of Peterswalde with two strong columns, and demanded possession of the village; but, on Prince Bragration answering that "he was there to give them welcome," they retired without firing a shot.

On the 31st General Bennigsen went to Heilsberg to examine a position which he was desirous to occupy, but, on the 2nd of April, returned to Bartenstein.

In the beginning of April the French made an assault on Graudenz, but were repulsed with great loss. It was said that the governor gave the enemy reason to suppose that he embraced a dishonourable offer made to him, and then suffered the columns to approach close to his works before he inflicted punishment.

General Platow continued to send in prisoners, and interrupt the foraging parties of the enemy, whilst he maintained, notwithstanding frequent attacks, the post of Ortelsburg. On requiring succours, he was reinforced by a regiment of dragoons, one of hussars, two battalions of infantry, and two of chasseurs.

On the 17th the Emperor and the King of Prussia arrived at Bartenstein, and on the 22nd they inspected the advanced guard of Prince Bragration, in front of Heilsberg, which was found in admirable order, and the huts, &c. arranged with an elegance that was quite unexpected. Their Majesties then advanced with three or four persons, and closely reconnoitered the enemy's posts, after which they returned to Heilsberg, where troops daily arrived from Russia, and amongst them the corps of guards under the Grand Duke Constantine, at the head of which, as the regiments successively entered, the Emperor always marched through the town.

The siege of Dantzic continued to be vigorously pressed: The Holme island, at the back of the city, on which the two Russian battalions were lodged had been carried with the loss of 400 men on their part. As the occupation of this island by the enemy completed the investment of the city, exposed every part to a bombardment, and intercepted all its communications with the Fair Wasser, and Weichselmunde, (where there are two forts at the mouth of the Vistula, about four miles from Dantzic), great anxiety prevailed for the place, then wanting ammunition, and having only a garrison of inferior description, being chiefly recruits raised in the Polish provinces occupied by the enemy; and as the place itself, notwithstanding Bonaparte's bulletins in compliment to Marshal Lefebre, can scarcely be rated in the second order of fortresses.

General Kaminskoy, on the 7th of May, was therefore ordered, with 6000 men, ta embark at Pillau, and proceed to the Fair Wasser, under convoy of the Falcon British sloop of war, and a Swedish ship of the line:—To favour this operation, General Tutchikow, who had replaced General Essen, was ordered to attract the enemy's attention, by demonstration of building bridges on the Narew and the Bug, and partial attacks; and the Emperor and the King, after reviewing the grand army on the 14th of May, proposed an attack on Marshal Ney's corps at Güttstadt.

The head of the column formed in the woods had already reached the *debouchure* on the plain in front of Peterswalde, where the Sovereigns and Commander in Chief rode on to reconnoitre. In about two hours the army received orders to retire into their cantonments, but the enemy alarmed, did not dismiss his troops for 36 hours.

Accounts were received from General Tutchikow, stating, that in conformity to his instructions, he had attacked the enemy by a corps under the command of General Wickenstein; that the General had passed the Narew on the 13th, and taken two pieces of cannon, several French officers and 60 men: and General Platow reported, that he had, on the 12th, with the same motive, attacked the Poles at Malga, killed several, and made three officers and 100 men prisoners; and that from thence to favour the attack on Guttstadt, he had on the 13th driven the enemy's posts into Allenstein, and cannonaded the town for the whole day. In the subsequent forward movements a great many bodies thrown into the Aller on this occasion, were found choking the bridges. Further advices from General Tutchikow stated, that the enemy having passed the Narew at Shiroz with several divisions of French and Bavarian troops, and some Polish horse, were immediately repulsed with the loss of several hundred killed, and three officers and 107 prisoners; and that another column which had passed the Narew in front of Pultusk had retired on the approach of General Tutchikow.

On the 15th of May General Kaminskoy made his attempt to enter Dantzic. The absence of the Swedish man of war, which had on board 1,200 of his men, had delayed his enterprise, and afforded time for Bonaparte to reinforce Marshal Lefebre by the bridge of Marienwerder, with more troops under Marshal Lasnes, amongst which was Oudinot's division.

The Russians, 4,400 strong, having to defile over the narrow bridge on the Vistula, which communicated to the Nehrung, were not ready to advance until two hours after day-break, when they moved forward in three columns, under an heavy cannonade, which immediately opened from the Holme island.

The columns, with the most daring resolution, entered the wood, and stormed the enemy's treble line of entrenchment, defended by Saxons, Poles and French, of whom they killed many, and took several pieces of cannon—they then advanced, but their order of formation being broken by the trees, they presented themselves on the plain at the extremity of the wood in disorder.

Here they were attacked by a very considerable body of troops, every moment reinforced from the left bank of the Vistula, when Marshal Lasnes found the point of attack was confined to the right bank. Unable to resist such a superiority, the Russians fell back, pressed by a large body of cavalry.—Rallying at the wood, they a second time attempted to advance, but after some success were again driven back, and the enemy entered the wood. A third time, impelled by desperation, they pushed on with the bayonet, and cleared the wood, killing many of the grenadiers; but a tremendous cannonade then beat them back, nor had they a gun to sustain them, and unfortunately all the zealous exertions of the British naval officers and crews of the vessels destined to co-operate were ineffectual, as the want of wind prevented their advance against the stream.

General Kaminskoy finding the force of the enemy so enormously superior, and their position impenetrable, ordered at eight o'clock his troops to retire, which movement was executed back to the range of the guns from Weichselmunde, without any loss, but the Russian soldiers with great reluctance quitted the works which they had so gallantly carried.

The loss of the Russians in killed and wounded was 45 officers, and 1,600 men, whilst the enemy stated their own to be but 25 killed, and 200 wounded. A whole Saxon battalion, (independent of the loss sustained by Oudinot's division, the French light infantry, Poles, &c.) had, however, been destroyed without mercy, and the French official report of the affair characterizes it as most daring on the part of the Russians,—for some time successful, and to the last, obstinate. This was afterwards regretted, as it would have surrendered; but the Russians, enraged at their own loss, fought with the greatest, ferocity on this occasion.

The British flotilla[18] had been unable to co-operate in the action; yet the laborious exertions; the ardent zeal, the affectionate interest with which they had toiled, and which now assured the relief and comfort of the wounded, were not only dwelt upon by the Russian officers and soldiers as honourable to the individuals and the British nation, but as a splendid and grateful proof of national attachment and sincerity in the common cause.

Whilst General Kaminskoy was endeavouring to advance by the Vistula, 2000 Prussians moved along the Nehrung from Pillau. They proceeded as far as Karlsberg, but here pausing in consequence of some intelligence, they were attacked by a considerable body of the enemy's infantry, and a brigade of dragoons, and routed with the loss of 600 men, two guns, and two vessels with provisions at anchor. A reserve on the narrow part of the Nehrung preserved the remainder, and it was fortunate for them that they had not pushed on beyond Karlsberg, as the enemy had prepared to cut off their retreat by crossing the Frisch Haff with a considerable force, and lodging it at that post.—Thus terminated this impracticable expedition.

---

18. The officers were Captains Strachey, Cheatham, and Saunders, commanding the *Valorous*, *Sally* and *Charles*, armed vessels—and Lieutenant-Colonel Bathurst, who was with General Kaminskoy, also particularly distinguished himself in the affair.

General Kalkreuth, after General Kaminskoy's unsuccessful enterprise, having repeated by telegraph his urgent want of ammunition, an English vessel—under the command of Captain Strachey—of 22 guns, armed with 32lb. carronades, on the 18th attempted the bold project of forcing her way into Dantzic, although the Vistula is a very rapid river, and not above 60 yards broad, with a boom thrown across.—Laden with 150 barrels of powder, and' having 50 chasseurs on board, she adventured; but she had scarcely gained the Holme, when a cannon shot injured her rudder, and her rigging being materially damaged, she became unmanageable and grounded—every effort to get her off failed, and after a gallant defence against nine batteries she was compelled to surrender.

Dantzic was now reduced to the last extremity, and General Kalkreuth had protracted the defence to a most extraordinary length—52 days open trenches. He had done all that ability and devotional loyalty could effect: he had applied, he had exhausted every resource, and could entertain no hope of succour. Therefore, as the enemy were preparing to storm the Hackelsberg,[19] he proposed to capitulate, if allowed to retire with his garrison and arms, on the condition of not serving, without being regularly exchanged, for one year, against France or her allies. As Bonaparte was fearful of being attacked whilst embarrassed with this siege, these terms were granted, and on the 27th the garrison, reduced to 9000 men, marched out for Koenigsberg. Marshal Lefebre then summoned the Weichselmunde, and Fair Wasser, which being no longer of any advantage, and if once besieged, incapable of being approached so as to save the garrison, were on the 26th evacuated by the Prussians.—General Kaminskoy had previously returned with his division to the army.

Bonaparte announced the surrender of Dantzic as the first glorious result of the victory of Eylau, but that battle did not supply him the means of laying siege to Dantzic. The surrender, *according to date,* followed, but was not by any means the *consequence of operations on the 8th of February.* Had his army never been disturbed in their original cantonments, the siege might still have been formed;

---

19. Dantzic is defended by two connected hills, rising from the town, called the Hackelsberg and Bichoffsberg. These taken, the town has no defence, for they domineer at 150 yards.

and if he had really driven the Russians behind the Pregel, with far greater probability of success. In one view, however, Bonaparte is correct. The siege of Dantzic was commenced to mitigate the impression of the lost battle. *Why he was permitted to prosecute the siege without interruption, is a question which the battle of Eylau creates, but not in confirmation of Bonaparte's pretensions to the victory.*

Accounts from Graudenz diminished the gloom of these ill tidings. The garrison had made a very successful sally—taken and disarmed two German battalions, and possessed themselves of several vessels laden with corn, rice, ammunition, and money, so that hopes were entertained of its being in a condition to hold out, notwithstanding its long investment, and the threatened siege of Marshal Victor.

On the 3rd of June, notwithstanding the surrender of Dantzic had disengaged 30,000 of the enemy's troops—notwithstanding the Russian means had not been subsequently augmented, General Bennigsen proposed a plan of operations by which he hoped to cut off Marshal Ney, (without doubt still hazardously adventured) and if successful, to fall on Marshal Davoust at Allenstein.

Circumstances retarded the attack until the 5th, when the Prussians, 10,000 strong, and the Russians, 75,000 strong,[20] immediately under the command of General Bennigsen, opened the campaign against an enemy who could oppose to that force 130,000 men,[21] and who had re-collected between the Vistula and the Memel, by the most vigorous exertions that Bonaparte had ever occasion to make, (exertions unparalleled in the history of Europe,) 190,000 men, including the garrison on Dantzic, whilst his cavalry had been reinstated, almost renewed, by considerable remounts drawn from Silesia and the country about Elbing.

The Prussians, on the 5th of June, feigned a serious attack on the bridge of Spanden over the Parsage, defended by the corps of Marshal Bernadotte, and protected by a strong *tête-du-pont*. After an action that lasted the whole day, in which the Prussians showed much gallantry, they desisted, according to the original plan of combined operation. The French, in their bulletins, boast of this voluntary retreat on the part of the Russians as the defeat of a *real* enterprise.

---

20. The Russians, besides this force, had on the Narew 17,000 men under General Tolstoy, who succeeded General Tutchikow.
21. Massena had under his command 45,000 men, including 15,000 Poles.

At the same time two Russian divisions commenced an affair at the bridge of Lomitten, defended by the corps of Marshal Soult, and, according to the same arrangement, engaged the attention of the enemy during the day, but on each side several hundred men were killed and wounded.

The real attack was directed against the posts of Marshal Ney's corps, 24,000 strong, whose stations were Altkirken, Ammt, Guttstadt, and Wolsdorf, whilst General Platow with 5000 men, including the brigade of infantry under General Knoring, was directed to pass the Aller between Allenstein and Guttstadt, to alarm the rear of Marshal Ney, and keep the corps of Davoust at Allenstein in check.

Unfortunately the different columns were directed to connect operations and attend upon each other, instead of having orders to press vigorously and reach the Parsarge with all possible expedition, so as to anticipate the arrival of the enemy, who, pursued by superior forces, could not deviate to undertake any operation that might delay his retreat. In consequence of this combined movement, and prescribed mutual progress, Marshal Ney was enabled to defend himself without any uneasiness for his flanks, and it was not until two o'clock that General Gartchikow could enter Güttstadt, where he took some magazines and 300 prisoners; but even then, when Marshal Ney was driven from the Aller, he was not urged back so as to throw his lines into confusion, but he was permitted to retire gradually Until night interrupted the action, when he withdrew his main body across the Parsarge at Deppen, (about six miles distant) where there was no *tête-du-pont*, and which was completely commanded by heights on the right bank; so that if the execution had been as well achieved as the plan was projected, Marshal Ney, with all the ability and means he employed, could not have prevented the complete loss of his corps.

The French bulletins estimate their loss, in these affairs, at 800 men, without including their killed and wounded at Spanden, or mentioning General Rozer taken, and General Dutiellis wounded; but Marshal Ney lost 1200 killed and wounded, the Russians several hundred, and the enemy 2000 prisoners in the general line of operation. Marshal Bernadotte was also wounded.

Whilst Marshal Ney had been defending Güttstadt, General Platow passed the Aller near Bergfried and surprised an enemy's post of 60 men. Count Strogonau then proceeding to Rezengarte, saw the enemy's baggage retiring, and charging the escort with a very inferior force, made 30 officers and 500 men prisoners, and captured a considerable booty.

The next morning, at six o'clock, the Russian army re-advanced, and the advanced guard under Prince Bragration drove the rearguard of the enemy across the bridge, where the Russians maintained the rest of the day a close and sharp fire of musketry and cannon on the French position and the village of Deppen,, which were completely commanded by the Russian guns.[84] At six, the action ceased; when part of the town had been consumed, and the bridge too much burnt for passage. This affair cost the Russians near 500 men, and the French certainly not less, for they resisted under every disadvantage, and some prisoners were made as they fell back upon the bridge.

During this action a regiment of Cossacks had swam the Parsarge, penetrated eight miles in the rear of the enemy, attacked and cut to pieces an escort of cavalry, broke the carriage of one gun that for want of horses they could not take away, destroyed thirty baggage wagons, and brought off an howitzer which they contrived to get safe across the river and deliver into the Russian camp.

On the 7th, the Russian army was about to move on Allenstein, when the Cossacks sent advice that they were in the town, and that Marshal Davoust had abandoned it to join Marshal Ney.

Some musketry and an occasional cannonade had occurred in the morning at the bridge of Deppen, but no enterprise of consequence was attempted by either side.

On the morning of the 8th, the French drew out their troops and made demonstration as if they would attack the Russians and pass at Deppen, which occasioned for two or three hours a very severe cannonade, and a partial fire of musketry continued through the day.

About midday Bonaparte had been seen to arrive, and the shouts of his army were distinctly heard. After inspecting the divisions, various movements were made, and cavalry and guns appeared to defile towards Osterode, but being attentively observed, they were seen to quit that route under cover of a wood, and retake the road in the direction of Liebstadt.

Towards the afternoon, General Ilavoiski with some Cossacks, sent in several hundred dragoons, that he had made prisoners, after killing as many, in an attack upon three regiments of French cavalry, and in consequence of information from the prisoners General Bennigsen determined to fall back with his army upon Heilsberg, leaving Prince Bragration to cover the retreat of his left, and General Platow the right. These movements were immediately commenced, and the Cossacks traversed from the left of the line to the right; but on reaching Lingnau, at day-break of the 9th, General Ouwarrow, with a brigade of heavy cavalry, was found there checking the advance of a body of the enemy lodged in a small wood in front of Elditten, and into which wood he had the evening before driven a party of their horse, with the loss of 150 killed and wounded.

From various indications, General Ouwarrow believed that the enemy were passing the bridge of Elditten in force, and covering their operations by the shelter of the wood, on the skirts of which small detachments were only seen; but before he withdrew, according to his orders, no serious augmentation of force was visible, and as the enemy remained quiet, a small advanced party was only left, and the main body fell back about two miles to refresh their horses, as the movement upon Heilsberg was to be deferred as late as possible, that the army might not; be interrupted in march so as to produce confusion.

Bonaparte, when he had heard of the serious attack on Marshal Ney, accompanied almost immediately by intelligence of his retreat upon the Parsarge, directed his army to assemble, and with the corps of Marshals Ney, Davoust, Lasnes, the guards, Oudinot's division, and the cavalry of reserve, passed at the bridge of Elditten, whilst the other Marshals crossed at Wuhsen, Spanden, &c.

The forces under the command of Bonaparte, being formed in close column within the small wood already noticed, concealed their operations until about mid-day, when the columns advanced upon the plain (bordered with woods to the right and left) in three lines, and with flanking columns, Whilst a considerable part of the cavalry marched in front, and a part in rear of the left. Over the first two miles he experienced no resistance; but when General Platow arrived and threw forward his Cossacks, which were supported by

Prince Bragation's cavalry,[22] the Russians resumed the offensive, charged the numerous skirmishers and supporting detachments that swarmed the plain;[23] and animated by success, pressed with so much daring vigour, that the French infantry halted, rapidly formed squares, and the whole cavalry (excepting such part as was driven in) consisting of the light, brigades of Generals Pajol, Bruyères, and Durosnel, and the division of heavy cavalry of General Nansouty, at full speed, rushed to the right.[24] in which direction the Russians were advancing, whilst volleys of musketry and artillery poured upon them, but with comparative little loss, for so soon as they found the, effort of the mass no longer expedient, they broke and separated over the plain,[25] whilst Prince Bragation covered them from pursuit by his artillery, and the judicious disposition of his infantry.

The Russian rearguard had, however, now nearly approached the extremity of the level ground, from whence an inclined plain descended to the town of Guttstadt and the Aller, over which river, and an arm of it, there were two bridges in the town, on which General Platow directed his troops, and three pontoon bridges had been formed on the left of the town, for the passage of Prince Bragation's division. The greatest resolution could alone save the troops, and any disunion of movements between the rearguards would infallibly have assured destruction. The cavalry seemed sensible of the importance of their exertions at this critical conjuncture, and by gallantry and active) manoeuvre so repelled the French advanced cavalry, that after various *rencontres*, in which they were always worsted, the latter) retired and paused until their infantry approached to their support; but during this time, Prince Bragration had crossed his infantry and guns, except guards for the *tête-du-pont*, and taken up his position, to cover the retreat of the cavalry, which now successively began to withdraw.

---

22. Prince Bragration had 1500 horse and 5000 infantry; General Platow, having sent away his infantry, only 2000 Cossacks and a regiment of hussars.
23. The Leib Cossacks particularly distinguished themselves; killing the colonel of cuirassiers, many dragoons, and capturing 100 horses at one charge,
24. It was afterwards known, that they bore down there to save Bonaparte, whom they apprehended to he in danger.
25. The Cossacks have the prudence, when advanced within the range o guns too highly elevated, not to rush back, but rather to close until they find opportunity to evade the line of fire altogether.

From the direction of the river, General Platow's distance from the town was not so great as Prince Bragation's, and he was earlier driven back towards the Aller, where his Cossacks being still hard pressed, began to retire with an irregular pace, and disorder was commencing. Platow, sensible of his duty to the general safety—fearful of a rush upon the town and the bridges, which would be fatal to the fugitives from their own tumult—apprehending that the enemy would be encouraged to profit of the confusion and carry the town, whilst his troops were unable to fight or fly in choked streets; dismounted from his horse, enforced order, and with the tranquillity of parade exercises, retired his Cossacks in small bodies with large intervals; and when he found that he could, without detriment to Prince Bragration, move upon the bridges, he, with his own rearguard, leisurely gained them, and remained until the whole were destroyed by the artificers who were stationed for that purpose.

Perhaps the enemy thought the town occupied by infantry, and feared to compromise themselves by an attack, for instead of advancing boldly upon it, the cavalry halted, and only the skirmishers and some flying artillery fired upon the retiring Cossacks, until the French infantry arrived upon the heights, when deploying from columns, the lines continued for some time to fire heavy volleys, and the artillery taking position, inundated with shot and shells the town, as well as the sand hills beyond, on which the Russians had stationed artillery to cover the rearguards, and through which fire, augmented when the enemy perceived them ascending, the rear-guards had to pass. The rearguards were obliged to fall back upon Güttstadt, as the enemy, from the disposition of their passage over the Parsarge, turned their right; moreover, it was a shorter line, and the intervention of the river, when once it was passed, afforded a better shelter—at the same time General Bennigsen wished to give the enemy a notion that he had altogether evacuated the left bank of the Aller.

Prince Bragration, with that courage, conduct, and fortune which characterize all his services, had also withdrawn his troops, and destroyed his bridges without any loss but a post of 150 infantry who had been thrown on the left, and who were charged approaching the river, and of whom 50 were drowned. Thus Bonaparte, with all his genius, vigour, and prodigious superiority of power, actually marching in the same field, suffered, in his own presence, the escape of a feeble rear-guard, which must have been overwhelmed if properly pressed and acted against. An escape far more extraordinary and more reproachful to his army than that of Marshal Ney on the 5th to the Russian reputation, since Marshal Ney had twenty-four thousand men under his command, and was sustained on his left by Marshals Soult and Bernadotte, who were actually engaged with the Russians, and by Marshal Davoust on his right, whom it was necessary to watch with four thousand men.

The enemy satisfied with possession of Güttstadt, and the left bank of the Aller, did not cross any troops over the river to pursue, but continued an heavy fire, whilst the Russians remained on the opposite bank, during which cannonade the main body of the French army moved along the left bank, in the direction of Launau. Towards night Prince Bragration fell back about half way to Heilsberg, and the Cossacks took post in his front.

On the 10th, the French being now concentrated, except the first corps commanded by Victor—Bernadotte having been wounded at Spanden, which was manoeuvring on the left and composed of the corps of Marshals Ney, Lasnes, Davoust, Mortier, Oudinot's division, the Imperial Guard, and the cavalry under Murat, advanced upon Heilsberg, and drove in the advanced posts of the troops stationed to observe their approach; but as the ground from Launau, for about a league towards Heilsberg was broken by transverse lines of high ridges, the Russians retired, but gradually, under the protection of artillery posted on the elevations, and disputed each tenable station, which gave time for the arrival of Prince Bragration about mid-day with his advanced guard, and which General Bennigsen had ordered to cross the river, when he found the enemy direct their march altogether on the left bank; but the Prince had been obliged to fall back as far as Heilsberg before he could cross on the pontoon bridges, so that he reached his station on the left bank only as the enemy had gained the uneven ground, and were beginning to deploy on the plain, which extended with partial interruption of wood, on their left flank, to the position of Heilsberg.

A corps of the enemy, Marshal Soult's, formed the advance, on the right of which two divisions drawn from the supporting corps marched, whilst another division extended the left to some commanding grounds bordered by woods.

Bonaparte seemed determined to retrieve his error on the 9th, and to crush the advanced guard of the Russians by weight of fire and cavalry attacks. The Russians, driven from the broken ground, in vain endeavoured to maintain their position on the plain—They were obliged to form alternate lines to sustain by fire their retrograde movements, yet the successive retreat of each was rapid, and the loss momentarily augmented. The Russian cavalry presented good countenance, but being so outnumbered, were unable to check the enemy. Prince Bragration sent for reinforcements. Some infantry were advanced to support him, and 15 squadrons of Prussian cavalry—five squadrons Auer dragoons, five squadrons Baczho dragoons and five squadrons Uhlans—with a battery of horse artillery, by their most gallant bravery, afforded him great relief, but still the enemy, by feeding his advanced lines proceeded; and about four in the afternoon, when Prince Bragration sent for further aid, General Bennigsen ordered forward more cavalry, and directed the Prince to keep retiring, and allure the enemy under the guns of this part of his position, armed with 150 pieces of cannon, and reinforced by all his troops, except the guards and some cavalry, from the position on the right bank. About six the enemy had approached sufficiently near, when the allied cavalry withdrew by the flanks, and a cannonade of extraordinary fury commenced, which compelled the enemy to recede from the reach of grape; but they threw their left in a small wood about five hundred yards in front of the Russian centre, and establishing their batteries, played upon all parts of the Russian lines, which extended from the river to the right about half a mile, whilst as night fell, swarms of tirailleurs advanced, and maintained an incessant and close fire—misprising darkness the commonly respected friend of humanity.

About seven the French columns suddenly again moved forward, and charging rapidly, carried the advanced work of the Russian position, with three guns. It was a critical moment; but Russia had officers and troops equal to the crisis.

Prince Gartchikow, commanding the right wing, instantaneously ordered the charge. The huzzas of his troops assured victory. They darted forward, overwhelmed all opposition, captured two eagles, and pursued until they threw their right upon the wood which the enemy had occupied. Then the cannon again thundered, and the musketry rolled, illuminating the atmosphere with continued flame—gradually the combat relaxed, and the Russian lines reascended to their position.

A little before ten at night, a deserter came over to the Russians, through the fire, and informed the General that another assault was preparing from the wood. Suitable arrangements had scarcely been made, when the dark bodies of the columns were seen sweeping forward. Again the batteries opened, and the fury of the battle again raged, but the assailants unable to force their progress, fled back wrecked and almost annihilated. The action became then more feeble, and about 11 o'clock, the enemy along their line of tirailleurs, shouted *"arrêtez le combat"*—cease the action—when this grand, and peculiarly rare scene closed, and the massacre (for no other term can be so properly applied) terminated; but the cessation of the tumultuous uproar of war was followed by a more melancholy din—the groans of wounded, who anticipating the morrow's renewal of the fight, or tortured by pain, in vain implored removal, relief, and even death.

Heavy rain fell in the early part of the night, and rendered the clayey ground behind the Russian batteries so slippery that the various arrangements of the night were greatly incommoded, and the troops experienced much distress.

Before day break the Russians again stood to their arms, momentarily expecting fresh efforts on the part of the enemy.

When light broke the, French were arrayed in order of battle, but a spectacle, indescribably disgusting, more engaged attention than the hostile dispositions.

The ground between the wood and the Russian batteries, about a quarter of a mile, was a sheet of naked human bodies, which friends and foes had during the night mutually stripped, although numbers of these bodies still retained consciousness of their situation. It was a sight that the eye loathed, but from which it could not remove. There is a painting abroad of the effects of the deluge, when, the waters had retired, and on which small canvas the artist has represented about 60 human corpses, which would give the best notion of the present scene, and if multiplied to 6000 carcases a very just one. The majority of the bodies were of the French grenadiers, which were easily distinguished from the other French regiments by their fine forms, and the white skins proved that the loss had been sustained by the enemy. The position of the bodies proved the desperate ardour of the attack. The ditches, the glacis were filled with them, to which they now served as a protection, unless Bonaparte's columns would or could have marched upon this pavement of their fallen comrades.

Towards ten the French, after some movements, a cannonade, and faint musketry, declined battle, and dismissed their troops, and each army now felt assured of a day's interruption to the work of slaughter; but the mutual positions still continued within cannon shot distance, and the interest consequent on the proximity of two such armies increased, whilst considerations of future movements and comparative means engaged serious attention.

The loss of the Russians had, during their retreat upon the position been considerable. One General had been killed, and four wounded; three battalions of chasseurs were almost destroyed; and altogether seven thousand men had been returned as killed or wounded in the battle. Lord Hutchinson had a narrow escape; his horse, and those of Colonel Eustace and Captain Hervey were wounded. The loss of the enemy had certainly not amounted to less than 10,000 men:[26] for even in the advance they had not proceeded with impunity, and the result of their assaults was not dependant on doubtful intelligence; still the effective force of the enemy in front of Heilsberg indisputably exceeded 100,000 men, and another corps was known to be manoeuvring against the Prussians on the left, so that the Russians had no equality of strength in the field, and no reserves to supply losses, except 30,000 men who had not passed the Russian frontier. The enemy had indeed been repulsed in his attacks, and therefore been defeated in the object of his enterprise on Heilsberg, but the victory had not an influence beyond the. moment, for the redundant power of the French was still unimpaired, and they could traverse by the right of the position, move on Koenigsberg, or, by throwing bridges over the Aller, surround and blockade the Russian army, who had not two days bread in their camp, or in those magazines, of whose capture

---

26. The French admit in their Bulletins above 3000, and the death or wounds of numerous general and staff officers. The loss, as is now ascertained on the best authority, was 12,000.

Bonaparte vaunts; whilst contagion from the putrid loads that polluted the atmosphere would have augmented the evils of famine. In the magazines of Heilsberg the enemy scarcely found any remnant. The Russians had not enough for three days to carry with them when they marched, and some barley grain which would have been abandoned was destroyed during the night by the Cossacks under the orders of the Attaman.

About mid-day a corps of the enemy (Marshal Davoust's) was seen in march upon the Landsberg road, and General Bennigsen conceived that the enemy were moving upon Koenigsberg, and that General Lestocq, who had been ordered in the morning to Zinten from Heiligenbeil, on which he had fallen back, might not be strong enough to resist the advance of the enemy, and cover Koenigsberg; he therefore detached General Kaminskoy with nine thousand men to join him, and ordered General Lestocq to fall back upon Koenigsberg with all expedition and maintain that city, as he was moving upon Wehlau with the army to support the line of the Pregel.

Fortunately General Lestocq had intercepted a courier with the order of Bonaparte to Marshal Victor, which directed him to attack General Lestocq on every point, and march direct to Koenigsberg; on which the General, with that decision and judgement which have rendered his name illustrious amidst the wreck of his country's fame, immediately determined to anticipate the enemy's object, and throwing himself between Victor, already at Muhlsack, and the city, gained it notwithstanding the enemy's movements and continued attacks; General Kaminskoy by extraordinary exertion also joined him during the march, and reached Koenigsberg; but a brigade on Lestocq's right, consisting of four squadrons of cavalry, two battalions of light infantry, and a. half battery of horse artillery, which had been posted to watch Braunsberg, was intercepted on march by the route of the Frischaff, and after a most gallant attempt to force a passage, 1500 men were obliged to surrender—the enemy make this force four thousand--when within two miles of Koenigsberg.

At night the Russian army began to cross the Aller, cheered by the assurance that they were not retiring, but moving to fight the enemy in a new position, for confident from their late victory, they still felt an abhorrence of retrograde operations, and recollected that Eylau had secured them a long and luxurious repose.

Day broke, and three divisions of infantry had still to pass the bridges, but the supine enemy, unaccountably, as the whole operation was under their view, within musket shot, made no movement, and the Cossacks did not retire until two hours afterwards, when they fell back upon the bridges. Here the Attaman stood to permit the passage of wounded men successively coming from the town until near seven o'clock, when some French yagers appearing, he ordered the first bridge to be cut away—waited to see the order executed—and in the same manner superintended the destruction of the second and the third, after which he retired unmolested, leaving the enemy but their mass of dead and wounded, and only Russians who from loss of limbs were unable to move.

The army on the 12th occupied Bartenstein, and Bonaparte's head-quarters were directed on Eylau, but his army was not put in movement before midday.

A division of dragoons, and two brigades of light cavalry followed the Russians cautiously on the right bank of the Aller, acting rather as a corps of observation than of pursuit.

On the 12th the Russian army moved on Shippenbeil, but some cavalry marched on the left bank of the Aller—As heavy rain had fallen, the roads were distressingly bad.

The French army on the 13th moved from Eylau. Murat was ordered to join Marshal Victor with his cavalry at Koenigsberg, and Marshal Davoust to support him. Marshal Soult marched upon Creutzburg, Marshal Lannes upon Domnau, the Marshals Ney and Mortier upon Lampasch.

When Bonaparte found that the Russians were marching upon Shippenbeil, he directed Murat, with the Marshals Soult and Davoust to move upon Koenigsberg, and, with the corps of Marshals Ney, Lannes, Mortier, and Victor, Oudinot's division, and the Imperial Guard, he in person marched upon Friedland.

On the 13th the Russian army in the evening reached Friedland.

During the morning, a body of French hussars had been in the town, (on the left bank of the Aller,) but had been driven out by a brigade of Russian cavalry.

From the information of the prisoners, General Bennigsen believed that Oudinot's corps, so shattered at Heilsberg, was alone stationed at Posthenen, about three miles in front of Friedland, on the road to Koenigsberg. Having occupied the town, and thrown forward some cavalry to cover it from insult during the night, he determined, at 4 o'clock in the morning, to fall upon Oudinot with a division and complete his extinction; accordingly he ordered a division to cross the Aller, and advance to the attack.

The enemy, at first, showed but a very small force, which encouraged perseverance in the enterprise, but by degrees resistance so increased, that another division was ordered to pass the Aller, and in addition to the town bridge, the construction of three pontoon bridges was directed.

An heavy cannonade soon commenced—the enemy's tirailleurs advanced—columns presented themselves—cavalry formed on the Russian right flank—and General Bennigsen, instead of a rencontre with a crippled division, found himself seriously engaged, not only with Oudinot, but the two supporting corps of Lannes and Mortier, sustained by a division of dragoons under General Grauchy, and by the cuirassiers of General Nansoutzy, whilst his own feeble army was lodged in a position that was untenable: From which—progress could not be made against an equal force;—nor retreat be effected without great hazard, and when no military object could be attained for the interests or reputation of the Russian army, whose courage had been sufficiently established, without tilting for fame as adventurers who have nothing to lose and every thing to win.

To confirm these remarks, and understand the future operations, a description of the ground is necessary.

Friedland is a considerable town situated on the left bank of the Aller; a long wooden bridge connects the town with the right bank—west of the town is a capacious lake—the country for a mile in the direction of Heilsberg forms a semicircle of apparent plain, but is cut by a deep and narrow ravine full of water, and scarcely fordable, which runs from Domnau into the lakes. Near the town, on the left of the plain, the ground abruptly descends, and woods border down to the Aller—a deep wood fringed the plain from the Aller to the village of Heinricksdorf, where there was a little interruption, but woods again closed round to the Aller, the banks of which were very steep, the fords subsequently used were unknown, and when discovered late in the evening scarcely practicable.

In the open space of the semicircle, between the Aller and the rivulet, and about half a mile in front of Friedland, General Bennigsen at first formed his troops in column, the cavalry being to the right of the Heinricksdorf road, and as the succeeding divisions passed the Aller, the right and part of the centre of his infantry were posted between that road and the rivulet, and that part of the centre was covered by a branch of the rivulet which terminated in a broad piece of water: thus his army was entirely exposed to fire, and every movement distinctly seen; whilst the enemy were sheltered from aim, and their force and operations were concealed until they chose to expose them; moreover, upon the right of their position they had the advantage of some rising ground, which commanded both banks of the Aller as far as the town.

After an heavy cannonade and much musketry, which the French maintained with their troops dispersed en tirailleur, the French cavalry and a body of infantry attempted to turn the Russian right by the occupation of Heinricksdorf. Thirty French squadrons bore down upon the twelve Russian squadrons stationed to the right of the village, advanced rapidly, charged, and obliged the Russians to break; but the Russian cannon and some columns of infantry moving forward, checked their progress, and compelled the retreat of the cavalry in confusion, and with some loss; during this attack, the enemy's chasseurs, with several pieces of cannon, had lodged themselves in Heinricksdorf, taken three pieces of cannon improperly advanced, and opened a battery from the village.

Soon afterwards the enemy being anxious to profit of the feeble fire of the Russians, yet scarcely established in their positions, advanced from the village in a column composed of 5,500 men to force the Russian right and gain Friedland. This column was suffered to approach close to the Russian cannon, when they opened a destructive fire of grape, which was irresistible. The column hesitated, and almost immediately gave way, the retreat commencing with the rear ranks, when the Russian infantry charged forwards, and captured the eagle of the 15th regiment. The column lost 1000 men. An attack on the Russian left had been attended with no better success, and the enemy was compelled to shelter their columns in the wood, but still they maintained in advance various batteries and an incessant tirailleur fire.

The Russian divisions had successively continued to pass, and about nine o'clock in the morning only one division remained on the right bank, and in its front about half a league, the Cossacks under General Platow were still stationed.

General Bennigsen, who, from some prisoners, was now acquainted with the force opposed to him, fearful that a corps of the enemy might be sent to seize the bridge, of Allenberg, which would intercept his retreat on Wehlau, and defeat the original plan of movement, concerted with General Lestocq; directed 6000 men, of which a regiment of the Imperial Guards composed a part, to recross the Aller, and march upon that town: this detachment added to General Kaminskoy's, deprived his army of 15,000 of his best troops, and left him but 40,000 men to defend the two banks of the Aller, and the probable destinies of Europe—40,000 gallant warriors, but almost exhausted by fatigue, and by want of sustenance.

About 11 o'clock the enemy gave way in every point, and great hopes were entertained that he was retiring altogether upon Eylau. General Bennigsen, therefore, ordered the Siberian chasseurs of the guards to lodge themselves in the wood at the extremity of the French right wing. They moved forward under the command of Colonel St. Priest in the most intrepid manner, drove or destroyed every thing before them, and pierced into the wood; but they could not long maintain themselves in that advanced position, for the enemy immediately moved his principal forces against them. Obliged to withdraw, they fell back with most perfect order, to half musket shot distance from the wood, where they threw their left upon the Aller and obtained the shelter of some farm houses.

The Russian cavalry had manoeuvred on the right to gain the rear of the enemy's left, by gradually encroaching into a new alignment. Having succeeded, a part charged the French dragoons and cuirassiers stationed in advance, who, at first, fled, but on a French officer riding down to them, they rallied, re-advanced, and met the Russians, who, daunted at this unexpected onset, receded until a Russian reserve moving to their succour, the French again yielded the ground. The remainder of the French cavalry then galloped forward, and the residue of the Russian cavalry also rushed into the combat, when a general melée ensued, which terminated in considerable loss to the enemy, especially his cuirassiers, and the temporary recovery of the village of Heinricksdorf, but which was again abandoned, as the enemy brought on a numerous artillery.

Thus far all had prospered, not indeed, as to the original project, which had been early abandoned, but as to the realisation of an hope that had succeeded of maintaining the ground until night. Under this confidence no precautions had been taken against disaster; no works were constructed to defend the entrances into the town and cover the retiring troops, if prematurely forced to recross the Aller; precautions that were perfectly easy of execution, as well as eligible, and which would have discomfited the ultimate efforts of the enemy.

About mid-day the enemy's fire, which had relaxed, resumed more vigour; the cannonade increased; the tirailleurs re-advanced greatly reinforced; and the cannon shot and the musketry continued unremittingly from that time a tremendous fire upon the Russians, who were totally exposed, and standing in columns with some infantry thrown forward to act as tirailleurs, whilst the French columns still remained in the woods, and the supporting lines of the advanced infantry, concealed themselves from direct aim by laying clown in long grass, or behind the favouring ground.

Never was resolution more heroic, or patience more exemplary than that now displayed by the Russians—never was a sacrifice of such courage more to be deplored.—Brave Russians! you indeed, exulting in the execution of your mandates, mourned not a devotion so fatal, but the hearts of your friends overflowed with the bitterest gall of affliction.

The enemy had continued to arrive with fresh succours, and the woods were now thronged by battalions which advanced upon the edge and there reposed.

About four o'clock in the afternoon Bonaparte was first noticed by the bustle and movement amongst the French troops, and soon afterwards he was distinctly seen giving directions.

A little before five the French army stood to their arms and the cavalry mounted. From the town of Friedland, the masses appeared, through the interstices of the trees, and the partial interruption of the wood, of enormous power and extensive depth, but the eye could not distinguish where the weight of the force was directing.

From the plain, the horizon seemed to be bound by a deep girdle of glittering steel.

It was in vain that General Bennigsen had notice, and saw, with his own eyes, the mighty preparation.—The ammunition of his artillery was exhausted, and not forty pieces could fire. He had not a single battalion in reserve, and as he had been obliged to pass the last division over the river, not a soldier but the Cossacks remained on the right bank of the Aller, and they half a league in advance. His columns, reduced by the loss of 12,000 men, were now so thinly scattered over the position, that they seemed rather advanced detachments than the army itself, and which impression deceived Bonaparte so as to suspend his ulterior efforts after the battle. Eight or ten of his generals also killed or wounded, and several hundred officers.

It was now that he regretted the absence of the 6,000 men detached in the morning to Allenberg—a detachment that the world has had cause, indeed, to deplore; for if these 6,000 men had been present at this moment on the left of the position, Russian courage would have maintained victory against the enormous superiority of hostile forces, and against their more ruthless destiny, which had seduced them into the plain of Friedland. At the same time, General Bennigsen had just cause to apprehend a movement of the enemy on Allenberg, and the preservation of that post was very important; but as his army was committed in a battle which he was resolved to continue, it was too weak to admit of such a diminution of its means. If he had not guarded Allenberg, and the enemy had moved upon it, he would have been unjustifiable. As it was, regret may be expressed without censure.

General Bennigsen in this extremity did all that his means and the time permitted. He directed six guns to take post on the elevation upon the right bank of the Aller, a little in front of his left, so as to flank the enemy's right in a forward movement. He closed up the wreck of his centre, and sent an order for his cavalry to quit the right wing of the position and support the centre and right of the infantry; orders which were, under the circumstances, most judicious; but, before the officer could reach the cavalry, the enemy's proposed attack was in execution.

About 5 o'clock the French army had taken its order of battle:—Marshal Ney on the right; Marshal Lannes in the centre;

Marshal Mortier on the left; Marshal Victor and the Imperial Guard in reserve; General Grouchy with his division of cavalry supported the left; General Lahoussaye's division of dragoons, and the Saxon Cuirassiers, the centre; General Latour Maubourg's division the right.

At half past 5 o'clock, 20 pieces of cannon, discharging salvo's gave the signal of attack, whilst another battery of thirty pieces opened upon the Russian left.

The report of the guns were scarcely heard when the French column started from the wood, and the right corps advanced in mass echelons at a quick step.

The chasseurs of the Imperial Guard greatly committed by an advanced station, fired some volleys and retreated. Several battalions of militia formed behind the chasseurs, and on the low garden ground near the banks of the Aller, also gave way, and streamed to the bridges, whilst the six guns upon the elevation on the right bank, overpowered by fire, were beat back out of action. Some Cossacks and cavalry, lately arrived from the right bank, so soon as the French column had quitted the wood, attempted to attack the rear of the right flank, but a division of French dragoons, sustained by infantry, repulsed them. General Platow attempted to cross the Aller in rear of the French army, but the wood was too strongly lined by infantry.

The enemy quickened their pace, animating each other to the assault by loud cheers, and driving everything before them, notwithstanding gallant efforts from a division of infantry in front of the guards, whilst the remaining French columns sallying from the wood could scarcely find space for the formation of their numbers.

The Russian Imperial Guard, impatient of the cannonade which tore them to pieces, rushed forward with fixed bayonets, but not in compact order. They, however, reached the enemy, pierced the leading column, exacted bloody revenge, and, for a moment, the corps of Marshal Ney retrograded in disorder; but General Dupont's reserve division advanced, obliged the guards to fall back, pressed on them, and, after a further obstinate contest in the streets forced the town.

During this contest the bridges were ordered to be fired. The flames rolled over them instantaneously; they were no longer passable for friends or foes, and were consumed, notwithstanding the efforts of the enemy to preserve them, so that a great portion of the infantry were obliged to plunge into the stream and escape by an almost impracticable ford.

The infantry of the centre and right wing had undauntedly kept their ground, and the enemy advancing upon the branch of the ravine, and with the existence of which they were unacquainted, suffered heavy loss during their embarrassment; but the Russian flank being exposed by the retreat of the guards, must have given way in disorder, if the Russian cavalry had not, in full speed, rushed at the enemy, now approaching also with his left wing, and trampled down two battalions of Lannes's corps of Oudinot's division, whilst the remainder were obliged to arrest their progress and assume a new formation.

The infantry, encouraged by this conduct of their cavalry, also advanced and covered its retreat. But when the smoke of the burning bridges darkened the atmosphere, then, indeed, further resistance to retrieve the day was acknowledged as hopeless, and destruction seemed inevitable; yet still resolved to preserve their honour from the impending ruin, cavalry and infantry adhered to each other's fortunes, and mutually scorned a safety that compromised a friend.

In solid order they retired; slowly measured back their march; charged whenever the encroaching enemy trespassed; and, in this manner, checking 50,000 men, they continued the action, unbroken and undismayed until near 11 o'clock at night, when the enemy desisted.

The Russian General then conceiving it too hazardous to continue his march upon the left of the Aller, explored the banks of the river until a ford was discovered, which did admit, with extreme difficulty, of the passage of his troops; but the infantry were obliged to wade through breast high, and the little remaining ammunition in the tumbrels was utterly spoiled.

General Bennigsen, who had been driven across the Aller, and who had rallied his left wing at the entrance of the wood, about a quarter of a mile north of the town, and on the right bank, covered this operation, and prevented for the night any interruption to the march of the artillery and retiring columns.

Thus, after 16 hours continued action, concluded the battle of

Friedland; a battle undertaken from an error of information, persevered in from an apprehension of retreat, but whose catastrophe was alleviated by the extraordinary valour of the officers and troops; a valour, which Lord Hutchinson (it may be permitted in this instance to quote from his official dispatch) declares, that he "wants terms sufficiently strong to describe, and which would have rendered their success undoubted, if courage alone could ensure victory, but, whatever may be the event, the officers and men of the Russian army have done their duty in the noblest manner, and are justly entitled to the praise and admiration of every person who was witness of their conduct."

Every disadvantage had oppressed the Russians, no food as usual, and the troops had been marching all night and for several days previous. The most unfavourable locality had been selected, and the immense superiority of the enemy prevented any useful result from victory even if victory had been possible. But although fortune could not produce a miracle to achieve for them triumph, nevertheless, she favoured the brave, and mitigate the evils that menaced. She overshadowed the judgement an enfeebled the energies of the conqueror, and rendered his laurel barren, and almost a memorial of reproach. A distinguished French General, whose name it would be a breach of confidence to mention, said, "It was a battle gained and a victory lost."

Had Bonaparte, when he saw the wasted condition of the Russian army on the left bank, and the naked unprotected state of the right bank and the bridges, on which their only security depended; had he passed across from his redundant forces but one corps, human courage could not have opened a passage for the Russians: or, had but one corps subsequently turned the right of the Russians by debouching from the village of Heinricksdorf: when the attack was made upon their left; or when the Russian right and centre by the loss of Friedland, were isolated, and wandering without a known point of preservation to bear upon, had the enemy even then gained their right and beat them with their artillery back upon the Aller, complete extinction must have been the consequence.

Why he did not direct the first operations, or his generals accomplish what his error had omitted, are circumstances inexplicable even at this time.

The loss of the Russians has been variously estimated, but the number of killed and wounded did not exceed 10 generals, 500 officers, and 12,000 men, and certainly not 500 prisoners. The loss of the enemy, at the lowest computation, was also a considerable proportion of officers, (several generals, &c.) 75000 men, and 400 prisoners. The French generals afterwards at Tilsitz (even Berthier) estimated it much higher.

The military trophies lost by the Russians were confined to 17 cannon,[27] and several of these unserviceable; not one pair of colours, whereas the enemy lost two eagles.

The preservation of the cannon in the day of Friedland was remarkable, but the ultimate preservation of these cannon, over the Pregel and Memel, and of the immense baggage which joined from Koenigsberg, is one of the most extraordinary incidents in military transactions.

The Russian army, on the morning of the 15th, unmolested, reached Allenberg, where they could find scarcely any subsistence—on the 16th Wehlau, where the Aller and the Pregel unite, and over which river is a long wooden bridge. To the right and left the ground is marshy, and the river not fordable without difficulty for cavalry, and in no case for carriages.

From an habitual, almost systematic, neglect of military police, the drivers of the guns, tumbrils, &c. were suffered to stop in the town, and proceed only at their own pleasure over the bridge. Towards the afternoon an alarm was given that the enemy was approaching, nay, even in the town, and some shots being fired, confirmed the panic. Horse, infantry, guns, carriages, &c. all rushed at the bridge, and as three streets equally filled, debouched upon it, a knot of confusion soon formed, which rendered all passage impracticable. A more terrible scene cannot be imagined. Friends became foes to each other, and the uproar, consternation, impediments, and danger, momentarily increased. Prince Dolgorucky, and a British officer who happened to be in the town, forced forward on foot, gained the bridge, and the front of the carriages contending for passage, arrested the struggle, collected some soldiers, formed a barrier, and, by menace, force, and perseverance, disen-

---

27. The French Bulletin has the audacity to say, "We believe that we have taken 120 pieces."

gaged the entangled carriages, and established order, by allowing six to pass out of each street successively, so that the town, towards night, was regularly cleared.

On the first alarm, some infantry had been thrown forward by Prince Bragration to support the Cossacks and Basquiers, who had just arrived, and who, swimming the Aller with the Cossacks, commenced instantaneous action, by discharging their arrows with some effect, charging some parties of the enemy, and making several prisoners.

Happily, Bonaparte had been satisfied, after such a battle as Friedland, with cutting off General Bennigsen's army from Koenigsberg. From *that* route on which if General Bennigsen had marched, he must, in a few days have capitulated;[28] and instead of pressing the defeated Russians, who, he states in the same bulletin to have lost 18,000 k*illed in the battle,* and whose total loss he afterwards states to be 60,000, of which 40,000 were prisoners, *(twenty thousand more men than in their army!)* the great Napoleon and the invincible grand army are satisfied with a manoeuvre to prevent *the re-appearance of the remnant on the left bank of the Aller!* A fact that could not be credible without his own admission in the 79th Bulletin, which states, "The next day, the 15th, whilst the enemy endeavoured to rally, and made retreat on the left bank of the Aller, *the French army continued their manoeuvres on the right bank to cut him off from Koenigsberg."*—A manoeuvre more imbecile and ignorant than has been paralleled in ancient or modern war.

Bonaparte himself, at the head of 4000 men, had occasioned the alarm in Wehlau, of which he did not profit, but was contented to rest a tame spectator of all the movements over the bridge, which was completely under his view within cannon shot distance, and in that inactive inglorious position he remained all night.

At six o'clock in the morning General Platow retired with his Cossacks over the bridge without interruption, and there waited to see it completely destroyed.

On the 17th the Russians moved to Polpitten, where the corps

---

28. He might perhaps have saved his cavalry by the route of the Frisch Haff, but even then with difficulty, for the route is nearly a desert, and the French might have reached Memel before them.

of Lestocq and Kaminskoy joined, with an immense equipage, having crossed the Domnau at Labian, in conformity with instructions sent after the battle of Koenigsberg.

Thus did General Lestocq successfully complete a most arduous campaign and service, in a manner that will ever do honour to his name; and thus were two corps of the French army, and Murat with his cavalry, unable to control the perilous movements of a handful of men, or to efface the disgrace of having been kept in check for four days before Koenigsberg by a corps unequal to the defence of one-third of the city, and which, although strengthened by some field-works, since the battle of Eylau, was perfectly untenable even as a post with thirty thousand men for its defence.

Koenigsberg was, however, a noble trophy of the battle of Friedland; and the exultation of the enemy, at its possession, under any circumstances, was excusable. But the higher value they attached to the capture— the greater importance they gave to the city, in so much more did they establish further proofs, (if proofs could be wanting,) that inability alone prevented their occupation of it after the battle of Eylau, at a time when the streets were only occupied *by a vanquished and fugitive soldiery,* and truly a timid population. But when, not satisfied with the real wealth of a large and commercial city,[29] with the means afforded for contributions and exactions, they boast of the spoil of immense public magazines, and one *hundred and sixty thousand* stand of British arms, they proclaim falsehoods of the most extravagant character, and which find no parallel but in the catalogue of their own compositions.

Notwithstanding many difficulties, and the incessant attack of the enemy, Generals Lestocq and Kaminskoy reached Koenigsberg on the 15th of June, but a Prussian brigade, as has been before stated,

---

29. General Lestocq had removed every thing from the city that was portable, by an immense equipage; and although some of the merchants had granaries, the Russians and Prussians had none of consequence; for they had no money, and no credit, and even the merchants' granaries were exhausted. There were no muskets lost. The supply for Prussia of cannon, arms, and ammunition, was sent to n Swedish port after the armistice by Lord Hutchinson, and the Russian muskets were landed at Riga and delivered to the Russian troops. The returns before the House of Commons will prove the fact relative to the arms. The British merchants of Koenigsberg can certify as to the former assertion.

which had been stationed at Brandenburg to defend the passage of the river Frisching, had continued so long at its post that the enemy occupied its only route to Koenigsberg. Major Gentegsky, who commanded, notwithstanding his force did not amount to 2,000 men, determined to attempt the daring enterprise of cutting his way through 15,000 men immediately opposed to him, but the survivors, after a gallant effort, in which the light artillery, commanded by Lieutenant Sowrisky, behaved with most meritorious conduct, were obliged to surrender at Duboisriche, two miles from the city.

When General Lestocq occupied Koenigsberg, he posted his infantry and artillery from the Brandenburg gate to the work of Fredricksburg, and General Kaminskoy was charged with the defence of the Friedland gate.

The enemy made several attempts to storm the Brandenburg gate, but were always repulsed with heavy loss; and, to prevent cover to their future approaches, the Nassegarten, suburb, and some fine mills before the Friedland gate, were set on fire and burnt.[30]

On the following day the enemy made an attempt to pass the Pregel River, but some horse artillery, supported by cavalry, drove them back.

On the 17th of June, at 4 o'clock at noon, General Lestocq having received advice of the battle of Friedland, ordered the garrison under arms with the pretext of making a sally, but when the troops were all ready at their posts, he directed the columns out of Koenigsberg towards Labian, leaving General Sutterheim, with two battalions of light infantry, to cover the retreat, who remained until midnight on the walls, when he retired, and on the morning of the 18th, the magistrates presented the keys to the enemy.

General Sutterheim was pursued and attacked near Baunwald, but his troops making an obstinate defence, the enemy could make no impression, and several hours after that the Russians had abandoned Wehlau.[31] Bonaparte threw a bridge across the Pregel, between Weh-

---

30. General Ruchel, one of Prussia's distinguished officers, killed at Jena by the 5th Bulletin, commanded the first day at Koenigsberg, but then retired that he might not supersede General Lestocq.

31. The French assert, that the Russians burnt considerable magazines upon the Aller; whereas, the Russian army was literally famishing, from not having established magazines in the line of retreat, and from not waiting long enough in a place to procure provisions from the inhabitants Of the district.

lau and Tapian; and Marshal Ney marched upon Insterbourg, in the direction of which place the Russian wounded had passed during the battle of Friedland, but he only overtook a *few* stragglers.

On the 18th, the combined army marched to Tilsitz and covered the passage of the guns, tumbrils, carriages, &c. over the single and long bridge of the Memel; but some of these guns were ordered back again to be put in position, as the enemy were reported to be advancing.

On the 19th, the army defiled all day and night across the bridge. For forty hours the column was passing, and for the last thirty in an uninterrupted succession, somewhat accelerated by the occasional fire of cannon.

The rearguard of the Russians, on the march from Polpitten, had been obliged occasionally to form against the French cavalry, and the Cossacks made several successful charges, lulling and wounding some officers, as well as many men, and making 2 or 300 prisoners.

When the French approached Tilsitz, notwithstanding the position was too extensive to be maintained even by the whole Russian army, and heights that could not be occupied by them, domineered the town and commanded the bridge, the French quietly suffered the retreat of the rearguard on the morning of the 20th, and the conflagration of the bridge about mid-day.

The Russian army was formed behind the Memel, in a very open country, and as the river was fordable in various directions, another conflict was expected; but on the 21st of June, in consequence of a proposition for an armistice, made by General Bennigsen, in the first instance, to gain time, hostilities ceased, and the ratification of the armistice took place on the 23rd at the Russian head-quarters, one league from Tilsitz. General Bennigsen wrote to Prince Bragration:

> After the torrents of blood which have lately flowed in battles as sanguinary as frequently repeated, I could wish to assuage the evils of this destructive war, by proposing an armistice, before we enter into a conflict, into a new war, perhaps still more terrible than the former. I request you, Prince, to make known to the chiefs of the French army this intention on my part, of which the consequence may have effects more salutary, as a general congress has already been proposed, and may prevent a useless effusion of human blood. You will afterwards transmit to

me the result of your proceedings—and believe me to be with the most distinguished consideration,

Your Excellency's most humble and most obedient servant,

B. Bennigsen

To which Prince Bragration replied:

General,

The General Commander in Chief has addressed to me a letter relative to the orders which his Excellency has received from his Majesty the Emperor, directing me to communicate its contents; I think I cannot better comply with his intentions than by transmitting to you the original. I request you, at the same time, to send me your answer; and accept the assurance of the high consideration with which I am,

General,

Your most humble and most obedient servant,

Bragration

By that armistice the left of the French army was applied upon the Currisch Haff, at the *embouchure* of the Memel river; and the right, under Massena, took up a position between the sources of the Narew and the Bug, on the borders of Polish Russia.[32] Bonaparte had demanded the surrender of Colberg, Pillau and Graudenz, but this proposition was peremptorily rejected, and the armistice, of which the basis was to be a negotiation for peace, was adopted.

Thus terminated the campaign and the war—a war in which Russia, with the feeble numerical aid of Prussia, and the partial aid of Sweden, had been opposed not only to France, but to Switzerland, Italy, Saxony, the Confederation of the Rhine, Holland, part of Poland, and even Spain;[33] a combination of force, of which the

---

32. Notwithstanding the great inferiority of force which General Tolstoy (who had succeeded to the command of the Russian army on the Bug) could oppose to Massena—(17,000 to 45,000) he resolved to alarm the enemy, so as to prevent any detachment to the grand army, and, on the 11th and 12th of June successively, he attacked the line of French posts, particularly at Donocgewo, carried several, and so imposed on the enemy, that they remained altogether on the defensive, and thus the left wing of the Russians maintained its original ground until the news of the armistice arrived, and which prevented General Tolstoy from executing further enterprizes which the reinforcements on march would have enabled him to undertake with vigour; Poland did not prove a field for the glory of Massena, nor did *fortune* even favour him.
33. The advance of the Spaniards enabled Mortier's corps to join the grand army.

Russians might have said, as the great Frederick, when enumerating his enemies—"I don't know that there will be any shame for me in being defeated, but I am sure that there can be no great glory for them in defeating me."

Thus closed this unequal war, which the Russian army had waged with such extraordinary courage and constancy, that Bonaparte had, during its progress, been induced frequently to solicit peace, and was finally compelled to conclude it on terms directly opposite to his professed policy, and most pernicious to the real interests of France.

It is true that he acquired too much when he attained the personal acquaintance of the Emperor Alexander; and peace was at that moment a boon of important advantage to him ; for he well knew that danger not only menaced from the increasing energies of England, but from the awakened sense of other powers, whose hostile movement must have determined the salvation of Europe. Yet, even at Tilsitz, although Bonaparte succeeded in some interesting objects, how different was his situation to that which he had anticipated on the banks of the Vistula; how different had been the event of the war to that which he had arrogantly predicted on his entrance into Warsaw, when he proclaimed—"Soldiers! We will not lay down our arms until a general peace has confirmed and secured the power of our allies—until it has restored to our commerce its freedom, and given back to us our colonies. On the Elbe and on the Oder we have re-conquered Pondicherry; all our possessions in India, the Cape of Good Hope, and the Spanish colonies. What right has Russia to hope that she shall hold the balance of destiny in her hand? What right has she to expect she should be placed in so favourable a situation? Shall there be a comparison made between the Russians and us? Are not *we* and *they* the soldiers of Austerlitz?"

He who had been accustomed to dictate peace in the conquered capitals of the hostile sovereigns—who had declared that he would plant his eagles on the towers of St. Petersburg, ere he condescended to treat with the humbled Czar of the Muscovites, had scarcely been able, after six months toil and sanguinary struggle, (which cost him above 100,000 men) to reach even the frontier of Russia, on whose boundary, in the character of a negotiator, he signed a treaty, augmenting the European empire of that sovereign, whose dominion he had resolved to reduce, and the majesty of whose dynasty he had sworn to degrade.

Such had been the achievements of the *contemptible soldiers of Austerlitz*. Thus had they justified Bonaparte's pretensions for his army to *superiority of courage*.

It cannot, however, be denied that all which concerned the interior economy of the service—the administration of the departments, and the elementary parts or strategy of war, were better regulated in the French army than in the Russian; and the exertions and talent of Bonaparte, by which he retrieved his embarrassments after the battle of Eylau, paralysed Austria, and collected a new, and still more formidable army in Poland, were splendid proofs of a powerful and unconquerable mind—but in the military operations of the field, directed by Bonaparte in person, there was nothing to astonish, and much to condemn.—Confiding merely in superiority of numbers, he impelled his forces on the Russians; but in these campaigns, and especially in the last, he did not act like a skilful artist, clothing the bloody trade of war in the beauteous garb of military science.

This censure of Bonaparte's military conduct will not be deemed unwarrantable or presumptuous by any one who, perusing the details of these campaigns, traces, on the map, the various movements of the armies from Pultusk to Tilsitz—and recollects the comparative strength of the Russian and French forces, and the favourable incidents that locality, error, or fortune, so frequently presented to Bonaparte.

Bonaparte indeed, formerly achieving victory by the influence of his name, had found a very different antagonist in the Russians—The gallantry which checked him at Pultusk—the desperate courage that rallied and defeated him at Eylau—that so sanguinely repelled him at Heilsberg, and the obstinate valour that maintained the plain of Friedland, might justly render him cautious and fearful of such an enemy; but his later caution exceeded prudence, and his fears amounted to weakness.

Some of his inconsiderate partisans would pretend that he permitted the escape of Lestocq and Kaminskoy, and the uninterrupted movement of the Russians behind the Memel, from a policy that he developed at Tilsit; but his own bulletins are at variance with this apology: and what policy could compensate his vanity for the loss of such military glory, or be equivalent to the advantage he would have obtained by the utter annihilation of the only army that Russia had between the Volga and the Aller?

This would have been a policy of a strange character, displacing himself from the station of a conqueror and dictator, to aggrandize and elevate to an equal altitude' and consideration, a subjugated enemy, who had no alternative but to surrender at discretion, and who, under such circumstances, could not have refused conditions, however loathsome, instead of *being in a situation to reject, with disdain, the hand offered to the lovely and dignified Catherine.*

Since that time Bonaparte has acquired new celebrity, and his passage of the Danube has been extolled as an immortal testimony of his military genius;—but there *is more than authority for insinuation; there is reason to assert, that when that operation is investigated, at a future period,* a development will be made public, to correct in future a too hasty and credulous admiration.

ESTIMATE OF THE COMBINED FORCES REUNITED ON THE BANKS
OF THE MEMEL AFTER THE BATTLE OF FRIEDLAND

	Men
Remains of corps actually engaged in that battle	28,000
General Kaminskoy's corps	9,000
Detached corps at Allenberg	6,000
Reinforcements of infantry joined on march to the Memel	3,000
At Olita	15,000
Exclusive of Cossacks and Basquiers	61,000
Prussian corps being reunited to its depots, but exclusive of the garrison of Dantzic	18,000
Russians with General Tolstoy on the Narew	18,000
On March to join him from Wilnau	15,000
Total of regulars	112,000

As soon as peace was made, the 400,000 militia were dismissed, and 200,000 men drafted into the line, which has enabled Russia to carry on the war in Finland—to cross the Danube with 80,000 men, and to maintain 100,000 on her Polish frontier.

The Russian Army

The infantry is generally composed of athletic men between the ages of 18 and 40, endowed with great bodily strength, but generally of short stature, with martial countenance and complexion ; inured to the extremes of weather and hardship; to the worst and scantiest food; to marches for days and nights, of four hours repose and six hours progress; accustomed to laborious toils, and the carriage of heavy burthens; ferocious, but disciplined; obstinately brave, and susceptible of enthusiastic excitements; devoted to their sovereign, their chief, and their country.—Religious without being weakened by superstition; patient, docile, and obedient; possessing all the energetic characteristics of a barbarian people, with the advantages engrafted by civilization.

Their defects as an army are but the consequences of their imperfect military system, and not of individual ineptitude. Their powers require but direction; their courage, experience.

Nature has provided in them the most excellent materials for a military establishment. No genius is required to create, method is only needed to arrange, and ability to command.

The bayonet is a truly Russian weapon. The British alone are authorized to dispute their exclusive pretension to this arm; but as the Russian soldier is chosen for the army, out of a numerous population, with the greatest attention to his physical powers, the battalions of the former have superior advantages.

The untrained Russian also, like the Briton, undaunted, whilst he can affront the danger, disdains the protection of favouring ground, or the example of his adversary, and presents his body exposed from head to foot, either to the aim of the marksman, or the storm of the cannonade.

No carnage intimidates the survivors; bullets may destroy, but the aspect of death awes not, even when a commander's evident error has assigned the fatal station.—"Comrades, go not forward into the trenches," cried out a retiring party to an advancing detachment; "retreat with us, or you will be lost, for the enemy are already in possession." "Prince Potemkin must look to that, for it was he who gave us the order: come on, Russians," replied the commander. And he and his men marched forward, and perished, the victims of their courageous sense of duty.

But, although Russian courage is in the field so pre-eminent, a Russian army in movements that are not in unison with the Russian principle of warfare and Suwarrow's practice, presents, to an enterprising and even inferior enemy all the advantages that may be derived from a state of disorganization of the military frame; and the most difficult of human operations to the year 1807, was the conduct of a Russian retreat.

When Bennigsen retired from Yankova, on the approach of Bonaparte, and sought to evade the enemy by forced marches in the dark nights of a Poland winter, although 90,000 men thundered on in close pursuit, the Russian murmur at retreat was so imposingly audacious, the clamour for battle so loud and reiterated, the incipient disorder was so frightfully extending, that Bennigsen was obliged to promise acquiescence to their demand; and to soothe their discontents, by an assurance that he was marching to reach an appropriate theatre of combat. Gratified in this request, they fought six long days to secure the undisturbed march of six longer, more painful, and more terrific intervening nights; but in which alarm, anxiety and disorder mingled to such a degree, and so shattered the military frame, that victory might have been achieved against them without the glory of a subdued resistance; yet when this army, wearied, famished, and diminished by the loss of 10,000 men, entered at Eylau, their alignment for battle, order regenerated as with the British at Corunna: the memory of former glories, and the confidence of approaching victory cheered even the most exhausted; and a spectator would have supposed that the joyous acclamations commemorated a success, instead of being an anticipation of the most sanguinary trial that was yet upon the records of this bloody war. Such was their vehement ardour to retrieve imaginary disgrace, and profit of a liberty to engage, that when in the evening before the battle, Bennigsen ordered the village of Eylau, which had been abandoned by mistake, to be recovered, and the columns were in motion to the attack, animated by an expression in the command, "that the Emperor expected his troops to execute the orders," but afterwards thinking it advisable, as the enemy was greatly reinforced, to desist from the enterprise, he sent his officers to countermand the service, "No, no," exclaimed every voice; the Emperor must not be disappointed." And they rushed forward, sheltering their gallant disobedience under the authority of an illusion created by their commander.

The desolating misery of a night passed without food, without any moisture to quench drought but the iced snow, without any shelter, without any covering but the rags of their garments, with bare and wounded feet, without fuel, without any consolation, and sleep interrupted by the groans of the dying, or preparations for action, not all this complicated bitterness of condition could humble the spirit or weaken the ardour of this illustrious host. Ere morning dawned they stood to their arms impatient for action; and in that most memorable day established a reputation, which immortalized their courage, and greatly influenced the preservation of their army, when its reduced numbers were unequal, without such impression, to secure its protection. Their valour, indeed, on that day had accomplished the prayers of mankind, and Bonaparte had been on the next an hopeless fugitive, if Bennigsen had yielded to the entreaties of every general in the field; but although the fruits of victory were by that decision wrested from their possession, not Bonaparte, nor France, can pluck the laurel from their brows, which truth and time will to the latest hour preserve with undiminished verdure.

The Russian, nurtured from earliest infancy to consider Russia as the supreme nation of the world, always regards himself as an important component part of the irresistible mass. Suwarrow professed the principle, and profiting of the prejudice, achieved with most inadequate means the most splendid success; and whilst he was more regardless of their blood than any of his predecessors or contemporaries, he was affectionately endeared to every soldier as his parent; and national pride and personal admiration have deified him as the still presiding God of their battles.

An acquaintance with the composition of his armies, a knowledge of their insignificant numerical strength, never exceeding 35,000, although operations were conducted on the scale for 70,000; and the court proclaimed, and the public believed the existence of that force. The assurance of the internal impediments that he had to encounter, certainly so augment the merit of his exploits, that he is entitled to the reputation of one of the first captains that ever appeared. His very eccentricities were characteristic of his superiority of intelligence. They affected his estimation amongst superficial observers; but he disdained the sneer of the less enlightened, and steadily persevered in the course that his wisdom had traced for the attainment of his patriotic ambition. His unmerited disgrace broke a heart whose vital principle was glory and loyalty; but not the misprision of the sovereign, not the *vultus instantis tyranni* could restrain the tears, or check the emotions of a soldiery who bewailed his loss as an irreparable affliction. Such was their enthusiastic affection for him, that when the coffin in which his body was conveying into the church of the citadel to be deposited near the remains of the great Catherine, fixed in the doorway, and instruments were ordered to wrench a passage—one of the grenadier bearers, indignant at the check, exclaimed—"What is all this?"

"*Nothing* could resist Suwarrow *living,* and *nothing* shall stop him *dead.*"

The sentiment was hailed as a just tribute to the invincible character of their chief. *That* consciousness supplied strength to zeal, and the remains of Suwarrow were forced triumphant to the grave!

Amidst the Russian qualities, the love of country is also preeminent, and inseparable from the Russian soldier. This feeling is paramount, and in the very last hour his gaze is directed towards its nearest confines. The wounded drag their mangled bodies over the field to expire with more satisfaction in the effort of approaching them; and the principle of patriotism threw a veil even over crime, in which sentiment the injured sympathized, and which principle was respected.

When General Bennigsen was retiring upon Eylau, considerable numbers of stragglers formed what they denominated corps of marauders, who, placing themselves under the orders of chiefs chosen by themselves, lived by violence until opportunity offered for a return to Russia.

A party of Russian officers, who had been taken at Landsberg, were marching to Prague on parole, but under the charge of some French officers; a corps of marauders surprised them, and after some violence the Russian soldiers were indiscriminately proceeding to dispatch the French, when the Russian officers interfered, and endeavoured to explain, that as these French were but an amicable escort to them, who had given their *parole,* their lives must not only be preserved, but that honour obliged the Russian officers to refuse the opportunity of release, and bound them to proceed as prisoners of war until regularly exchanged. The marauder captain stepped forward—"Will you," addressing himself to the Russian officers, "join and command us, and conduct us to our country? If so, we are bound to obey you, but with this annexed condition, that you do not interfere with our intention of putting to death the French who are in your company."

"No, we cannot," was the answer; and arguments were urged to justify the propriety of their decision. The marauders then assembled as a court-martial; and, after some deliberation, the captain re-advanced, and delivered its sanguinary decree.

"The French, for their atrocious conduct to Russian prisoners on every occasion, have merited death—Execute the sentence."

Obedience was immediate, and the victims were successively shot. This lawless assassination completed, silence was again ordered, and the leader resumed his harangue—"Now, degenerate Russians, receive your reward; you, forgetting that you were born so, that your country has a prescriptive right to your allegiance, and that you have voluntarily renewed it to your sovereign, have entered into new engagements with their most hated enemies; and you have dared to advance in your defence, that your *word* must be binding in *their* service, when you violate the *oath* you have sworn *against* them. You are therefore our worst enemies; more unnatural, more wicked, than those we have slain, and you have less claim upon our mercy. We have unanimously doomed you to death, and instant death awaits you."

The signal was immediate, and fourteen officers were thus massacred for a persevering virtue, of which history does not record a more affecting and honourable trait. The fifteenth (Colonel Arsinoeff, of the imperial guards) was supposed dead, the ball of the musket having entered just above the throat. He was stripped, and the body abandoned on the frozen and freezing snow. Towards night, after several hours torpor, sense returned; and whilst he was contemplating the horror of the past and present scene, identified, not only by his own condition, but still more painfully by the surrounding corpses of his mangled friends, and momentarily becoming more terrific, from the apprehension of an horrible and unmitigable death, he perceived a light, towards which he staggered with joyous expectation; but when he approached the hut, a clamour of voices alarmed his attention. He listened, and recognized his carousing murderers! He withdrew from imminent destruction to a fate, as he then supposed, not less certain, but less rude and revolting. He had still sufficient strength to gain the borders of a no very distant wood, where he passed the night without any covering on his body, or any application to his open wounds. The glow of a latent hope, perhaps, preserved animation, his fortune did not abandon him, his extraordinary protection was continued; and as the day broke, he perceived a passing peasant girl, who gave him some milk, finally sheltered him, and obtained surgical relief, He recovered, and went to Petersburg. The Emperor ordered him to pass the regiments in review, that he might designate the offenders.

He declined to do so, observing that "he thought it inadvisable to seek an occasion for correcting such a notion of indefeasible allegiance. That it was better to bury in oblivion a catastrophe that could not be alleviated, than by an exemplary punishment hazard the introduction of a refined polity and manners, which, by denationalising, the Russian, prepared him for foreign conquest; that Russia was menaced by-an enemy, who could only triumph by the introduction of new theories, generating new habits; and although he had suffered from an effort of more liberal philanthropy and respect for the laws of war, he would not at such a moment be accessory to innovations which removed some of the most impregnable barriers to the designs of France."

But the Russian soldier in general is extremely subordinate, and attached to his officer, who treats him with peculiar kindness, and not as a machine, but as a reasonable being whose attachment he ought to win, although he has authority to command his service.

Punishment is not so frequent as in other armies, nor is it very severe; and the Russians have had occasion to express astonishment at the character and frequency of punishment amongst the troops of their allies. Their spirit of manhood is not prostrated by irreparable disgrace; although born in vassalage, their mind is not humiliated, and even in the presence of their sovereign, whom they obey as an omnipotent, they bear themselves as men and soldiers, honouring as well as honoured.

Their deportment is martial and noble; their answers frank and disembarrassed; and, whilst expressing homage or gratitude, they preserve a dignity which increases the value of their sentiments and duty.

They exercise with great precision, and march well, changing pace instantaneously as if all worked from one pair of hips. Their evolutions are generally the formations of columns and squares, rapidly executed, arid they are not fretted and tormented by goose-step attitudinarians, who consider war to be the science of mountebanks, and victory the prize of distortion.

The design of their dress is good; but the materials are bad, and the allowance too moderate for active service. Their pay is about half-a-guinea a year. Their appointments are cumbersome, and their arms so heavy and coarse, that on 60,000 British stand being distributed, they were given or reserved as distinctions for meritorious soldiers.

In the late war they carried no tents, and constantly bivouacked without shelter in the depth of the severe winter of 1797, nor had they any additional covering to their ragged great coats, in which they always marched.

Their regular food is of the plainest and coarsest quality; and their commissariat was so ill-arranged, that even this issue was precarious, and their subsistence depended on their own diligence, or rather rapine, through a country where terror had induced every inhabitant to fly, and the anticipation of famine had buried many feet deep under snow and ground the pittance destined for the future maintenance of the peasantry; but even with this miserable and uncertain provision they existed, without murmur; and occasions were frequent where they shared their insufficient meal with some starving wretch whose humid eye implored what his power of utterance was almost too feeble to solicit. At Heilsburg, the inhabitants subsisted almost entirely on the bounty of the soldiery, but one third perished in six weeks from actual want and its consequences. Through the other towns of Poland, the distress was as great.

The wear and tear however of a Russian army is enormous, in consequence of these bad arrangements; and the Emperor might have increased his army one third solely by the establishment of an improved system. In that campaign such an addition would have been decisive of victory. Frederic the Second observes, that the Russian armies, in the seven years, although they had been in only four great battles, lost 120,000 men; whilst Prussia, who had fought 16 great battles, lost only 180,000, and Austria, in ten battles, with two garrisons, lost only 140,000.

The recruiting of the Russian infantry is not by volunteer enrolment. The magistrates select the most efficient young men according to the required number. The day of nomination is passed in general grief, and each family is in unaffected affliction at the approaching separation of a son or a brother. But no sooner is the head of the reluctant conscript shaved, according to military habit; no sooner is he recognised as a defender of his country, than the plaints and lamentations cease, and all his relatives and friends present articles of dress or comfort to the no longer reluctant recruit; then revel, with the music and the dance, takes place, until the moment arrives when he is to abandon his native home, and the adored tomb of his fathers; with cheers the eternal farewell is mutually expressed, and the exulting soldier extends his regards to his country, and devotes his new life to the glory and prosperity of his sovereign and Russia.

This moral death, this military resuscitation, is a phenomenon generated and perpetuated by patriotism, the fundamental principle of Russian action, which cheers him in hardship, and animates him in danger.

The soldier, however, does not enter into a new state, with which his domestic habits had been at variance. From earliest infancy, he has been accustomed to sports of manly and warlike character, and his body has been hardened by exposition to the elements and the use of his national bath—first, he goes into an apartment heated by bricks kept moist, so that the chamber is full of vapour, he then rushes naked into the air, although his body is in the highest perspiration, and rolls himself in snow, returning into the bath he enjoys his *summum bonum* of artificial gratification—whilst no intemperance has vitiated his constitution, no unhealthy employment has impregnated the germ of a premature decay.

Religious, perhaps superstitious—but not a bigoted intolerant, the Russian believes that heaven is a palace with many gates, and whilst he respects his own faith, he gives himself no concern whether he shares his ration with a Mohammedan, a Protestant, or a Pagan. He professes no concern about any soul but his own; he invades not the right of option to any form of worship, and presumes not to select for the Almighty those who shall only find favour in his sight.

LIGHT INFANTRY

The Light Infantry is augmenting since the late war; and as Russia possesses a population well adapted for this service in various parts of her empire, she ought to extend it considerably.

The regiments of Light Infantry, hitherto formed, are of an excellent description, and it is impossible to imagine a more beautiful body than the Chasseurs of the Guard, who, it is said, come chiefly from Siberia; indeed, this is the province where the best marksmen and of the hardiest race are recruited, although, in general, the men are lighter. They know their service perfectly: and as many of these men, in common with other regiments, had marched more than three thousand miles to join the army; as the vicissitude of a Siberian winter, and the raging heat of Asiatic deserts were familiar to them, they possessed a natural training and stamina which qualified them in the highest degree for the service they were required to encounter.

THE IMPERIAL GUARDS

It cannot be doubted but that the picked men of such a population as Russia, a country where man is so well grown, must compose a superior body of foot guards, whose numbers do not exceed 7000. There cannot be a nobler corps, or one of more warlike description, and the simplicity of dress gives to the man the full character of his figure and mien. On every occasion the Guards have distinguished themselves: and it is singular in this service that the whole army prides itself in their majesty and excellence. All extol; all joy in their perfections; and the sentiment of jealousy is unknown.

At Tilsitz the guards of France, of Russia, and some of Prussia, paraded in the same town. Those of France, whatever may be their military merits, made but a very indifferent appearance, and, being generally small men, the grenadier high cap had an effect contrary to ornament or grandeur.— Those of Prussia were too much ruined to be estimated justly, yet the stature and proportion were better than those of France; but the guards of Russia surpassed both as daylight doth a, lamp. They exhibited a combination of form and stature, of manly expression and warlike simplicity, of martial character and beauty which was not only unrivalled, but elevated above all comparison.

Ipse, inter primos, prsestanti corpore Turnus
Vertitur arma tenens, et toto vertice supra est.

The Russian Cavalry

The Russian cavalry is certainly the best mounted of any upon the continent; and as English horses never can serve abroad in English condition—at least so long as the English cavalry are nurtured to require warm stables, luxuriant beds, etc., efficiency abroad is sacrificed to appearance at home—it is the best mounted in Europe.

Hungary and Turkey may perhaps produce horses as well adapted for the hussar and irregular services, but the heavy Russian horses are matchless for an union of size, strength, activity and hardiness; whilst formed with the bulk of the British cart-horse, they have so much blood as never to be coarse, and withal are so supple as naturally to adapt themselves to the manège, and receive the highest degree of dressing.

They are chiefly bred in the plains of the Don and the Volga; but as the native breed of those countries, and of the surrounding nations is of inferior size, it is not improbable that they are descendants of the celebrated Cappadocian breed, introduced into Europe by the Romans, and (which is, remarkable,) into Nubia, by a present of three hundred from the Emperor Constantine to one of the African princes, where they seem to have preserved all their character and powers, whilst the influence of European climate or food has somewhat degenerated their stature. Bruce, when in Nubia, first noticed this gigantic and peculiar species, but the statement increased the charges of invention against this much wronged traveller; and Bruce, not recollecting the Roman present, dated their introduction to the time of the Saracen conquests, which origin not being supported by any collateral evidence, was too vague for such a remarkable exception to the race of Arabia, Egypt, and Abyssinia: but it was reserved for the period of the Egyptian expedition to vindicate Bruce by the corroboration of the fact of the existence of such a breed of horses.

After the battle of Eylau, when the Imperial cavalry of the guards were ordered from St. Petersburg to join the army in Poland, the men were sent in wagons as far as Riga, and the horses accompanied at the rate of 50 miles each day. From thence they were ridden, and proceeded to their station at the rate of 35 miles each day; after a march of 700 miles, so conducted, they appeared not only in excellent comparative order, but in such high condition, that the regular garrisons of any capital in Europe could not present a finer cavalry parade. The hussar horse has nothing remarkable, except that he is generally stronger loined than the Hungarian, with equal blood, and force of constitution.

During Bennigsen's retreat, and from that period to the disappearance of the snow in June, no cavalry ever encountered greater hardship.

For above six months in the severity of the extremes! Poland winter, they were always at the piquet post without any shelter; and for three months, or more, they had no other sustenance than what the old thatch, stripped from the roofs of the cottages, supplied; and in consequence of this necessity Poland was progressively rendered uninhabitable, and war assumed her most frightful aspect.

The mortality certainly was great, but it did not render the cavalry inefficient or feeble for the service of the most active and laborious campaign which succeeded.

The appointments are of the best quality, superior to most of the continental nations; but latterly, France has applied so much attention to the improvement of her cavalry equipment, that she may dispute the preference.

The Russian dragoon is entirely an artificial cavalier; for the habits of the country do not prepare and train for horsemanship, but art and attention prevail, and their success attains the essential objects: the graces indeed are not sufficiently considered with regard to the toes, according to equestrian laws in the best schools, for they generally are at right angles, with their knees: but the seat is firm, the hand light, and the body well placed.

The dress of the cavalry is simple, yet handsome. The casque of the Imperial guard was particularly martial and becoming: but the miserable and deplorable connexion with Bonaparte introduced a Franco-mania, which threatened a serious revolution in the national costume, favourable to the policy of the French projects, and of course injurious to Russian interests.

The care taken by the dragoons of their horses was very great and more commendable, from the little acquaintance that a common Russian has with this animal, so as to attach him self by early habits to his consideration and treatment.

In war they are alert and intelligent, in battle brave and capable of every evolution and operation, they charge with rapidity and union, and in all the actions their loss from gallant enterprise and efforts was considerable. At Eylau they sustained the tremendous fire with heroic fortitude, and made some desperate and successful attacks. At the battle of Friedland, when Bonaparte, by the superiority of numbers, had forced the Russian left, and gained possession of the town of Friedland, with the bridges over the Aller; notwithstanding their losses on a day where they had repeatedly charged, notwithstanding the position in which they were now exposed, and the ruin that threatened by delay in the field; animated with a generous resolution to save the centre and right wing of their army, they rushed across the plain, charged the advancing centre of the enemy, and by their daring efforts and bold countenance, enabled the retreat of the infantry, with all their cannon, through an almost impracticable ford, in the presence of Bonaparte and 80,000 men; and subsequently so covered the march upon the Aller, which was to be passed again at Wehlau, and over the Memel, (upon each of which rivers there is but one bridge, and from Friedland an intervening open country of about 120 miles,) that Murat and Bonaparte could effect nothing against a defeated force, reduced to 34,000 men, and after Lestocq's union, encumbered with above 500 pieces of cannon and 10,000 carriages, of which they lost not one, whereas, the French cavalry, who were obliged to remain united, with all their caution, experienced loss and disgraced.

The officers of the Russian cavalry attend to their various duties with great zeal and diligence, and the whole interior economy is well regulated and administered.

The proper employment of this delicate, but important arm, is alone required to insure its good service. No cavalry is more used, on all occasions, or more steadily maintains a passive position under the most destructive fire; but the genius of the master, the eye of the great captain which infallibly seizes those occasions that fortune or adverse error may present, to lance on the enemy's lines with irresistible impression, and the brilliant and decisive effect of cavalry's successful operation, is here no more common than in the other armies of Europe.

ARTILLERY

The Russian artillery is of the most powerful description. No other army moves with so many guns and with no other army is it in a better state of equipment, or is more gallantly served.

The piece is well formed, and the carriage solid, without being heavy. The harness and the rope-tackling is of the best quality for service, and all the appurtenances of the gun complete and well arranged. The draught horses are small, but of great muscular strength, strongly loined, and with high blood. Four draw the light field-pieces, and eight the twelve pounders; the latter have sometimes indeed ten horses; but then the roads must be such as are only to be met with in Poland before the frost sets in, or when it breaks up, and which, during the last campaign, were in such a state that Bonaparte said he had discovered, by crossing the Vistula, *the new element of mud.* The power of these animals is however so great, that on taking up positions, they will plunge through the ditches filled with yielding snow, although so deep as to cover their back, and bury the guns altogether; and when the centre and right wing retired through the Aller, after the battle of Friedland, at a point discovered on the emergency, they were partly swimming, and afterwards compelled to ascend the banks, which were almost perpendicular. If the horses had possessed less strength or activity, the whole must have fallen into the hands of the enemy; but the Russians seem well aware of the importance of horsing their artillery well, and the Russian government is wise enough to spare no expense that may be necessary for its efficiency and security.

The drivers are stout men: like all other drivers, they require superintendence in times of danger, to prevent their escape with the horses, but on various occasions they have also shown great courage and fidelity; and they have the essential merit of carefully providing subsistence for their horses. Neither gun, tumbrel, nor cart belonging to the artillery is ever seen without forage of some kind, and generally collected by the prudence and diligence of the drivers, which might be improper where the issues are assured under regular authority, but which, according to the practices of continental nations, is very commendable and necessary. The artillery-men are of the best description, and the non-commissioned officers equal, but the artillery officers of inferior rank have not the same title to estimation as in the other European services, for their education is not formed with the same care, and their service does not receive the same encouragement. To them is the toil and responsibility, but the honour is by no means assured them. Some favourite officer, completely ignorant of the science and practice of the artillery, is frequently in the day of action appointed for the day to the command of their batteries, and the credit is in the dispatches given to him for a service which depended on long previous systematic arrangements and laborious attention, with which he never was acquainted: an injustice mortifying to the corps, injurious to the individual artillery officer, and gravely detrimental to the general interests.

The horse artillery is no less well appointed, and the mounted detachments that accompany the guns ride excellent powerful horses, and form both in real character and appearance, a corps not inferior to any in the European services.

When the Russian army was in Poland, above 500 pieces of field-cannon moved with it generally, and were actually in the battle of Eylau. Bennigsen had indeed left in his previous movements towards the Bug 120 pieces, chiefly of 12 pounders in reserve, which fortunately escaped Bernadotte's column, and only entered the field in the evening before the general action. Its safety may indeed be owing to the capture of the courier, which gave Bennigsen notice at Mohrungen of Bonaparte's intention to assemble his army and attack him, whilst by the interception of the dispatches Bernadotte's orders to manoeuvre on his right and in his rear were delayed two days—important days, for they preserved the Russian army, as well as the reserve cannon, by enabling them to reach Eylau without such further impediment. This number was certainly out of proportion to the infantry, which at the outset never amounted to 80,000 men, and was particularly inconvenient and embarrassing in countries and seasons when forage was not to be assured. In the latter part of the campaign, when the infantry was by sanguinary actions greatly reduced, the number of guns was a real disadvantage, and endangered the safety of the army by the delays it occasioned.

During the late campaigns the Russians lost very little artillery. At Pultusk some few after the action were completely smothered in the mud, and the French lost as many of theirs in the same way.

In the retreat from Yankova to Eylau, notwithstanding the daily serious conflicts, they did not lose ten pieces. At Eylau, they left the next morning 12 pieces that had been damaged, but withdrew above 30 of the enemy's guns. At Heilsberg they lost in the retreat of Prince Bagration, and previous to the attack on the position three or four, at Friedland only 17. And at Austerlitz their cannon fell into the enemy's hands, from an error in the road, and not from the achievements of victory in that field, although Bonaparte in his dispatches announces their capture as so many trophies gained oh that day.—According to the French bulletins indeed, the Russians lost 300 pieces of cannon from December to June, of which above 200 pieces were lost at, and previous to the battle of Eylau; but the falsehood was so gross, that to account for their disappearance, he shrewdly ordered them to be melted for the erection of a bronze statue to the memory of General Haultpoult, an excellent officer of cavalry, killed at Eylau, but the 64th bulletin of the French army, out-Herods Herod—"On this subject it has been remarked, that the Emperor has never lost any cannon in the armies he commanded, whether in the first campaigns of Egypt, whether with that of the Army of Reserve, with that of Austria and Moravia, or in Prussia and Poland."—If this fact is to rest on French authority, certainly none was or ever will be lost; but a more impudent falsehood was never published for French credulity.

The Russians, however, wisely do not attach too much reputation or disgrace to the possession or loss of a gun. They think that it is better to fight it to the last moment, and let an enemy gain it dearly, than withdraw it too soon for a preservation that also preserves the enemy.

The Cossack artillery, worked by Cossacks, which is a late institution, consisted of 24 pieces, extremely light, and the carriages were fashioned with a care and nicety which did great credit to Russian workmanship. This park joined at Heilsberg, after the battle of Eylau, and in a march of 3000 wersts, one werst, ¾ of an English mile, in the course of 14 weeks, not one horse was disabled or died, and it was soon afterwards brought into action, and did considerable execution on the enemy near Allerstein, nor was one piece lost during the whole campaign.

THE COSSACKS

The Cossacks are a description of troop peculiar to the Russian army. Amalgamated in the Russian empire, the natives of the Don and the Volga still preserve a constitutional independence which is possessed by none of the other provinces of Russia. Regulated by their own laws, exempt from taxes, and governed under the immediate authority of their own Attaman, or chief, chosen from amongst themselves, they are relieved from all impositions of conquest, but the obligation for every male to serve gratuitously for five years with the Russian armies, and some interior services connected with their own police. Blessed with a country of rich plains and noble rivers, which nature covers with the glorious canopy of a fine climate, and fills with redundant food, the Cossack still maintains his warlike character, and unites with the most enthusiastic admiration of his country, and a disposition to profit of its enjoyments, the ambition of martial service, and an errant spirit of adventurous and foreign enterprise. In the land which gave him birth he is the peaceful and civilized inhabitant, natural in his affections, and domestic in his habits; but in other countries he is the lawless Scythian, respecting no property or rights.

Proud of his national comparative freedom, he bears himself as one conscious of superiority and privilege, and yet he tempers the haughty sense of these advantages with an Asiatic grace of manner that renders the expression inoffensive to his associates and grateful to the stranger. Of late years the Attaman has lost some of his power and consequence at St. Petersburg, but as yet no serious encroachment has been made on the independence and character of the nation. He was almost an independent prince; but is now more subject to the laws and will of the Autocrat. He has been deprived of some of the appendages of royalty, and is perhaps more pliable to the views of Russia in the character of one of her generals; but still the Cossacks remain a people with the worth to deserve and the resolution to maintain their freedom or sacrifice themselves in the effort.

In the qualities of private character, the Cossack is to no man inferior—affectionate to his family; faithful to his friend; hospitable to the stranger, and generous to the distressed; with graceful simplicity of manners, and a candour that commands confidence. His military virtues are splendid in common with the Russian nation; but hereditary habits of war, and perhaps a natural talent for that species of it in which they are engaged, adds an acute intelligence and capacity that is not generally shared. By the stars, the wind, and an union of the most ingenious observations, he travels over countries unknown to him, through forests almost impervious, and reaches his destination, or tracks some precursor that he is directed to pursue with the assurance and the indefatigable ardour of the instinctive blood-hound. Nothing can elude his activity, escape his penetration, or surprise his vigilance. Irreparable disgrace would dishonour the Cossack whose negligence offered an advantage to the enemy. The crimes of the passions, cowardice itself would not attach so fatal a stigma; for, in the words of their Attaman, "This offence would not only sacrifice the army to the swords of the enemy, but entail a reproach on all, and distrust of all, that no valour or service could retrieve." And such is the general impression of its base character that no instance of a surprise is on record.

Mounted on a very little, ill-conditioned, but well-bred horse, which can walk at the rate of five miles an hour with ease, or, in his speed, dispute the race with the swiftest—with a short whip on his wrist (as he wears no spur)—armed with the lance, a pistol in his girdle, and a sword, he never fears a competitor in single combat; but in the late war he irresistibly attacked every opposing squadron in the field. Terror preceded his charge, and in vain discipline endeavoured to present an impediment to the protruding pikes. The Cuirassiers alone preserved some confidence, and appeared to baffle the arm and the skill of the Cossack; but in the battle of Pruess Eylau, when the Cuirassiers made their desperate charge on the Russian centre, and passed through an interval, the Cossacks instantly bore down on them, speared them, un-horsed them, and, in a few moments, five hundred and thirty Cossacks re-appeared in the field equipped with the spoil of the slain. Many more were killed, and cuirasses were found even three weeks afterwards. But they did not propose to cover their bodies with this iron harness in future combats; they were sensible that an heart fortified by courage requires no coat of mail. They were worn but for the day, to make them more valuable to those for whom they were destined, and then, by subscription, they paid the expense of their conveyance to the Don and the Volga, where they are suspended as memorials of their prowess, and respect for the pride of their kindred, and the glory of their nations.

When Murat, after the battle of Eylau, advanced with the French cavalry to menace the Russians, and induce Bennigsen to evacuate Koenigsberg, the Cossacks attacked his posts in every direction, killed a very considerable number, and made prisoners, in the course of the succeeding 10 days, of 1,600 dragoons and hussars, which loss obliged Murat to retire, and Bonaparte to abandon Eylau and the open country in front of Guttstadt. They afterwards, in the Russian retreat, (being supported by some squadrons of regular cavalry,) made such desperate attacks, that Bonaparte was obliged to form squares with his infantry, and was himself in such danger that the whole French cavalry was brought down in full gallop to cover him.

It was in this retreat that their Attaman Platow evinced a trait of that superior mind which attained his station, and which, if he had received a liberal education, would have rendered him one of the first men of the age, as indisputably he is one of the most eminent warriors. After Bonaparte had brought up a second corps of his army—the brigades of Pajol, Durosnel, and Bruyères, and the division of heavy cavalry under the orders of General Nansouty—supported by the whole body, he advanced with rapidity, resolved to overwhelm the rear guards of Platow and Bagration; before they passed the bridges of the river, which flowed behind them, and to which they had to descend.

The Cossacks saw the impending danger, and began to press back in confusion. Platow checked, but found the disorder increasing. He immediately sprang from his horse, exclaiming to the Cossacks, "Let those who are base enough abandon their Attaman." The corrected lines paused. He gradually moved; with a waving hand kept back those who trespassed; sent his orders with calmness; reached the town in order; halted at the bridge until every man had passed, destroyed it, and still on foot, proceeded on the other side of the town, struggling above ankle deep through the heavy sand; nor could the most tremendous cannonade, and the incessant fire of the French battalions, crowning the opposite heights, and who commenced their volleys as they formed successively, accelerate his pace, or induce him to mount his horse, until the object was attained, and superior duty obliged him, for the direction of other operations. His mien, his venerable and soldier-like appearance, his solemn dignity of manner, combined, with the awful incidents of the scene, to render this one of the most imposing and interesting sights that could be witnessed.

But although the Cossacks, on some occasions, have discomfited; by direct attacks, regular cavalry, it must not be supposed that they are calculated to act generally in line. Their service is of a different character, which requires a greater latitude and liberty of operation. They act in dispersion, and when they do re-unite to charge, it is not with a systematic formation, but *en masse,* or what in Germany is called the swarm attack; but even then the order should originate from their own officers, who best know their genius and powers, or, which is frequently the case, be the effect of a voluntary impulse that simultaneously animates the whole body, and which is expressed by a yell of excitement more frightful and terrific than the war-hoop of the Canadian savage.

Dexterous in the management of an horse that is guided only by the snaffle, they can twist and bend their course through the most intricate country at full speed, and Platow, in front of Heilsberg, when Bonaparte was retiring on the Parsarge at the head of his regiment, charged into a pine wood filled with French infantry *en tirailleur,* (who had, during the whole day, disputed possession with 4,000 Russian infantry,) carried it in an instant, and decided the affair.

Notwithstanding, however, their military services, the security which their vigilance assures their army, and the distress their enterprises and stratagems occasion the enemy. The following is an instance of their ingenuity:—The French cavalry were afraid to remain at night in the out-posts, and withdrew, to the long mortification of the Cossacks, who thus had no opportunity to achieve any enterprise against them. A party came one day to the officer of artillery, and requested a loaded shell, which was given them. They went when night fell, and having observed where the enemy's posts by day lighted their fires, they buried it under the ashes. The unsuspicious foe returned in the morning, and, after their patrols, rekindled the usual flame, round which they collected; in a short time the fuse was en-flamed, and the fatal explosion killed and desperately wounded seven men, whilst the exulting Cossacks rushed from their ambuscade to secure the horses of those who could not escape. They are injurious in countries where the good-will of the inhabitants is of immediate importance, or where moderation and regularity can alone provide the armies with their subsistence. Then the Cossacks are too frequently scourges of terror and desolation, more fatal to friends than foes; sweeping and devastating in the lawless thoughtlessness of barbarian invaders, without any consideration of future necessities.

Their obligation to maintain their own horses and themselves; the number of reserve horses that march with them; and the habits of their Turkish wars, produce this counteracting inconvenience to the employment of the Cossacks, and there are many obstacles to the introduction of a system that might regulate their licentious practices without serious innovation on the character of the nation which supplies, (at least,) thirty thousand voluntary and equipped warriors to the empire, and whose various services, not double the number of regular cavalry could execute, without a waste of man and horse that no resources of the Russian empire could supply.

There has, indeed, been lately some incipient attempts at reformation, by regimenting the Cossacks, and by the introduction of distinctive dress to each corps; but the evils are of too complicated and ancient a date to be so superficially remedied, and not only dependent upon the improvement of Cossack habits, but the ability of Russia to provide the necessary indemnifications which a change of system would render necessary. More order, indeed, might be introduced, by diminishing the numerous detachments of the Cossacks, and collecting them in a body, under the immediate superintendence of their Attaman, whilst the concentration would assure the most decisive superiority over the French cavalry, and enable the Attaman to fulfil his engagement, "that with ten thousand Cossacks not a French horseman should, with impunity, advance from under the covering fire of the infantry." An engagement which, even with his dispersed corps, was so far accomplished, that from the loss sustained, after the battle of Eylau, and apprehension of Cossack prowess and enterprise, all the French cavalry posts were withdrawn, and the duty performed by infantry, who deserted daily, and who, if proper measures had been taken, would have come over in battalions.

Every general officer wishes to have Cossacks in front of his line, but as they have no authority, no funds, and a commissariat so wretchedly arranged as to admit of no increased burthens, they cannot pretend to interfere with the interior economy of the Cossacks. Yet their own Attaman, embracing the general interests, without alarming their jealousy of encroachment on national prerogatives—without indiscreetly restraining and checking their enterprise, could adopt salutary regulations to diminish the waste of provisions, and mitigate the anxieties of the peasantry by the establishment of a judicious discipline.

The character of the Cossacks certainly never before attained so high a military reputation; but as they fought under the eyes of their Attaman, the pride of distinction, the hope of reward, animated the humblest to the most splendid efforts, until by success they acquired an irresistible confidence! So enthusiastic was the ambition to march with their chief, so emulous were the warriors of the Don to re-engage the French, that old and young flocked as volunteers, and even a patriarch of 100 years of age joined the array, and couched his lance in the fields of Poland.

The Attaman, the generals, and officers, presented also not only an example of courage, but of the successful career of merit in a service where each had obtained his station by individual exertion. Platow himself had once served in their ranks, and his successor will be like him—the most distinguished soldier of his nation; but proud and happy indeed may that nation be if she always finds a chief with equal mind and virtues.

Those who have not seen the achievements of the Cossacks, may, perhaps, from the impression of former opinion, hesitate to credit their superiority in cavalry attacks; but what body, armed with sabres, can resist a lance projecting above six feet beyond the horses heads, sustained by the firmest wrist, and impelled with the activity of the race horse? The Cossack is not first armed with the lance when he proceeds to war, or when he attains manhood: it is the toy of his infancy,, and the constant exercise of his youth; so that he wields it, although from 14 to 18 feet in length, with the address and freedom that the best swordsman in Europe would use his weapon. In hands less familiarized to this arm, it would be the *telum imbelle sine ictu*, but in his direction, under the guidance of an horseman so powerful and dexterous, it becomes invincible but by fire, and the presuming enemy, who rashly adventures an unequal contest, will perish or obtain an inglorious experience.

The Russian cavalry has swam the Danube and the Vistula in regular lines as well as the Cossacks; but no cavalry has power, like them, to march for days and nights, climbing hills, swimming rivers, and winding through vallies without interruption to the prescribed order of gradual progress, and, therefore, by a combination of power, properties, and habits, there is no Cavalry more serviceable or formidable if suitably directed. Ten thousand such warriors would, against more than equal numbers, command in every field, or, in the course of a campaign, ruin their adversaries by mere excess of duty and movement.

Bonaparte, unwilling to allow any merit to his opponent beyond the common quality of courage, and that quality always inferior to his own troops, has, in the *Official Collection of Bulletins*, (not documents,) *Memoirs, &c. of the Campaigns in Prussia, Saxony, and Poland,* admitted "that the Cossacks are brave, active, dexterous, and high-minded warriors." He accuses them of cruelty in action. They at first gave no quarter, but the Emperor offered a ducat for every living prisoner, and several thousand French are now evidences of their mercy; yet it was only in the battle's heat they were sanguinary. They did not murder in cold blood—they did not cut down the sick and the infirm, or glory in butchering, with a division of cavalry, a few dispersed sharp-shooters—vide the account of the massacre of Jaffa, the bulletin in Spain, when General Moore was retreating, and Massena's bulletin of the attack on General Craufurd. Accusations of inhumanity from Bonaparte!!—Scripture quotations from the Devil!!

They and their horses have alike constitutions of iron temper; no toil, no weather, no distress seems to affect their efficiency or impair their service.

Ten thousand such Cossacks, under Paul, were ordered to join the army destined for the invasion of India. They were actually on march to the frontiers, when that monarch ceased to exist.

Amongst the Cossacks there was no dislike to a service from which they know Thomas Kouli Khan returned with a spoil of near 60 millions sterling, and which has been described, with truth, rather as a party of pleasure than an expedition of war; nor could they dread a want of sustenance through a country where a million of camels may be procured for forty shillings a head; a hundred pounds of wheat for fifteen pence; as much salt for two-pence; an ox from six to eight hundred weight for twenty shillings; and a sheep of 200lb. for four shillings; but they dreaded those bad arrangements which impede Russian success, and which more than the forces of Persia have hitherto resisted their Asiatic progress.

The equipment of the Cossack's horse is light—a snaffle, a halter, of which the rein is always held in the hand that he may be instantly attached on dismounting, be or led with facility, the tree of a saddle, on which is bound a cushion stuffed with the Cossack's property, and on which he rides—form the whole of his accoutrements and baggage.

His dress is equally simple; a blue jacket, (with a white frog on the cuff or cape,) fastened with hooks; a pair of loose trousers, plaited so as to cover and conceal the opening in front; a pair of short boots, a black cap made of the unborn lamb, from which depends a red pandour sack, a plume on the side of the cap, or, what is more common, except in the Attaman's regiment, merely a cloth cap with a kind of sack hanging behind, in which he stuffs his provision or other articles—and a white or black hair Circassian short cloak,—is the costume of the Cossack on service and of his country.

But still an Asiatic taste for the embellishment of warlike accoutrements is blended with the simplicity of this equipment. He disdains the ornament of artificial metals, and solid silver is wrought throughout upon his arms and appointments.

The Cossacks of the bodyguard, who are always with the Emperor, indeed, clothe themselves with a magnificence, which, corresponding with their extraordinary proportion and stature, renders them the most superb corps of cavalry that can be imagined. Their dress is red with French grey trousers: they are all nearly six feet high, some much higher, with broad shoulders, and graceful form. Every person who has been at Petersburg can verify the fact.

The admiration of ornament is not however selfishly confined to the decoration of their own persons. The Cossack in his wars never forgets his home, never disconnects his thoughts from his family; with avidity he seeks for tokens of his recollections; he estimates money but as the means of obtaining these more valued objects, and he exchanges for female trinkets, even at an exorbitant depreciation, the spoil that he pursues with eagerness, and acquires with hazard.

When the King of Prussia was anxious to find some further distinction for Platow, who by a series of great and gallant services had exhausted the usual means of royal recompense—he already had received the red and black eagles—for military achievements, the Queen graciously discovered the compliment that would be most grateful to him, and presented into his hands a beautiful heron's plume, rendered inestimable to all who admire beauty, and every female accomplishment that could distinguish a woman and a sovereign, by having herself once worn it. Platow received it with enthusiastic and grateful emotions; but on his knee solicited permission that his "wife might wear it on the most solemn occasions, as he should contemplate it with suitable veneration, when so borne by one who was more worthy than himself of this honour."

The Cossack officers are by no means ignorant or devoid of manners, and education is rapidly extending; but their application to the French language is not congenial to Russian interests.

Amongst the common Cossacks is also frequently found a chivalrous spirit, a delicate sense of honour that would grace the very age of chivalry, and be worthy the records that eternise illustrious actions of fidelity and valour.

When a British officer was observing the retreat of Marshal Ney from Guttstadt, his dress and telescope attracted the attention of the enemy, who directed some cannon at him: the first ball struck the moist earth under his horse, and covered the animal and rider with the sods;—a second ball was fired with similar accuracy, when the attendant Cossack rushed up to him with resentment in his features, and pointing at his helmet, desired him to change it with his cap; and on the officer's refusal, he attempted to snatch it from his head and substitute his own, but during this contest a shower of musket balls rendered the horses wild, and they flew apart. When the Cossack was afterwards asked by the Attaman, with feigned anger, for his own explanation of such disrespectful conduct;—he replied, "I saw that the enemy directed their fire at the English officer on account of his casque and plume—I was appointed by you to protect him—I knew you had marched with many Cossacks, but only one stranger; it was therefore my duty to avert mischief from him by attracting it to myself, and by so doing preventing the sorrow you and every Cossack would feel at the loss of a guest perishing in your service."

When opportunity is favourable, the Cossack indulges in festivity, and revels with the dance and the song; the former is peculiar to the nation, but is something like an English hornpipe, but when women become their partners, they dance English and French country dances with spirit and skill, the latter is truly martial melody—the notes are wild, and enthusiastically inspiring, and their choruses are thundering peals of musical power and barbaric sublimity. Like the Russians, however, they are not insensible to the fascinating harmony of softer strains, and many of their airs are tinged by that spirit of melancholy which Kotzebue unwarrantably attributes to a repining sense of servitude in the Russian nation.

The Cossacks however alone sing sarcastic songs expressive of their regards or dislikes, of the merits and demerits of the the persons introduced; and they mix considerable humour with their freedom, which, like English caricature, is no respecter of persons. There is always a species of buffoon singer who performs with the most extravagant gestures, and changes the notes of his voice in the most extraordinary ventriloquial manner.

Established amongst the Cossacks, with whom they intermarry, are 30,000 Calmucs, who furnish 5,000 soldiers, armed as the Cossacks. Their broad Chinese inanimate countenance, with small eyes, immediately distinguishes them, and they have a greasiness of complexion peculiar to themselves, but although they are Mahomedans, Pagans, &c—although they eat horse flesh, even when tainted, they are in their natural character mild, docile, and inoffensive, and in war they are brave and active. Amongst them are jugglers, who pretend to fortune-telling; but General Bennigsen having asked one to divine what was to happen; he answered, "that he always wrought on a roasted shoulder of mutton, and if one was placed before him, he could give some important intelligence, but otherwise he was unable to trace the destinies." They also have their festivities, but the monotony of their tones, and the expression of their countenance when singing, will not find a parallel in any other nasal performance.

THE BASQUIERS

The 1,500 Basquiers, with helmets of steel, and coats of chain mail, after a march from Grand Tartary, joined the army at Wehlau, on its retreat from Friedland, and in time to discharge a flight of their arrows with some effect upon a squadron of the enemy; but although the Basquiers are personally brave, and might on occasions usefully employ their silent arms, nevertheless their service in European armies (with any number) can never have any great military advantage.

At the same time some benefits might be derived from the example of their habits, and the troops who could like them banquet on horse-flesh, dressed or raw, sweet or tainted, requiring not either bread or wine for sustenance, might indeed be called savages, but would soon have at their command all the luxuries of other nations, to lose again when they adopted the polished manners of the conquered.

The difficulty of procuring and removing the bulky commodity of corn is an impediment to the progress of all armies, and the great embarrassment which controls genius and force; but where a soldiery will feed indifferently on the flesh of those animals that have been killed for the table, or have died of disease; where they will devour with peculiar greediness horseflesh, which in every age and country has been proscribed by the civilized nations of Europe and Asia, military operations must be facilitated.

The Basquiers, like the Cossacks, move with numerous reserved horses, but the latter only employ them for their military duties, whilst the former use them to satisfy their hunger or accelerate the rapidity of their movements, enabling them, as Voltaire describes,

On trembling nations from afar
To breathe a living cloud of war.

The manners and customs of these people have been uniformly represented as the same, from the earliest historian to the present time; but, before fire-arms were introduced, the ancients held their bows and arrows in high estimation: and Alexander reminds Caesar that Crassus and Anthony had felt the Persian arrows, and that the Romans, in a war of 300 years, had not yet subdued a single province of Assyria.

THE OFFICERS

The officers of the guards are, generally, noblemen of rank, but who began their service as private soldiers, which regulation has lately been very properly modified through the army; for although the service of the soldier is not disreputable, and the acquaintance with his duty and hardships most useful, still many inconveniences result from a constant intercourse with a. class whose manners and pursuits are not adapted to the rank in which an officer is to move, and whose uncultivated minds are not calculated to promote a desire of knowledge. The principle was good, but the practice imperfect,[1] and the soldiery, without benefiting solidly, or even imaginably, lost much of that respect for the future officer which is the most satisfactory basis of all discipline; whilst parents with fear committed their children. to the hazard of such dangerous initiation to manhood.

The dress of the officer of infantry is martially plain, and yet handsome, but that of the hussars of the guard rich and splendid to the greatest degree of brilliancy. It is singular that this description of troop, whose service is characterised by the endurance of all the severities of warfare, and whose accommodation admits of no attention to nicety of dress, should, in all services, nevertheless, be more decorated with gold and silver lace than any other; yet such is the unaccountable fact, and the hussars of all royal guards exhaust invention, fancy, and ornament, to rival their comrades; but the same emulous spirit, it must in justice be remarked, animates them to attain more valuable excellencies and distinctions.

The officers of the cavalry of the Russian army are, generally, unexceptionable; and as many are introduced as cadets very young, and go instantly on service, a considerable portion of experience is disseminated. The condition and service of the Russian cavalry is an unequivocal proof of good interior arrangements, and that the officers are entitled to confidence and respect.

The officers of infantry are but in the higher ranks such as ought to fill those stations. With partial exceptions, the inferior officers are disqualified by the neglect of education, and the absence of those accomplishments which should distinguish officers as well as the sash and gorget.

The qualifications of zeal and courage, which they have but in common with the soldiery, are not sufficient to command the

---

1. It would be very advantageous if every officer were obliged to do the duty of a soldier for three months—march with the same appointments, &c. so that he should, when he gave orders, have an experience by which he might judge of the general ability to execute them, and also be instructed in the useful lesson of meting out duty with proper consideration for the man.

respect of superiors or inferiors, and, consequently, the society in the infantry regiments is generally so little worth, that the nobility of the country commence their career in the guards or the cavalry, until they are eligible for those ranks in the infanttry battalions of the line which assure them a better association—a system which is one of the fatal causes of the condition which it proposes to evitate. The poverty of the pay, and the little encouragement afforded previously to officers, without birth to attract consideration to merit, were also more premature and serious causes of this bad composition, but, in addition, it must be remembered, that Russia is a new empire, which, by the genius of her princes has, in the course of a century, established an European dominion that demands immense armies, and that whilst the outline has been drawn with gigantic features, there has not been sufficient time to fill up the interstices by an equal progress in society and civilization. Freedom has been advancing but gradually, and education has extended but slowly against the barriers raised by obstinate ignorance, prejudice, and inveterate habits. Until the sage dispositions of the Government, for the amelioration of the peasantry and the diffusion of instruction, have had time to operate, the chasm must exist between the highest and the lowest classes, and the chain of gradual connection cannot attach the vassal to the lord. That time, however, would, in the natural course of human institutions, be very remote, and the Russian armies would have long to suffer if remedies could not be supplied by the improved financial measures of their Government, and the dispersion through their regiments of the better educated youth of the conquered provinces of Sweden and Poland. Numerous foreigners already are in the Russian service, and are universally encouraged without any regard to country or religion; but then these foreigners are placed in situations where their presence and example have little influence on the character of the mass of Russian officers. The want of regimental officers is more felt in this army than in any other in Europe, and it is marvellous how well the troops behave under such incapacitating circumstances. If the Russian troops had better regimental aids, they would, from their disposition to obedience and habits of temperance,' be as distinguished for their discipline as they are for their courage.

In this view alone the acquisition of Poland would be of infinite value to Russia. Her officers would supply the proportion that is required, to render the Russian army equal to every operation to which its force could at this time pretend; whilst the native officers of the empire would form upon these models, and a general improvement rapidly erase the recollection of former deficiencies, provided the Government at the same time afforded those encouragements, which would be for the interest of the state, and which are the just right of the meritorious subaltern as well as of the chief.

It has before been remarked, that the officers are kind to their men. The higher officers are particularly considerate of them, and promote every occasion for their solace or encouragement. They share every hardship with a gallant spirit of example that cheers the soldier, and which would afford a valuable model to other armies. They enjoy pleasures within their reach, but they make no prearrangement to secure them, or murmur at a deprivation; and with astonishment foreigners must regard the abstinence, the endurance, the total indifference to accommodation, and even the common decencies of the better order of society, with which the high nobility, accustomed to every luxury, in Petersburg and Moscow, proprietors of palaces and royal revenues, encounter the rudeness of the most severe campaigns.

Their courage is worthy of Russian soldiers; the *amor patriae, mdumque immensa cupido* is ever present in their thoughts, and the stimulus to constant exertion. With these feelings is united an ardent ambition of distinction, that cheap defence of nations; and when stars and honours are distributed after gallant actions, they express their joy and exultation with a vehement satisfaction and pleasure which are particularly remarkable in a service where military honours are not rare.

The most cordial friendship, the most liberal hospitality unite the officers, and form a bond of brotherhood. Their generosity is so enlarged, that whatever one possesses is alike the property of the friend or the stranger, and the banquet or the solitary loaf is equally partaken by the invited or uninvited guest. The custom of the capitals of Moscow and Petersburg are continued in the camp, and the spirit of munificent hospitality is not impaired by the diminution of means and the pressure of necessities.

The high sense of their country's pretensions is no less the sentiment of the officer than it is the creed of the soldier, and he is jealous of every remark or incident that might admit an inferiority.

The superior officers are liberal gentlemen, of kind dispositions, affable manners, and honourable conduct, with high independent feelings. They speak several languages fluently, and particularly French; but they by no means are pleased with the familiar use of that language in their camps, or even at court; and when a British friend was ridiculing some incorrect idiom of his comrade whilst speaking French, the same Count Ostreman, with the cheering approbation of a large society, defended him by observing that "it would be more creditable for every nation to be no better acquainted with the language of foreigners than would be sufficient for communication or common courtesies; but it was rather a reproach than otherwise, to speak it nationally so well as to afford cause for censuring an individual, when he was not acquainted with its refinements; and that as a Russian he felt ashamed and alarmed to observe the French language so preferred as to be rapidly superseding his own."

The mischievous habit of gambling is but too prevalent. It is indeed the constant employment of the leisure hours, and all orders on that subject have hitherto been inefficient even to check the practice. There are some few eminent persons, who, having received a better regulated education, pass their time in more worthy occupations; but the great majority abuse their leisure moments by this unsatisfactory and unprofitable pursuit, yet, although they play with the spirit of professed gamesters, they encounter fortune with a placid equanimity which prevents many of the injurious consequences that too frequently are connected with the gaming table, and they do not scruple to confess the impropriety of the custom, or to assign to it the real cause. They are, indeed, so sensible of their error, that they applaud those who have forbearance to refrain; and such was their disdain of corrupting others, that during the course of a twelve-month's residence, there was not one instance of a proposal to any of the British officers serving with the army to participate in their game, although they were living together as members of one family.

Generous by nature, prodigal by military habits, they seem eager to acquire, but to distribute. Satisfied with the present, heedless of the future, they are thoughtlessly profuse, but their good qualities are inseparable from their character. Their faults are but excrescences which time and an improved system will eradicate. The vice of drunkenness does not degrade them. They are, when they have the means, gay and convivial at table, but they have no Bacchanalian orgies, where rank and humanity are confounded and degraded.

The Russian officer, although frequently making the greatest physical exertions, is, however, inclined to indolent habits when not on actual duty; loves his sleep after food, and dislikes to walk or ride far. His general mode of conveyance is in a wagon, even when passing from one cantonment to another; and the number of these carriages with the Russian army is one of the serious impediments to its movements, and a great reduction of the effective strength of the battalions under arms.

Amongst the present Russian officers there is no deficiency of talent; there are, indeed, many excellent generals of brigade and division, but an uninterrupted succession of Suwarrows cannot be expected. The want of truly great captains is universal. Even Bonaparte at Tilsitz, when giving the character of his present marshals, described one as a washerwoman, another as a mere bavard, &c. &c. &c. and observed, "If I should die before them, you will find my account verified, and Europe will be astonished at the miserable insufficiency of my aids."

RUSSIAN STAFF

If regularity of manuscript could organize an army, the Russians long ago would have attained excellence; but much more than sedulous penmanship in the transmission of orders is required for the conduct of this department.

The executive superintendence is of far greater importance to troops in the field; but that superintendence must be united with ability, experience, and its authority; or method in the formation and collection of returns and reports will prove unprofitable, and a chancellery of plans and regulations but useless encumbrances.

In no service is there a greater attention to departmental minutiae, and the lowest Cossack officer, from his saddle or the snow is obliged to send his information with such care about the paper, the wording, folding and address, as if the report was destined to be preserved as a document in the archives of St. Petersburg; but the more essential duties of the departments are very unequally administered, and do not appear in progress of amendment, notwithstanding a diligence most indefatigable; the superior genius of direction is still to be found, and without that head, zeal and regularity are insufficient.

The officers of the Quarter-Master-General Staff draw well,, rapidly, and accurately—take up ground quickly and judiciously; but they have too complicated duties to perform, and many of them prejudicial to their consideration, and which would be better performed by persons whose talents and time were not so valuable. These and other improvements are, however, but minor, the great desideratum is proper chiefs. Their instruments to work with are ready, and of malleable quality.

It has been said that armies, led by officers of other nations, would conquer the world. Certainly, if the Russian army had an Austrian *état* major, it would be adequate to attempt the greatest enterprises even without other amelioration.

The Russians were sensible of the need of an experienced director of this department, and wished General Anstruther to be appointed. They had, in Hanover, learnt to appreciate his merits and abilities, and there satisfied themselves that his reputation, although so great, did not exceed his real qualifications.

The Commissariat

The Commissariat is wretched, but not from the neglect of the commissaries. Magazines and transports are only to be provided with money. The Russian treasury was exhausted, and British aid amounting to eighty thousand pounds, was hardly obtained.

Whilst armies are advancing rapidly, the food of the inhabitants can be seized and may prove sufficient; but when the seat of war becomes permanent, as was the case in Poland, in consequence of Russian valour, famine must destroy the population, and disorganization and disease consume the army, unless, arrangements are made to ensure the regular supplies from un-exhausted countries. As the Russian soldiery are satisfied with less than perhaps any soldiers in Europe, great facilities are afforded for the establishment of sufficient supplies; but, unless those supplies are, in the first instance, redundant, the convoys will always be intercepted by the famishing divisions in route, and rapine and violence will destroy all the resources which might be collected, under a proper direction, from the immediate country in which the army may be acting. As it was, no derangement could be greater, no effect more distressing, and no misery more continual, and it is only extraordinary that the array did not disperse, not from mutinous spirit, but actual necessity.

Russia has the best description of carriage for the transport of provisions. The native and trustworthy Russian, with his powerful pair of horses and cabitka, under good direction, under such direction as Count Pahlin gave when with the Turkish army, ensures the most ample means of transport either for moveable or fixed magazines.

HOSPITALS

At Friedland, for the first time, the wounded were dressed in the field of battle; and the humanity of the Emperor, aiding the zeal of the Surgeon-General, has introduced new regulations[2] in the medical department, which promise to be beneficial: but Russia has not the means to supply a sufficient number of medical officers fit for their appointment; and as the pay is too moderate to invite strangers, the immediate effect must be partial, and the progressive extension of it very slow. It must also be stated, that the care of grievously wounded men, so as to be disabled from future service, has never till lately been in the policy of Government; for the finances of the empire did not admit of this burthen; and even at Friedland it was remarked by an officer of high rank and of most humane character, "that a cannon ball was the best doctor for men without limbs."

When Platow was asked by the Emperor if he would have more medical assistants, as he had but one to his corps, "God and your Majesty forbid," he answered; "the fire of the energy is not half so fatal as one drug."

---

2. M. Wildie, surgeon to the Emperor, has the merit of this improvement, and most active and gallant service; for the wounded were necessarily dressed under the fire of cannon.

After the battle of Eylau the wounded Russians and French did experience, at Koenigsberg, the kindest treatment, and ten thousand men in the hospitals were regularly dressed, but then with Prussian assistance; yet the numbers who perished by horrible lingering deaths in the former actions, and in that battle, from the want of surgical aid, was prodigious, and the most terrible series of irremediable distress were constantly presented.

The Russian soldiery had, however, at last began to be dissatisfied with neglect. Perhaps the residence of many in France had expanded their sense of rights, and as the Emperor was passing through Riga a circumstance occurred that at first occasioned some uneasiness.

Several of the neglected wounded, who had struggled under their sufferings in that place, had often sought to speak with the Emperor, and had as often been driven away. Resolved on seeing him, they took post at the church door through which he was to pass. They were commanded to retire. One who had a severe wound in his arm advanced, and, without any embarrassment, demanded to be heard. "For nine months I and my comrades have endured, without a murmur, all the ills of the most severe campaign; We starved, we marched, we fought, nay *we even retreated* without complaint. We wished to serve our Emperor faithfully, and not augment his difficulties. I call God to witness that for seven days these soldiers and myself had nothing to eat but a piece of hide steeped in water that we might be enabled to chew it when softened, and yet for eighteen hours we remained in the field of battle, until, at the same instant, we were struck with grape.

Now that we have passed our frontiers, and are returned to our own country, we know that the Emperor cannot profit by our ill treatment. Look at this arm; undressed for 17 days, and a burrow for worms ! Look at our bodies worn down with fatigue, and wasting for food. The Emperor may want us again, we are ready to serve him, but he shall know our condition that we may have his redress.

The representation of the indelicacy of intruding on their Emperor at such a moment induced them to withdraw; but the Emperor heard the story, ordered instant relief, and to his honour recompensed the bold but still loyal orator.

Such are the character and state of the Russian armies. Such are the materials with which Peter the Great established his European empire; with which Suwarrow undeviatingly triumphed, and which, under the orders of Bennigsen disputed, and successfully disputed, the power of France. Such is the army which conquered at Pultusk, Eylau, and Heilsberg, and which maintained its honour unimpaired in the unequal battle of Friedland. Materials fully equal to execute whatever ambition proposed, or a conqueror achieved, and which sooner or later, and at no remote period, will re-establish that ascendancy which the errors of policy may defer, but cannot destroy. There is a living active principle of growth and power in the Russian empire; a self-impetus that will break through all restraints which a cabinet would unnaturally oppose; a national spirit of superiority that would resist and ultimately control any humiliating policy of an imbecile or degraded government. But hitherto Russia has been advancing with fleet and gigantic strides in the career of aggrandizement, and consolidation of power. Each Ukase, ever since the treaty of Tilsitz, has announced some important acquisition, either by treaty or the sword, and Catherine never more industriously pursued the views of the aspiring Peter, (as traced in his speech after the naval victory near Aland, over the Swedish fleet,) than has the present ruler of the empire during his short reign.

At Tilsitz the Emperor Alexander might descend from his dignity, and suspend his just estimation in Europe, by a contaminating connexion of personal amity with Bonaparte ; but even in that fatal moment he was not senseless to his duty as protector of Russian interests (for the sake of which he indeed consented to the revolting sacrifice); and although he humiliated his own majesty, he enriched the sway and essentially strengthened the throne of succeeding autocrats.

Peace was not degrading to Russia; the mode of affiancing with France could only render such peace a reproach.

After the glorious and sanguinary resistance that she had alone opposed to Bonaparte with all his means, she was warranted in sheathing an un-dishonoured sword, if her situation and immediate interests required some repose. She had engaged, in the campaign as an ally of Prussia: She had prepared, only as an auxiliary, and to support a sovereign who could bring into the field above 200,000 soldiers of high military character; whose country was covered with strong fortresses; and who had the means of abundantly providing every supply. By the loss of one battle, and a series of unparalleled treasons and misfortunes, Prussia was in a few days annihilated, and the conquerors, confident in numbers, and presumptuous from victory, appeared on the Vistula, with the declared intention of planting their eagles on the towers of St. Petersburg.

The Russian army, inadequate in numbers, unprepared for such a contest, reinforced by no more than 10,000 dispirited Prussians, instead of the victorious multitude that they anticipated to join on the banks of the Rhine—with a knowledge of their immediate wants—without the hope of succour for many months—conscious, but always indignant at the disasters of Austrelitz, resolved to resist the menacing torrent: and by a combination of extraordinary courage and endurance, they not only arrested its progress, but preserved the Russian territory from the foot of an invader, and finally maintained an attitude which obliged Bonaparte to treat their country with a consideration that no hostile power had ever before experienced in his negotiations. Had Alexander but refused for a *third* time that interview which Bonaparte so eagerly urged, and sent his ministers to treat for a peace which the exigencies of Russia, might have rendered generally desirable; such peace would have been sanctioned by honour, and although not in unison with the wishes of England, England would have had no right to remonstrate with asperity or reproach the termination of a war which Russia had alone sustained. If Alexander had not yielded a final acquiescence to councils repugnant to his own feelings; if, in that extremity, he had collected around him the wise, the patriotic, the loyal and the brave, who were ready to support him, and were devoted to his interest, his dignity would have been preserved, and his ministers would have been enabled to maintain a tone commanding terms so favourable, that the assurance of a prosperous continuation of the war could scarcely have offered equal advantages to Russia.

The acquisitions in Poland were of infinite importance to Russia, by extending and confirming her influence over a country with which she can never be disconnected without the utmost danger to her own existence as an European power. The extinction of those hopes that had been excited of a Polish monarchy regenerated under the auspices of Bonaparte, was in itself a momentous result that no statesman in Europe could have anticipated when the French obtained possession of Warsaw, and which so intimately involved the glory and interests of Bonaparte, that even the temporary suspension of that project must be considered as a most important trophy conceded to the still apprehended power of the Russian arms.

The subsequent possession of Finland was a measure that may be condemned for its immorality, but which has placed the most valuable gem in the Russian diadem; and Bonaparte in consenting to the conquest, abandoned the real interests of France *in perpetuo*, for the advantage of a temporary expedient which is approaching to its date. Finland is a province that would have been cheaply purchased by the expense and blood of a long war. It is more than useful; it was necessary for the safety of Petersburg; and in the hands of Sweden it gave to her an offensive attitude, an instrument of menacing terror, which controlled the policy and enfeebled the efforts of Russia.

The anxiety and check were too intolerable for the endurance of a great power; and had the gallant Gustavus[3] been well advised, he would have long before secured the amity of Russia by negotiating for a possession which irritated a formidable neighbour, but which he could not by force maintain. He might have designated territorial equivalents more natural to the present condition of Sweden, and at all events he would, have diminished the ills that a wrested conquest entails.

Fifty thousand men, which the province of Finland[4] will supply from its population, added to the Russian army, and the reduction

3. Gustavus, when the war pressed on Alexander, pledged himself to take no advantage of the nakedness of the Russian dominions—the guards in consequence marched to Poland—Gustavus kept this word—he is now deprived of his throne and his family expatriated.
4. The river Torneo forms the line of demarcation, and the acquired country is in every respect valuable and improvable. The islands of the Gulph of Bothnia ceded to Russia are peculiarly beautiful, and extremely populous. Perhaps Aland ought not to have been required, because the possession does not come within the defensive line to which Russia had pretensions, but is an offensive station, menacing Stockholm, where a fleet may arrive in 24 hours.

of the Russian cordon, are the least of the benefits that its acquisition assures; and whilst every Russian estimates the annexation to be invaluable, even foes must admit that the seizure was instigated by a more rational policy than ambition ordinarily suggests, and that any protraction would have been fatal to the extraordinary opportunity presented for its execution.

The possession of Moldavia was less necessary, but still Moldavia is an important province that pierces deep into her empire, exposes a large frontier, and over which she had long advanced specious pretensions. Moldavia is situated between Wallachia, Transylvania, Hungary, Poland, and the provinces of Oczakow, Budziak, and Bulgaria. It is bounded on the north and east by the Neister and a part of the river Bath; on the south by the Danube, and on the west by the Buckoize. It is 90 leagues in length, and 60 in breadth. Its revenue is calculated at three millions of francs, and the Turks receive an annual tribute of 1,200,000. The Russians conquered it in 1769, restored it 1774, when a part called the Buckoize was added to Austria. The Hospodar or Governor was a general sometimes named by Russia. Bessarabia, the ancient desert of the Getae, belongs to Moldavia, and is only valuable for completing the frontier of the Danube, by which it is bounded on the South.

The Turks, indeed, from their weakened condition, were not likely to be offensive neighbours, but those who are acquainted with the Turkish nation well know that *there* are embers which the genius of one man might kindle, and powers to support the enthusiastic excitement. Turkey is an impoverished, not an exhausted country, and the Mussulman banner may yet wave in a career of victory and ambition beyond the Ottoman boundaries, and the calculations of many European politicians. It is not therefore very inconsistent that Russia should have sought the Danube as her limits and protection from an enemy whose invasions would be characterized with the rapidity of surprise, and whose progress would be traced by the most destructive desolations.

The possession of Wallachia is not indeed so advantageous to Russia, since she removes a neighbour from the Austrian frontier who excites less jealousy, and places herself, who must awaken every suspicion, and thus, even if her intentions are not hostile, diminishes the disposable power, and augments the expenditure of the Austrian monarchy by indispensable precautions; but possession enables exchange, and other arrangements that otherwise might be difficult, if not impracticable; and having value at her disposal, she negotiates with more consideration, and augments the chances of her more serious and warrantable pretensions. Wallachia is bounded on the north by high mountains which separate it from Moldavia and Transylvania—on the east and south- by the Danube—on the west by Transylvania. It has 90 leagues in its extreme length, and 50 in its greatest breadth. The Wallachians make good soldiers.

The line of the Vistula has become the natural boundary of Russia, either by actual incorporation or undisputed influence; and Bonaparte, in the fervour of his connexions with Russia, or of hatred to Prussia, declared at Tilsitz that "he foresaw that Russia would advance to that point;—That it was her natural boundary; although Alexander might then decline the offer, influenced by motives of friendship, a term which he did not recognize in the vocabulary of sovereigns under the head of state affairs." Bonaparte returned Prussia to Alexander, not to the King. Alexander transferred the gift with a little diminution not injurious to Prussia.

The Acquisitions in Galicia from the House of Austria were a continuation of the most propitious fortune, and further established that policy, which, if successfully pursued, will seat the sovereign of Russia on a more military and durable throne than was ever erected by Northern Invaders. Some Russians are of opinion that such an arrangement would only add dignity to the crown, hut be injurious to the power of Russia, whose interests require the incorporation of the Polish provinces, and the extinction of Poland as a nation. If the spirit of the people could be extirpated, perhaps entire amalgamation would be more simple; but the Poles never will forget their rights, and never cease their efforts to recover them. By a wise administration of their government, connecting public and private interests with the fortunes and establishments of Russia, Poland would be not only a feather in the crown, but a most solid pillar for the support of the Russian empire.

Poland, impatient for a monarchy which might reunite her dismembered provinces, and re-establish her in the history of nations—sensible that she alone had not sufficient resource—that her geographical position, girded by great military powers, did not admit of her entire independence or repose; but that applied upon one of these powers, with her interests amalgamated with theirs, she might preserve her integrity, her laws and her dignity, proposed to Russia, whose dominion the subjugated provinces preferred, to invest her sovereign with the regal title, in perpetual fief to her Emperors. The apprehension of adding Austria to the number of her enemies, instead of her active friendly co-operation, as was then expected, deferred the adoption of this proposal, until the fortune of war had created more embarrassing impediments. But Poland—Poland is still the true, the only object about which Russia has now to concern herself. On her will—on her word depends the fiat which not only ensures her prosperity, but which anticipates hostile intentions, that if realised by the previous occupation and disposal of Poland, will shatter the whole power of the Russian empire, south of the Volga, into disunitable fragments. United with Poland her destinies are fixed, and her attitude commands the tranquillity of her rivals. Warring from her positions, and with her population, the conquests of Bonaparte would fleet as rapidly as they were obtained.

The last war has diffused a mass of invaluable experience through the Russian armies. The loss of men was considerable; but the knowledge that the war has disseminated was still cheaply purchased, and when Russia again enters the field, she will have learned by experience of former errors how to proportion her means to her objects : she will support her advanced line of operations with adequate reserves; and not, with a population of near 50 millions, rapidly increasing, set her destinies on the bayonets of one hundred and twenty thousand men, without a depot of recruits between Moscow and their ranks.

It has been indeed insisted, that the population of Russia is so dispersed, that she cannot collect and concentrate her disposable means but such arguments can only be used by persons ignorant of the powers of systematic direction, and who are not habituated to contest with difficulties. Distance is of no consequence if an advance be gained upon the need ; and it must be presumed that Russia has not neglected to profit of the opportunity. An augmented expenditure is indeed a consideration of great weight, and the finances of Russia are embarrassed, but she can never *again* experience pecuniary difficulties when she adopts a policy suitable to her character, and consonant with her legitimate views.

The war with England has counterbalanced some of the advantages of the peace of Tilsitz, and its continuation is injurious to Spain, a nation in whose welfare Alexander ever professed a deep interest, since the mere cessation of hostility would engage the attention of France in the North, and weaken her exertions to conquer the peninsula; but this war being now impolitic, unwarrantable, and unpopular, would not be of long duration, even if collateral incidents did not render an expeditious renewal of amicable relations the essential policy of the Russian government. The declarations of Bonaparte respecting the guarantee of Turkish interests—the alliance with Austria—the appointment of Bernadotte, admit no longer a doubt of his resumed intention to repel the European progress of Russia, and to contend for the recovery of her late acquisitions.

Alexander must see that "in state affairs Bonaparte recognizes no amity amongst sovereigns" and he must be sensible that the hostile projects of Bonaparte *(which he never for a moment could imagine to be abandoned)* are now developing into action, He will be judicious enough to anticipate the designs of his enemy, and not wait until they are matured by the unimpeded occupation of their offensive positions—He finds in Spain an ally who engages near two thirds of the power of France, and a national war not dependant on the caprice, the weakness, or the treachery of continental governments: He has directed attention to England, and has witnessed the phenomenon of a considerable military power created almost with magic rapidity by the spirit of the people in unison with the views of the government—He has seen a kingdom that He was induced, too warrantable, to suppose incapable of employing the force of a petty German state out of her colonies, disembark at one moment near one hundred thousand native troops on the continent, not puny whipsters, not undisciplined rabble, but warriors whose characters are traced in the memorable fields of Maida, Vimeiro, Corunna, and Talavera.

England will embrace, in the true spirit of amity, a nation whose hostility she never feared, but which she has regretted as incompatible with mutual interests, as an interruption to that intercourse, which is founded on the base of admiration and esteem, as well as reciprocal advantage; she will bury in oblivion the recollection of a temporary aberration, or never refer to it but as a lesson to cement more firmly the ties of union.

Bonaparte and the French nation have witnessed and felt the courage of Russian armies, and their efforts under the most distressing and enfeebling circumstances. He has seen their desperate valour retrieve almost irretrievable errors, and he has found that superior force alone can retrograde their columns; that the Russian shrinks not from the French bayonet, the sabre, or the fire, and the battles of the late campaign have engraved an indelible respect and awe for Russian courage and prowess.

We never can want men for such an expedition so worthy of old England. Every man capable of bearing arms, would volunteer to achieve again the exploits of our fifth Henry. Assuredly it is a greater chimera for Bonaparte to propose the capture of London, than for us to take advantage of his situation, and enterprise for Paris. He has often said, that could he but disembark 60,000 men he would conquer us in our very citadel. He had 45,000 at Talavera; and if Massena with 70,000 men, has not in three months taken Lisbon, defended by a very inferior force, England has not much reason to apprehend the loss of London, protected by several hundred thousand bayonets, and British courage, over which, when has France ever established her superiority? It would be well for the world if Bonaparte, with 100,000 men were landed on our shores; The British government should give them free passage over the Channel. But upon the question of invasion the spirit of England should, and now does mount to retort the menace, and reply—

What! shall France seek the lion in his den?
And fright him there, and make him tremble there?

Estimate of the French Forces in December, 1806 on March to the Vistula

	Combatants
Marshal Lannes, between Wraelewic and Plontzk	20,000
Marshal Davoust, Warsaw	30,000
Marshal Augereau, on march to Warsaw	20,000
Marshal Ney, at Thorn	18,000
Marshal Soult, in position, extending from the Higher Warthe towards Pilize	25,000
Marshal Bernadotte, in advance of Warsaw	30,000
Marshal Mortier, on forced march from Berlin	12,000
Marshal Lefebvre, corps of reserve, formed by different corps of the Imperial Guard	12,000
General Oudinot's Corps of Grenadiers, formed at Berlin by companies of his ancient corps that served in Austria, and from reserve on the Rhine	8,000
Grand Total, (exclusive of cavalry under Murat)	175,000

Moreover, Poland agreed to furnish 60,000, to be assembled between Lowicz and Warsaw, (and of which 40,000 actually were in the field.)

Besides the Bavarians, the Saxon, the Baden, the Darmstadt, the Nassau, and the Wirtemberg contingents.

APPENDIX 2

French Army Bulletins

36TH BULLETIN OF THE FRENCH ARMY

Posen, 1st December, 1806

The head-quarters of the Grand Duke of Berg were, on the 27th of November, at Lowicz. General Beningsen, who commanded the Russian army, had, in the hope of anticipating the French, entered Warsaw, and pushed forward an advanced guard to take positions along the river Drizura. On the 26th, the out-posts of the respective armies fell in with each other, and the Russians were thrown into confusion. General Beaumont passed the Drizura to Lowicz, killed and wounded several Russian hussars, and made a regiment of Cossacks prisoners, and pursued the enemy to Blonie. On the 27th, some skirmishing took place between the advanced posts of the cavalry of both armies, when the Russians were pursued, and some taken prisoners. On the 28th, towards evening, the Archduke of Berg entered Warsaw with his cavalry, and on the 29th, the corps of Marshal Davoust advanced to the capital. The Russians had retreated over the Vistula, and had burnt the bridge after they had passed. It would be difficult to describe the enthusiasm of the Poles. Our entrance into the capital was quite a triumph, and it is impossible to form an idea of the zeal which the Poles of every rank display. Patriotism and national spirit have not diminished in the hearts of this people, but have acquired new force amidst misfortune. The most fervent desire, the only wish of the Poles, is to become again a nation. The powerful abandon their castles, and come to implore with earnestness the restoration of their nation, and offer their children, their fortunes, and all their influence towards accomplishing that end. This spectacle is indeed interesting. They have already every where resumed their ancient dress, and their former customs. Shall the Polish throne be re-established, and shall the Great Nation secure for it respect and independence? Shall she recall it to life from the grave? God only, who directs all human affairs, can resolve this great political question. But certainly, never did more memorable, more important, events arise. From a con- geniality of sentiment, which does honour to the French, the few stragglers, who were guilty of excesses in other countries, have ex- perienced so good a reception from the people here, that no severe regulations have been necessary to make them conduct themselves with propriety. Our soldiers often observe that the solitary wilder- nesses of Poland are very different from the smiling fields of their own country—but they immediately add, that the Poles are good. Indeed, the people of this country exhibit themselves in such a light, that it is impossible not to take an. interest in their destiny. The day after this bulletin was published, namely, the memorable 2nd of December, there was addressed, in the name of the Em- peror, to the grand army, the following proclamation:

Imperial Headquarters at Posen
2nd December, 1806
Soldiers!
A year ago, at this same hour, you were on the memorable field of Austerlitz. The scared cohorts of Russia fled defeated before you, or, surrounded, laid down their arms at the feet of their conquerors. To the moderation, and the (perhaps) blameable generosity, which overlooked the criminality of the third coali- tion, is the formation of a fourth to be ascribed. But the ally on whose military skill their principal hope rested, is already no more. His principal towns, his fortresses, his forage and am- munition magazines, 280, standards, 700 pieces of cannon, are in our power. Neither the Oder nor the Warta, the Deserts of Poland, nor the rude season of winter, have been capable of ar- resting for a moment our progress. You have braved all dangers, have surmounted them all, and every enemy has fled on your approach. In vain did the Russians wish to defend the capital of ancient and illustrious Poland. The French eagles hover over

the Vistula. The unfortunate, but brave Poles, on contemplating you, fancy they behold the celebrated legions of the Great Sobieski returning from a military expedition. Soldiers! we shall not lay down our arms until a general peace has confirmed and secured the power of our allies; until it has restored to our commerce its freedom, and given back to us our colonies. On the Elbe, and on the Oder we have re-conquered Pondicherry; all our possessions in India) the Cape of Good Hope, and the Spanish Colonies. What right has Russia to hope that she shall hold the balance of destiny in her hand? What right has she to expect she should be placed in so favourable a situation? Shall there be a comparison made between the Russians and us? Are not we and they the soldiers of Austerlitz?

(Signed) *Napoleon*

37TH BULLETIN OF THE FRENCH ARMY

Posen, 2nd December, 1806

The following are the particulars of the capitulation of fort Czentoskaw: 600 men of the garrison, 30 pieces of cannon, and some magazines, have fallen into our hands. A treasure has been found, consisting of a number of valuables which had been dedicated by the Poles to the Holy Virgin, as the tutelary guardian of the country. This treasure the Emperor has ordered to be given up to the original proprietors. The part of the army at Warsaw remains fully satisfied with the patriotism of the people of that city. This day the city of Posen gave a ball in honour of His Majesty, who remained present an hour. *Te Deum* was also performed to day, in consequence of its being the anniversary of His Majesty's coronation.

38TH BULLETIN OF THE FRENCH ARMY

Posen, 5th December, 1806

Prince Jerome, who commands the army of the allies, after having closely blockaded Glogau, and caused batteries to be constructed around that place, proceeded with the Bavarian divisions of Wrede and Deroi towards Kalitsch, to watch the Russians, and left General Vandamme and the Wirtemberg corps to continue the siege of Glogau. The mortars, and several pieces of cannon, arrived on the 29th of November; they were immediately placed in battery. After a few hours bombardment, the place surrendered, and a capitulation was signed. The allied Wirtemberg troops have displayed great gallantry. 2,500 men, considerable magazines of biscuit, corn, powder, nearly 200 pieces of cannon, are the results of this conquest, which is so important, particularly on account of the excellence of the works and the situation of the fortress. It is the capital of Lower Silesia. The Russians have refused battle on this side of Warsaw, and have repassed the Vistula. The Grand Duke of Berg has passed that river in pursuit of them, and has taken the suburb of Praga. The Emperor has consequently given orders to Prince Jerome to advance on his right, towards Breslau, and to invest that place, which must also soon fall into our power. The seven fortresses of Silesia will be successively attacked and blockaded. When the temper of the troops which are in those places is considered, no one can expect them to make a long resistance. The little fort of Culmbach called Plassenburg, has been blockaded by a battalion of Bavarians. Being furnished with provisions for several months, there was no reason to expect that it should have surrendered soon. The Emperor ordered artillery to be prepared at Cronach and Forchein for battering this fort. On the 24th of November, 22 pieces of cannon were placed in battery, which determined the governor to surrender the place. M. de Beckers, colonel of the 6th Bavarian regiment of the infantry of the line, who commanded the blockade, displayed much skill and activity in the situation in which he was placed. By the articles of capitulation of Plassenburgh, the Prussian garrison were to remain prisoners of war, at the disposal of the King of Bavaria; the officers to be released on their parole; the sick soldiers to remain till recovered; the invalids to retain their allowances, and to be removed to Bayreuth; all the pictures and genealogical tables relative to the royal family of Prussia were to be preserved in the depôt for the King of Prussia. There were found in Plassenburg, 68 pieces of cannon, 64 quintals of powder, 600lb. of saltpetre, 400 quintals of lead, 40 quintals of bar iron, 1144 muskets of different kinds, 700 old muskets, 74 carbines, 200 pistols, 200 sabres, 29 pair of old colours, 29 old standards, 46 new standards,

150 cartouche boxes, 8000 flints, 2,700 hedge bills, 8 caissons, 14 trains, 9 forges, 9 kettle drums, &c. &c. The troops consisted of Major General Baron D'Uttenhosen, 4 majors, 7 captains, 7 lieutenants, 600 privates of the line, and 150 invalids.

39th Bulletin of the French Army

Posen, 7th December, 1806

A courier has arrived with intelligence to the Emperor, that the Russians have declared war against the Porte; that Choczim and Bender are surrounded by their troops; that they have suddenly passed the Dneister, and advanced as far as Jassy. It is General Michelson who commands the Russian army in Wallachia. The Russian army, commanded by Gen. Beningsen has evacuated the Vistula, and seems inclined to bury itself in the interior. Marshal Davoust has passed the Vistula, and has established his headquarters before Praga; his advanced posts are on the Bug. The Grand Duke of Berg remains at Warsaw. The Emperor still has his head-quarters at Posen.

40th Bulletin of the French Army

Posen, 9th December, 1806

Marshal Ney has passed the Vistula, and entered Thorn on the 6th. He bestows particular encomiums upon Colonel Savary, who, at the head of the 14th regiment of infantry, and the grenadiers and voltigeurs of the 96th, and the 6th light infantry, was the first to pass that river. At Thorn he came to action with the Prussians, whom, after a trifling affair, he compelled to evacuate the place. Some were killed, and 20 made prisoners. This affair gave occasion to a very singular exploit. The river, 200 roods in breadth, was covered with ice; the vessel occupied by our advanced guard stuck fast and could not be moved, when a number of Polish seamen from the other side of the river evinced a disposition to venture through a shower of balls, in order to get the vessel afloat. In this intention they were opposed by some Prussian sailors, and a battle with fists ensued between them. The Poles succeeded in throwing the Prussians into the water, and brought the French vessel to the other side. The Emperor has inquired respecting the names of these brave fellows, to reward them. This day the Emperor received the deputation from Warsaw, consisting of M. Gutakouski, Grand Chamberlain of Lithuania, Knight of a Polish Order; Gouzeuski, Lieutenant-General, and Lubenski, Knights of the same Order; and Alexander Potocki, Knight of the Orders of St. Stanislaus and Lusweski.

41ST BULLETIN OF THE FRENCH ARMY

Posen, 14th December, 1806

The General of Brigade Belair, of the corps of Marshal Ney, left Thorn on the 9th, and advanced upon Galup. The 6th battalion of light infantry, and Captain Schoeni, with 60 men of the third regiment of hussars, met a party of 400 cavalry belonging to the enemy. The two advanced bodies immediately came to an engagement. The Prussians lost an officer and 5 dragoons taken prisoners, and had 30 men killed, whose horses we took. Marshal Ney praises highly the conduct of Captain Schoeni on this occasion.—On the 11th, at six in the morning, a cannonade was heard on the side of the river Bug. Marshal Davoust had ordered General Gauthier to pass that river at the mouth of the Urka, opposite the village of Ukunin. The 25th of the line and the 89th having passed, were already covered by a *tête-du-pont,* and had advanced half a league farther, to the village of Pontikuwo, when a Russian, division, presented itself, for the purpose of storming the village. Its efforts were useless, and it was repulsed with considerable loss. We had about 20 men killed or wounded.—The bridge of Thorn, which is constructed upon wooden piles, is re-established. They are now busied in re-establishing the fortifications of that town. The bridge from Warsaw to the suburb of Praga is completed: it is a bridge of boats. They are forming an entrenched camp at the suburb of Praga. The General of Engineers Chasseloup has the chief direction of those works.—On the 10th, the Marshal Augereau passed the Vistula, between Zakroczym and Utrata. His detachments are employed upon the right bank, in covering themselves by entrenchments. The Russians appear to have forces at Pultusk. Marshal Bessieres advanced from Thorn with the second corps of reserve of the cavalry, composed of General Tilly's division of light cavalry, of the dragoons of General Grouchy and Sanue, and of the cuirassiers of General Hautpoult. Messrs. Lucchessini and De Zastrow, Plenipotentiaries of the King of Prussia, passed through Thorn on the 10th, to join their Master at Koenigsberg. A Prussian battalion, of the regiment of De Klock, has deserted in a body from the village of Brok: it arrived at our posts by different roads. It is composed partly of Prussians and Poles. All are indignant at the treatment that they receive from the Russians. "Our Prince,!" they say, "has sold us to the Russians; we will not go with them."—The enemy has burned the fine suburbs of Breslau : many women and children have perished in the flames. Prince Jerome has given succour to those unfortunate inhabitants. Humanity has triumphed over the laws of war, which prescribe, that one should drive back again into a besieged town those useless mouths that the enemy wish to send away. The bombardment has been commenced; General Gouvion is named Governor of Warsaw.

42ND BULLETIN OF THE FRENCH ARMY

Posen, 15th December, 1806

The bridge over the Narew, at its confluence with the Bug, is now finished: the *tête du-pont* is finished, and protected with cannon. The bridge over the Vistula, between Zakroczym and Utrata, is also finished: the *tête-u-pont,* protected by batteries, is a formidable work. The Russian armies come in the direction of Grodno and Bielock, along the Narew and the Bug. The head quarters of their divisions were on the 10th at Poltusk, upon the Narew. General Dulauloi is Governor of Thorn. The 8th corps of the grand army, commanded by Marshal Mortier, is advancing. Its right is at Stettin, its left at Rostock, and its head quarters at Anclatn. The grenadiers of the reserve of General Oudinot are arriving at Custrin. The division of, cuirassiers, lately formed under the command of General Espagnac, is now at Berlin. .The Italian division of General Lecchi is to join at Magdeburgh. The corps of the Grand Duke of Baden is at Stettin. In fifteen days it may be placed in the line. The hereditary Prince has constantly followed the head quarters, and was present at every affair. The Polish division of Zayenscheck, which was organised at Haguenau, is 6000 men strong : it is now at Leipzic, to get its clothing. His Majesty has ordered a regiment to be raised in the Prussian states, on the other side of the Elbe, which is to assemble at Munster: Prince Hohenzollern Sigmaringen is Colonel of that corps.—Peace with the Elector of Saxony, and with the Duke of Saxe Weimar, has been signed at Posen. All the Princes of Saxony have been admitted into the Confederation of the Rhine. His Majesty has disapproved of the levy of contributions in the States of Saxe Gotha and Saxe Meinungen: he has ordered the restitution of what has been raised. Those princes who have not been at war with France, and who have not furnished contingents to Prussia, were not subject to war contributions. The army has taken possession of the country of Mecklenburgh. This is a consequence of the treaty signed at Schwerin, on the 25th of October, 1805. By that treaty the Prince of Mecklenburgh granted a passage to the Russian troops commanded by General Tolstoy. The season is astonishing: it does not freeze; the sun appears every day, and it is quite autumn weather. The Emperor sets out this night for Warsaw.

43RD BULLETIN OF THE FRENCH ARMY

Kutno, 17th December, 1806

The Emperor has arrived at Kutno, at four o'clock in the afternoon, after having travelled all night in the *calochees* (a sort of carriage) of the country, as the thaw makes it impossible to travel in the common carriages. The caloche in which Duroc, Grand Marshal of the Palace, travelled, was overturned. That officer has been severely hurt in the shoulder, but his hurt is not dangerous. This accident will oblige him to keep his bed for eight or ten days. The *tête-du-pont* of Praga, of Zakroczym, of Narew, and of Thorn, are acquiring every day a greater degree of strength. The Emperor will arrive at Warsaw to-morrow. The Vistula being extremely broad, the bridges are every where three or four hundred *toises* in length, which makes the labour very considerable.

Warsaw, 21st December, 1806

Yesterday the Emperor inspected the works of Praga, where eight fine redoubts, with palisadoes, bastions, &c. enclose a space of 1500 toises, and form, upon the whole, the entrenched camp. The Vistula is one of the largest rivers in the world. The Bug, though considerably smaller, is still larger than the Seine. The bridge over the Bug is completed. General Gauthier, with the 25th and 85th regiments of infantry, occupies the *tete-du-pont*, which General Chasseloup has fortified with great skill: so that this *tête du-pont*, which is nearly 400 toises in extent, together with the morasses and the river, enclose an entrenched camp which is capable of covering the whole army upon the right bank, and protecting it from any attempt by the enemy. A brigade of the light cavalry of the reserve has skirmishes with the Russian cavalry every day. On the 18th Marshal Davoust felt the necessity of strengthening and improving his camp upon the right bank t)f the river, and likewise occupying a small island at the mouth of the Urka. The enemy perceived the convenience of this post, and a heavy fusillade immediately commenced between the advanced posts; however, the conquest of the island remained with the French. Our loss consisted of a few wounded. The officer of engineers, Clouet, a young man of great promise, received a ball in the breast. On the 19th, a regiment of Cossacks, assisted by the Russian hussars, endeavoured to surprise the piquet of light cavalry at the *tete-du-pont* of the Bug; but the piquet had taken such a position as secured it against any surprise. The 1st regiment of hussars, and a Colonel, with a squadron of the 13th, immediately coming to the assistance of the piquet, the enemy were thrown into confusion. In this trifling affair we had three or four men wounded, but the Colonel of the Cossacks was killed and 30 men; 25 horses fell into our hands. There are no men so wretched and cowardly as the Cossacks; they are a scandal to human nature. They pass the, Bug, and violate the Austrian neutrality every day, merely to plunder a house in Gallicia, or to compel the inhabitants to give them brandy, which they drink with great avidity. But since the late campaign, our cavalry is accustomed to the mode of attack made use of by these wretches; and notwithstanding their numbers, and their hideous cry on these occasions, they await them without alarm, and it is well known that 2000 of these wretches are not equal to the attack of a squadron of our cavalry. Marshal Augereau passed the Vistula at Utrata. General Laivesse entered Plonsk, after drawing out the enemy. Marshal Soult passed the same river at Vizogrod. Marshal Bessieres was at Kikol on the 18th, with the second corps of the cavalry of reserve. His advanced guard is at Serpez. There have been several affairs between our cavalry and the Prussian hussars, of whom a great number have been made prisoners. The right bank of the Vistula is quite cleared. Marshal Ney, with his light corps, supports Marshal Bessieres: and his right, at the same time, extends to that under the command of Marshal the Prince of Ponte Corvo. Thus every corps is in motion, and if the enemy, remains in his position, a battle will take place in a few days. With God's help, the issue cannot be uncertain. The Russian army is commanded by General Kamenskoy, an old man about 75 years of age. The Generals Buxhowden and Bennigsen command under him! General Michelson has, beyond a doubt, penetrated into Moldavia; and there are accounts that he arrived at Jassy on the 29th of November. We are assured that his generals took Bender by storm, and put every one to the sword. Here behold war declared against the Porte without reason or pretext! But at St. Petersburg it was thought that the moment had arrived when France and Prussia, the two powers who had the greatest interest in preserving the independence of the Porte, being at war, was the most favourable period for subjugating the Turkish empire. Still the events of one month have defeated that project, and to these events the Porte shall be indebted for its preservation. The Grand Duke of Berg has a fever, but he is better. The weather is as mild as at Paris in the month of October, but rainy, which makes it inconvenient. We have taken measures for the delivery of a sufficient quantity of wine, in order to support the vigour of the troops. The palace of the King of Poland, at Warsaw, is a fine edifice, and well furnished. There are several noble palaces and private houses in this city. Our hospitals are well established, which is ho small advantage in this country. The enemy seems to have a number of sick; they also lose greatly by deserters; and of the Prussians we hear nothing, for even whole corps of them have deserted, to avoid that continual contempt which they might expert among the Russians.

45th Bulletin of the French Army

Paluky, 27th December, 1806

The Russian General Bennigsen had the command of an army which was estimated at 60,000 men. At first he intended to cover Warsaw; but he took a lesson from the intelligence of the occurrences which had taken place in Prussia, and determined to retreat towards the Russian frontiers. Without having been compelled almost to fight a single battle, the French entered Warsaw, passed the Vistula, and occupied Praga. In the mean time Field-Marshal Kamenskoy joined the Russian army, just at the moment when General Bennigsen's corps formed a junction with that under Buxhovden. He was indignant at the retreat of the Russians, conceiving that it tended to sully the honour of his country's arms, and he accordingly made a movement in advance. Prussia remonstrated with the most earnest importunity; and complained, that, after all the promises of support made to her, she was abandoned; representing, that the way to Berlin was not by Grodno, Olita, or Brezsc; that her subjects had begun to abate in their zeal for their sovereign; and that the habit of beholding the throne of Berlin hi the possession of the French was dangerous to him and favourable to the enemy. The Russians not only ceased their retrograde movement, but they again began to advance. On the 5th of December, General Bennigsen moved forward his head quarters to Pultusk. The orders issued were, to prevent the French from passing the Narew, to retake Praga, and to occupy the banks of the Vistula until the moment when more important offensive operations could be adopted. The junction of Generals Kamenskoy, Buxhovden, and Bennigsen, was celebrated at the palace of Sierock with rejoicings and illuminations, which were descried from the steeples of Warsaw. Nevertheless, at the moment when the enemy were cheering themselves with festivals, the Narew was passed. Eight hundred Frenchmen having suddenly crossed the Narew at its junction with the Ukra, entrenched themselves the same night; and when the enemy appeared next morning, with the intent of forcing them back into the river, they found themselves too late. The French were secure against every event. Being informed of this change in the enemy's operations, the

Emperor left Posen on the 10th; at the same moment he put his army in motion. Every report which had been received of the movements of the Russians gave him to understand that they designed, to resume offensive operations. Marshal Ney had been for several days master of Thorn: he united the different corps of his army at Gallup. Marshal Bessieres, with the second corps of the cavalry of reserve, consisting of the divisions of dragoons of Sahuc and Grouchy, and the division of Hautpoult's cuirassiers, marched from Thorn to proceed to Biézun. The Marshal Prince of Ponte Corvo marched with his corps to support them. Marshal Soult passed the Vistula opposite Plock; and Marshal Augereau passed at Zakroczyn, where the utmost exertion was made to establish a bridge. The same activity was exerted in constructing that on the Narew. On the 22nd the bridge on the Narew was completed. All the reserve of cavalry instantly passed the Vistula at Praga, on their march to the Narew, where Marshal Davoust had collected the whole of his corps. At one o'clock in the morning of the 23rd the Emperor set out from Warsaw, and passed the Narew at nine. On reconnoitring the Ukra, and the considerable entrenchments thrown up by the enemy, he ordered a bridge to be thrown across at the confluence of the Narew and Ukra. By the zeal of the General of Artillery the bridge was completed in two hours.

46TH BULLETIN OF THE FRENCH ARMY

Golymin, 23rd December, 1806

Marshal Ney, charged with executing the manoeuvres by which he was to drive the Prussian Lieutenant-General Lestocq from Wkra, to outflank him, and by these means to cut of his communications with the Russians, has executed these movements with his accustomed ability and intrepidity. On the 23rd, General Marchand's division moved to Gurrzno. On the 24th, the enemy was pursued to Kunzbrock. On the 25th, the division came to an action, by which the enemy's rear suffered some loss. On the 26th, the enemy having collected at Soldau and Miawa, Marshal Ney was determined to advance and attack him. The Prussians were in possession of Soldau, with 6000 infantry, and about 1000 cavalry, and, being defended by morasses and other obstacles about the place, they thought themselves secure against any attack. All these difficulties, however, were surmounted by the 69th and 76th regiments. The enemy defended themselves in all the streets of the place, and were every where driven with fixed bayonets. General Lestocq, observing the small number of the troops that had attacked him, wished to retake the place. In the course of the night he made four successive attacks, without effect. He afterwards retired to Neidenburg. Six pieces of cannon, some colours, and a great number of prisoners, are the effects of this affair at Soldau. Marshal Ney praises General Vonderweldt, who was wounded. He also makes particular mention of Colonel Brunn, of the 69th, whose behaviour was highly encouraging. On the same day the 59th marched to Lauterburg. During the action at Soldau, General Marchand's division drove the enemy from Miawa, where also a great action took place. Marshal Bessieres had already taken possession of Biézun, with the second corps of cavalry on the 19th. The enemy, feeling the importance of this post, and observing that the left wing of the French army wished to cut the Prussians off from the Russians, made an attempt to retake the place : this gave rise to the engagement at Biézun. On the 23rd, at o'clock, the enemy approached by various ways. Marshal Bessieres had placed the only two companies of infantry he had upon the bridge; when seeing the enemy approach in great numbers, he ordered General Grouchy to advance with his division to meet them. The enemy had already made himself master of the village of Carmeden, into which he had already thrown a battalion of infantry. Being attacked by General Grouchy's division, the enemy's line was soon broke; the Prussian infantry and cavalry, 9000 strong, were thrown into confusion, and driven into the morasses. Five hundred prisoners, five pieces of cannon, and two standards, are the fruits of this attack. Marshal Bessieres bestows the highest encomiums upon General Grouchy, General Rouget, and his Chief of the Staff, General Roussel; Renie, the Chef d'Escadron of the 6th dragoons, distinguished himself. M. Launay, Captain of the select company of that regiment, is killed.

47TH BULLETIN OF THE FRENCH ARMY

Pultusk

The affair of Czarnowo, that of Nasielsk and Kursomb, that of the cavalry and Lapoczyn, have been followed by that of Pultusk, and by the complete and precipitate retreat of the Russian army, which has finished the present year's campaign. Marshal Lannes first arrived on the morning of the 26th, directly opposite to Pultusk, where, during the night, the whole of General Bennigsen's corps had assembled. The Russian division, which had been defeated at Nasielsk, had arrived about two in the morning at the camp of Pultusk, with the third division of Marshal Davoust's corps in close pursuit of them. At ten o'clock Marshal Lannes began the attack, having his first line composed of the division of Suchet, the second of Gazan's, and that of Oudin, of the 3rd light corps under the command of General Dauttaue, on his left wing. The engagement was obstinate; after various occurrences, the enemy was completely routed. The 17th regiment of light infantry, and the 34th, covered themselves with glory. Generals Vedel and Claperede were wounded. General Treilhard, commandant of the light cavalry; General Bouslard, commandant of a brigade of dragoons under General Becker; and also Colonel Barthelemy, of the 15th dragoons, were wounded with grape shot. Volsin, *aid-de-camp* to Marshal Lannes; and M. Curial, *aid-de-camp* to General Suchet, were killed, and both have fallen with glory. Marshal Lannes was likewise grazed by a ball. The fifth corps of the army gave a proof of every thing that could be expected from the superiority of the French infantry over that of other nations. Marshal Lannes, though he had been for six days indisposed, persisted in following the corps. The 85th regiment sustained several charges of the enemy's cavalry with great coolness and success. During the night the enemy beat a retreat, and reached Ostrolenka.

48TH BULLETIN OF THE FRENCH ARMY

Warsaw, 3rd January, 1807

General Corbineau, *aid-de-camp* to the Emperor, had set off from Pultusk, in pursuit of the enemy, with three regiments of light cavalry. After occupying Brok, he reached Ostrowiel, on the 1st instant. On his march he picked up 400 Russian soldiers, several officers, and a great quantity of baggage wagons.—Marshal Soult, with three brigades of light horse, part of Lasalle's division, has taken a position along the banks of the little river Orcye, in order to cover the cantonments of the army.—Marshal Ney, the Prince of Ponte Corvo, and Marshal Bessieres, have cantoned their troops on the left bank. The light corps, under Marshals Soult, Davoust, and Lannes, continue to occupy Pultusk and the banks of the Hug. The enemy's army continues to retreat. The Emperor arrived at Warsaw on the 2nd of January. We have had snow and frost for two days in continuance; but it has begun again to thaw, and the roads which were becoming somewhat better, are now as bad as before. Prince Borgheze has incessantly been at the head of the 1st regiment of carabineers which he commands. The brave carabineers and cuirassiers testified the most anxious desire to meet the enemy ; but the division of dragoons which came first into action, by carrying every thing before them, left the former no opportunity of attacking the enemy. His Majesty has appointed General Lariboissiere a general of division, and given him the command of the artillery of the guards. He is an officer of the highest merit. The troops of the Grand Duke of Wurtzburgh compose the garrison of the city of Berlin. They consist of two regiments which make an excellent appearance. The corps under Prince Jerome continues to besiege Breslau. That beautiful city is in ashes. A disposition to wait the course of events, and the hope of being relieved by the Russians, have prevented the garrison from surrendering, but the siege makes progress. The Bavarian and Wirtemberg troops have merited the praise of Prince Jerome, and the esteem of the French army. The Governor of Silesia had collected the garrisons of the fortresses not yet blockaded, and formed out of them an army of 80,000 men, with which force he had commenced his march to interrupt the operations of the army besieging Breslau. Against this force General Hedouville, the chief of Prince Jerome's staff, detached General Montbrun, commandant of the Wirtemburghers and General Minucci, commandant of the Bavarians. They came up with the Prussians at Strenien, put them to flight, and took 400 men, 600 horses, and several convoys of provisions, which the enemy intended to send into the fortress. Major Herscher, at the head of 150 of Leningen's light horse, attacked two Prussian squadrons, and completely routed then, making 36 of them prisoners.

Breslau has surrendered. The capitulation has not yet been received at the head-quarters; neither has the inventory of the magazines of subsistence, or of the clothing and artillery, yet come to hand. They are, however, known to be very considerable. Prince Jerome must have made his entry into the place. He is going to besiege Brieg, Schweidnitz, and Kusel. General Victor, commander of the 10th corps of the army, has marched to besiege Colberg and Dantzic, and to take these places during the remainder of the winter. M. de Zastrow, *aid-de-camp* to the King of Prussia, a wise and moderate man, who had signed the armistice which his master did not ratify, was, however, on his arrival at Koenigsberg, appointed Minister for Foreign Affairs.—Our cavalry is not far from Koenigsberg.—, The Russian army is continuing its movements towards Grodno. We learn that in the last engagements it had a great number of generals killed and wounded. It evinces great discontents against the Emperor of Russia and the court. The soldiers say, that if their army had had been judged strong enough to fight with advantage against the French, the Emperor, bin guards, the garrison of Petersburg, and the generals of the court, would have been conducted to the army by the same security which brought them to it last year; that if, on the contrary, the events of Austerlitz and those of Jena made it be thought that the Russians could not obtain successes against the French army, they ought not to have been engaged in an unequal struggle. They also say, "the Emperor Alexander has compromised our glory. We had always been vanquishers; we had established and shared the opinion that we were invincible. Things are greatly altered. For these two years past we have been led about from the frontiers of Poland to Austria, from the Dniester to the Vistula, and made to fall every where into the snares of the enemy. It is difficult not to perceive that all this is ill managed."—General Michelson is still in Moldavia. There is no news of his having marched against the Turkish army, which occupies Bucharest and Wallachia. The fears of that war are hitherto confined to the investing of Choczim and Bender. Great movements are taking place throughout all Turkey to repel so unjust an aggression.—General Baron Vincent is arrived from Vienna at Warsaw, with letters from the Emperor of Austria for the Emperor Napoleon.—There had been a great fall of snow, and it had frozen for three days. The use of sledges had given a great rapidity to the communications, but the thaw has just began again. The Poles assert, that such a winter is unexampled in this country. The temperature is in reality milder than it generally is at Paris at this season.

50TH BULLETIN OF THE FRENCH ARMY

Warsaw, 13th January, 1807

The troops found at Ostrolenka several sick Russians, whom the enemy had been unable to take off with him. Independent of the loss of the Russian army in killed and wounded it has suffered still greater losses by the illness which increases in it from day to day.—On the 8th of January the garrison of Breslau, consisting of 5,500 men, defiled before Prince Jerome. The town has sustained considerable damage. From the first moment it was invested, the Prussian governor caused the three suburbs to be burned. The fortress was regularly besieged; we were already battering it in breach when it surrendered. The Bavarian and Wirtemberg troops distinguished themselves by their intelligence and bravery.—Prince Jerome is now investing and besieging, at the same time, all the other fortresses in Silesia; it is probable that they will not hold out long. The corps of 10,000 men, whom the Prince of Pless formed of the garrisons of the fortresses, were cut in pieces in the engagements of the 29th and 30th of December. General Montbrun, with the Wirtemberg cavalry, went to meet the Prince of Pless, near Ohlau, which he took possession of on the 28th, in the evening. On the following morning, at five o'clock; the

Prince of Pless ordered him to be attacked. General Montbrun, taking advantage of the unfavourable position of the enemy's infantry, made a movement to the left, turned and killed a number of men,, made 700 prisoners, took four pieces of cannon, and as many horses.—The principal forces, however, of the Prince of Pless, lay behind on the side of Neis, where he assembled them after the engagement of Strechlen. He left Schurgalt, and marching day and night, advanced as far as the night camp of the Wirtemberg brigade, which were drawn up in the rear of Hube, under Breslau. At eight in the morning he attacked, with 600 men, the village of Griesten, occupied by two battalions of Infantry, and by the Lilange light-horse, under the command of the Adjutant Commandant Duveyrier; but he met with so vigorous a reception, that he was forced to make a speedy retreat. Generals Montbrun and Minucci received orders immediately on their return from Ohlau to cut off the enemy's retreat. But the Prince of Pless made haste to disperse his troops, and made them return by detachments into the fortresses, abandoning in his flight a part of his artillery, a great deal of his baggage, and several horses. He had a number of men killed in this affair, and left us 800 prisoners.—Letters received from Bucharest give some details concerning the preparations for war making by Baraycter and the Pacha of Widdin. On the 20th December, the advanced guard of the Turkish army, consisting of 15,000 men, were on the frontiers of Wallachia and Moldavia. The Prince Dolgorucky was also there with his troops. They were thus in the presence of each other. In passing Bucharest, the Turkish officers appeared to be very much animated; they said to a French officer who was in that town, "the French shall see what we are capable of; we form the right of the army of Poland; we shall show ourselves worthy to be praised by the Emperor Napoleon the Great."—Every thing is in motion through this vast empire; the Sheiks and Ulemas give the impulsion, and every one flies to arms in order to repel the most unjust of aggressions. Count Italinsky has hitherto only avoided being sent to the Seven Towers, by promising that on the return of his messenger the Russians will have received orders to abandon Moldavia, and restore Choczim and Bender.

Warsaw, 14th January, 1807

On the 29th of December, the annexed dispatch of General Bennigsen was received by the King of Prussia at Koenigsberg. It was immediately published and posted up throughout the town, where it excited the greatest transports of joy. The King was publicly complimented on the occasion, but on the 31st in the evening intelligence was given by some Prussian officers, corroborated by other advices from the country, of the real state of things. Sadness and consternation were now so much the greater, as every one had abandoned himself to joy. It was then resolved to evacuate Koenigsberg, and preparations were accordingly made for that purpose. The treasure and most valuable property was immediately sent to Memel. The Queen, who was still ill, .embarked on the 3rd of January for that town; the King set out from thence on the 6th. The remains of General Lestocq's division also departed for the same, after leaving at Koenigsberg two battalions and a company of invalid The King of Prussia's ministry is composed in the following manner:—General Ruchel, still ill of the wound he received at the battle of Jena, is appointed Minister at War. Till President, Sagebarthe, is appointed Minister of the Interior.—The present forces of the Prussian monarch are as follows:—The King is attended by 1500 troops, both foot and horse. General Lestocq has scarcely 5000 men, comprising the two battalions left at Koenigsberg with the company of invalids. Lieutenant General Hamburger commands at Dantzic, where he has a garrison of 6000 men. The inhabitants have been disarmed, and it has been intimated to them that in case of alarm the troops will lire on all those who shall quit their houses. General Guzadon commands at Colberg with 1800 men. Lieutenant General Couhiere is at Gradentz with 3000 men. The French troops are in motion to Mirround and besiege these fortresses. A certain number of recruits whom the King of Prussia had caused to be assembled, and who were neither clothed nor armed, have been disbanded, because there was no method of keeping them in order. Two or three English officers were at Koenigsberg, and caused hopes to be entertained of the arrival of an English army. The Prince of Pless has in Silesia 12 or 15,000 men shut up in the fortresses of Breig, Neis, Schweidnitz, and Konell, which Prince Jerome has caused to be invested. We shall be silent concerning the ridiculous dispatch of General Bennigsen; we shall only remark that it contains something inconceivable. This General seems to accuse his colleague, General Buxhovden; he says that he was at Mokow. How could he be ignorant that Buxhovden was gone to Golymin, where he was beaten; he pretended to have gained a victory, and nevertheless he was in full retreat at ten at night, and this retreat was so hasty that he abandoned his wounded? Let him show us a single piece of cannon, a single French standard, a single prisoner, but twelve or fifteen men who might have been taken here and there in the rear of the army, while we can show him 6000 prisoners, two standards, which lie lost near Pultusk, and 3000 wounded whom he abandoned in his flight. Should General Bux-hovden have given, on his side, as true a relation of the engagement of Golymin, it will be evident that the French army was beaten, and that in consequence of its defeat it took possession of 100 pieces of ordnance and 1600 baggage wagons, of all the hospitals of the Russian army, of all its wounded, and of the important position of Sieroch, Pultusk, Ostrolenka, and obliged the enemy to fall back 80 leagues. With regard to the inference attempted to be drawn by General Bennigsen, from his not having been pursued, it is sufficient to observe, that good care was taken not to pursue him, because our troops outstretched him by two days march, and that but for the bad roads that hindered Marshal Si ink from following this movement, the Russian General would have found the French at Ostrolenka. It remains for us only to seek what could be the intention of such a relation ? It is the same, no doubt, that the Russians proposed to themselves at the battle of Austerlitz. It is the same, no doubt, as that of the Ukases, by which the Emperor Alexander declined accept-ing the grand insignia, because, he said, he had not commanded at that battle, and accepted the small insignia for the success he had obtained in it, although under the command of the Emperor of Austria. He says furthermore, he had the Grand Duke of Berg and Davoust against him, whilst, in fact, he had only to cope with the division of Sachet, and the corps of Marshal Lannes; the 17th regi-ment of light infantry, and 34th of the line, the 64th and 88th are the only regiments who fought against him. He must have reflected very little on the position of Pultusk, to suppose that the French would take possession of that town, commanded within pistol shot. There is, however, one point of view under which the relation of General Beningsen may be justified. No doubt but apprehensions were entertained of the effect which the truth might produce throughout Prussian and Russian Poland, which the enemy were to cross, had it readied those countries previous to his being enabled to place his hospitals and scattered detachments safe from insult. These relations, so evidently ridiculous, may still produce the advantages for the Russians of delaying for some days the ardour which faithful recitals will not fail to inspire the Turks with; and these are circumstances in which a few days form a delay of some importance. Experience, however, has proved, that all wiles defeat their end, and that in all things simplicity and truth are the best means in policy.

52nd Bulletin of the French Army

Warsaw, 19th January, 1807

The 8th corps of the grand army, commanded by Marshal Mortier, has detached the second battalion of light infantry to Wollin; three companies of the same regiment had scarcely arrived there, when before break of day they were attacked by a detachment of 1000 foot, and 150 horse, with four pieces of cannon, from Colberg. The French, not appalled by the enemy's great superiority of number, carried a bridge, took four pieces of cannon, and made 100 prisoners. The rest were put to flight, leaving behind a number of slain and wounded in the city of Wollin, the streets of which were covered with them. The city of Brieg, in Silesia, has surrendered after a siege of five days. Poland, rich in grain and provisions, affords us a plentiful supply; Warsaw alone furnishes 100,000 rations per day. No diseases prevail in the army, nor is it possible to take more care of the health of the soldiers than is done; although the winter season is already so far advanced, no severe frost has hitherto been experienced. The Emperor is daily on the parade, and reviews the different corps of the army, which, as well as the detachments of conscripts who arrive from France, are supplied with shoes and other necessaries out of the magazines of Warsaw.

Considerable magazines of provisions were found at Brieg. Prince Jerome continues his campaign in Silesia with activity. Lieut.-General Deroi has already surrounded Kosel, and opened the trenches. The siege of Schweidnitz, and that of Neisse, are pushed at the same time. General Victor, being on the way to Stettin, in a carriage, with his *aid-de-camp* and a servant, was taken prisoner by a party of 25 chasseurs, who were scouring the country. The weather has grown cold; it is probable, that, in a few days, the rivers will be frozen; the season, however, is not more severe than it usually is at Paris. The Emperor every day parades, and reviews several regiments. All the magazines of the French army are in a train of organization; biscuit is made in all the bake-houses. The Emperor has given orders, that large magazines be established; and that a,great quantity of clothing should be made in Silesia. The English who can no longer gain credit for their reports, that the Russians, the Tartars, and the Calmucks, are about to devour the French army, because it is well known, even in the coffee-houses of London, that these worthy allies cannot endure the sight of our bayonets, are now summoning the dysentery, the plague, and every kind of epidemical disease, to their assistance. Were these calamities at the disposal of the cabinet of London, not only our army, but also our provinces, and the whole class of manufacturers of the continent, would, doubtless, become their prey. As this is not the case, the English content themselves with circulating, and causing their numerous emissaries to circulate, in every possible shape, the report that the French army is destroyed by disease. By their account, whole battalions are falling like those of the Greeks at the siege of Troy. This would be a very convenient way of getting rid of their enemies; but they must be made to renounce it. The army was never more healthy; the wounded are recovering, and the number of dead is inconsiderable. There are not so many sick as in the last campaign; nay, their number is even inferior to what it would have been in France in time of peace, according to the usual calculations.

54TH BULLETIN OF THE FRENCH ARMY

Warsaw, 27th January, 1807

Eighty-four pieces of cannon, taken from the Russians, are ranged before the Palace of the Republic at Warsaw. They are those which were taken from Generals Kaminskoy, Bennigsen, and Buxhowden, in the battles of Czarnowo, Nasielsk, Pultusk, and Golymin; and are the very same that the Russians drew along the streets of this city with so much ostentation, when lately they marched through them to meet the French. It is easy to conceive the effect which the sight of so grand a triumph must produce upon a people delighted with seeing the humiliation of enemies who have so long and so cruelly oppressed them. There are several hospitals in the country which the army occupies, containing a great number of sick and wounded Russians. 5000 prisoners have been sent to France, 2000 escaped in the first moments of confusion, and 1500 have entered among the Polish troops. Thus have the battles with the Russians cost them a great part of their artillery, all their baggage, and from 25,000 to 30,000 men, killed, wounded, or prisoners. General Kaminskoy, who had been represented as another Suwarrow, has just been disgraced. It is reported that General Buxhowden is in the same situation : hence it appears, that General Bennigsen now commands die army. Some battalions of light infantry belonging to Marshal Ney's corps had advanced twenty leagues from their cantonments; the Russian army took the alarm, and made a movement on its right. The battalions have returned within the line of their cantonments, without sustaining any loss. During this period, the Prince of Ponte Corvo took possession of Elbing, and the country situated on the borders of the Baltic. The General of Division Drouet entered Christbourg, where he took 300 prisoners from the regiment of Courbieres, including a major and several officers. Colonel Saint Genez, of the 19th dragoons, charged another of the enemy's regiments, and took 50 prisoners, among whom was the Colonel Commandant. A Russian column had gone to Liebstadt, beyond the little river the Passarge, and had carried off half a company of the voltigeurs of the 8th regiment of the line, who were at the advanced posts of the cantonment. The Prince of Ponte Corvo, informed of this movement, left Elbing, collected his troops, advanced with Rivaud's division towards the enemy, and met them near Mohring. On the 25th at noon, the enemy's division appeared, 12,000 strong. We soon came to blows. The 8th regiment of the line fell upon the Russians with inexpressible bravery, to repair the loss which one of its posts had experienced. The enemy were completely routed, pursued four leagues, and compelled to repass the Passarge. Dupont's division arrived just as the engagement was concluded, and could take no part in it.—An old man, 117 years of age, has been presented to the Emperor, who has granted him a pension of 50 Napoleons, and has ordered him a twelve-month's allowance in advance. The weather is very fine. It is no colder than it should be for the health of the soldiers, and the amendment of the roads, which are becoming passable. On the right and centre of the army the enemy are more than 30 leagues from our posts. The Emperor is gone on horseback to make the tour of the cantonments. He will be absent from Warsaw eight or ten days.

55TH BULLETIN OF THE FRENCH ARMY

Warsaw, 29th January, 1807

The details of the battle of Mohringen are as follow:—The Marshal Prince of Ponte Corvo arrived at Mohringen with the division of Drouet, on the 23th, at eleven in the morning, at the very moment when the General of Brigade Pactod was attacked by the enemy. The Marshal Prince of Ponte Corvo ordered an immediate attack of the village of Pfarresfeldeben, by a battalion of the 9th of light infantry. This village was defended by three Russian battalions, which were supported by three others. The Prince of Ponte Corvo caused also two other battalions to march, to support that of the 9th. The action was very sharp. The eagle of the 9th regiment of light infantry was taken by the enemy; but on the aspect of the affront with which this brave regiment was on the point of being covered for ever, and from which neither victory, nor the glory acquired in an hundred combats, would have purified it; the soldiers, animated with an inconceivable ardour, precipitated themselves on the enemy, whom they routed, and recovered their eagle. In the mean while the French line, composed of the 8th of the line, of the 27th of light infantry, and of the 94th, were formed, and attacked the Russian line, which had taken its position on a rising ground. The fire of the musketry was very brisk, and at point blank distance. At this moment General Dupont appeared on the road, with the 32nd and 96th regiments. He turned the right wing of the enemy. A battalion of the 52d rushed upon the enemy with its usual impetuosity, put them to flight, killing several of them. The only prisoners they made were those who were in the houses. The Russians were pursued for two leagues, and were it not for the coming on of night, the pursuit would have been continued. Counts Pahlen and Gallitzin commanded the Russians. They left 1200 dead on the field of battle, and lost 300 prisoners and several howitzers. Laplanche, General of Brigade, distinguished himself. The 19th dragoons made a fine charge against the Russian infantry. It is not only the good conduct of the soldiers, and the talents of the Generals, which are most worthy of remark, but the expedition with which the troops broke up from their cantonments, and performed a march which would be reckoned extraordinary for any other troops, without a man being missing in the field of battle. It is this which eminently distinguishes soldiers who have no other impulse but that of honour. A Tartar is just arrived from Constantinople, which place he left on the 1st of this month. He has been dispatched to London by the Porte. On the 30th of December war with Russia had been, solemnly proclaimed. The pelisse and the sword had been sent to the Grand Vizier: 28 regiments of Janissaries set out for Constantinople; and several others passed from Asia to Europe. The ambassador of Russia, his whole suite, all the Russians in that city, and all the Greeks belonging to them, to the amount of seven or eight hundred, quitted Constantinople on the 29th. The English Minister and two English ships remained spectators of these events, and appeared to wait the orders of their government. The Tartar passed through Widdin the 15th of January. He found the roads covered with troops, who marched with alacrity against their eternal enemy; sixty thousand men were already at Rudschuk, and twenty-five thousand, composing the advanced guard,, were between that town and Bucharest. The Russians halted at Bucharest, which they occupied with an advanced guard of fifteen thousand men Prince Suzzo was proclaimed Hospodar of Wallachia. Prince Ypsilanti was proclaimed a traitor, and a price set upon his-head. The Tartar has met the Persian ambassador on the road, half way from. Widdin to Constantinople, and the ambassador extraordinary of the Porte beyond this last city. The victories of Pultusk and of Golymin were already known in the Ottoman empire. The *Tartar courier* heard the recital from the Turks themselves before he arrived at Widdin.

56TH BULLETIN OF THE FRENCH ARMY

Arensdorf, 5th February, 1807

After the combat of Mohrungen, where the advanced guard of the Russian army had been beaten and routed, it fell back upon Liebstadt; but the day after but one (the 27th of January), several Russian divisions joined it, and all marched forward to carry the theatre of war on the Lower Vistula.

The corps of General Essen had arrived from Moldavia, where it had been destined to serve against the Turks, and several regiments which were in Russia, and had been put in march for some time from the extremities of this vast empire had joined that corps of the army.

The Emperor ordered the Prince of Ponte Corvo to retreat, and to favour the offensive operations, by attracting it to the Lower Vistula. He ordered, at the same time, the establishment of his winter quarters.

The 5th corps, commanded by General Savary, Marshal Lannes being sick, was united on the 31st of January, at Brok, to check the corps of Essen, stationed upon the High Bog.

The 3rd corps assembled at Maysiniez.

The 4th corps at Willenberg.

The 6th corps at Gilginburg.

The 7th corps at Neidenburg.

The Emperor quitted Warsaw, and arrived in the evening of the 31st of January at Willenberg, where the Grand Duke had for several days been reuniting all his cavalry.

The Prince of Ponte Corvo had successively evacuated Osterode and Jobree, and had thrown himself upon Strasburg.

Marshal Lefebvre had reunited the 10th corps at Thorn, for the defence of that city, and the left of the Vistula.

On the 1st of February the army marched. At Passenheim it met the advanced guard of the enemy, which was proposing the offensive, and was directing itself upon Willenberg. The Grand Duke, with several columns, charged and carried the town by assault.

The corps of Marshal Davoust marched on Ortelsburg.

The Grand Duke of Berg marched on Allenstein, with the corps of Marshal Soult.

The corps of Marshal Bernadotte marched on Wartzburg.

The corps of Marshals Augereau and Ney arrived on the 3rd at Allenstein.

On the 3rd, in the morning, the enemy's army, which had retrograded with precipitation, seeing itself turned on the left flank, and thrown upon that Vistula over which it had boasted so much to pass, appeared ranged in order of battle. The left appeared on the village of Moudthen, the centre at Yankowo, covering the great road to Liebstadt.

COMBAT OF BERGFRIED

The Emperor went to the village of Gettkendorf, and arranged his order of battle ; the corps of Marshal Ney on the left, the corps of Marshal Augereau in the centre, the corps of Marshal Soult on the right, and the Imperial Guard in reserve. He ordered Marshal Soult to post himself on the road to Güttstadt, and to carry the bridge of Bergfried—thus to debouch on the rear of the enemy with all his army—a manoeuvre, which was giving to this battle a decisive character. Conquered—The enemy was lost without resource.

Marshal Soult sent General Guyot with his light cavalry to take possession of Güttstadt, where he also took a great quantity of baggage, and successively made 1600 prisoners. Guttstadt was the enemy's central depot; but at the same instant that Marshal Soult was directing himself upon the bridge of Bergfried, with the divisions Leval and Legrand, the enemy, who perceived that this important position protected the retreat of his left flank, defended the bridge with twelve of his best battalions. At three o'clock, p. m. the cannonade commenced. The 4th regiment of the line, and the 24th of light infantry had the glory to reach the enemy first. They sustained their ancient reputation. These two regiments alone, and a battalion of the 28th in reserve, were sufficient to dislodge the enemy. They then passed the bridge *au pas de charge,* pierced the twelve Russian battalions, took four pieces of cannon, and covered the field of battle with dead and wounded.

The 46th and the 55th, who formed the second brigade, being behind, were impatient to deploy; but already the routed enemy, terrified, abandoned all his fine positions. A happy presage for the events of next day.

At the same time Marshal Ney carried a wood where the enemy had lodged his right. The division of St. Hilaire carried the village in the centre, and the Grand Duke of Berg, with a division of dragoons placed in the centre, passed the wood, and swept the plain, in order to clear the front of our position. In these little partial attacks the enemy were repelled, and lost one hundred prisoners. Night overtook the two armies, thus in presence of each other.

The weather is superb for the season. There are three feet of snow. The thermometer is at two or three degrees of cold.

At daybreak of the 4th, the General of Cavalry Lasalle, scoured the plain with his hussars. A line of Cossacks and cavalry instantly opposed him. The Grand Duke of Berg formed his cavalry in line, and marched to meet the enemy. The cannonade commenced. But very soon we had the assurance that the enemy had profited of the night to retire, and had only left rearguards on his right, centre, and left. These were instantly attacked, and driven, fighting, six leagues. The enemy's cavalry were several times overthrown, but the difficulties of the mountainous, and unequal ground opposed the efforts of the cavalry. Before day closed the advanced guard of the French reposed at Deppen. The Emperor slept at Scklett.

The 5th, at daybreak, all the French army again moved. At Deppen the Emperor received the intelligence, that a column of the enemy had not yet passed the Aller, and thus found itself turned by our left, whilst the Russian army slept entirely on the roads of Arensdorf and Landsberg.

His Majesty ordered the Grand Duke of Berg, and Marshals Soult and Davoust to pursue the enemy in this direction. He ordered the corps of Marshal Ney, reinforced with General Lasalle's division of light cavalry, and a division of dragoons to pass the Aller, and attack the corps of the enemy which was cut off.

Combat of Watersdorff

The Grand Duke of Berg arrived upon the heights of Watersdorff, and found himself in presence of eight or nine thousand cavalry. Several successive charges were made, and the enemy retired.

Combat of Deppen

During this time Marshal Ney commanded, and was engaged with the corps of the enemy, which was cut off. The enemy wished for a moment to attempt to force a passage, but they came only to find death in the middle of our bayonets. Overwhelmed *au pas de charge,* and completely routed, they abandoned cannon, colours, and baggage. The remaining divisions of this corps seeing the fate of their advanced guard, beat a retreat. At night we had already made several thousand prisoners, and taken 16 pieces of cannon. Nevertheless, by these movements the greatest part of the communications of the Russian army have been cut off, and its depots at Güttstadt and Liebstadt, and a part of its magazines on the Aller have been taken by our light cavalry.

Our loss has been inconsiderable in all these little affairs. It amounts to 80 or 100 killed, and 3 or 400 wounded. General Gardanne, *aide-de-camp* to the Emperor, and Governor of the pages, has received a severe contusion on the breast. The Colonel of the 4th regiment of dragoons has been severely wounded. The General of Brigade Latour Maubourg has been shot in the arm. The Adjutant Commandant Lauberdiere, charged with the detail service of the hussars, has been wounded in an attack, and the Colonel of the 4th regiment of the line has been wounded.

57th Bulletin of the French Army

Prussian Eylau, 7th February, 1807

At six in the morning the army began its march in pursuit of the enemy. The Grand Duke of Berg with the corps of Marshal Soult, moved upon Landsberg, Marshal Davoust's corps on Heilsburg, and Marshal Ney's on Wormditt, to prevent the escape of the corps cut off at Deppen.

On arriving at Glandau the Grand Duke of Berg met the rearguard of the enemy, and charged it between Glandau and Hoff. The enemy deployed several lines of cavalry, which appeared ready to sustain this rearguard, composed of twelve battalions, formed on the heights of Landsberg. The Grand Duke of Berg made his dispositions, after different attacks upon the right and left of the enemy, applied upon a wind-mill and a wood. The dragoons and cuirassiers of Hautpoult's division made a brilliant charge, overthrew, and annihilated two Russian regiments of infantry. The Colonels, the colours, the cannon, and the greater part of the officers and soldiers were taken. The enemy's army made a movement to support the rearguard. Marshal Soult was arrived. Marshal Augereau took position upon the left, and the village of Hoff was occupied. The enemy perceived the importance of this position, and marched ten battalions to retake it. The Grand Duke of Berg executed a second charge with his cuirassiers, took the enemy in flank and broke them. These manoeuvres are proud deeds of arms, and render the greatest honour to those intrepid cuirassiers. This day merits a particular relation; a part of the two armies passed the night between the 6th and 7th in presence. The enemy filed-off during the night. At daybreak the French advanced guard again marched, and met the rear-guard of the enemy between the wood and the little town of Eylau. Several regiments of chasseurs á pied who defended it were charged, and part taken. We did not delay to arrive at Eylau, and to discover that the enemy was in position behind this town.

58TH BULLETIN OF THE FRENCH ARMY

Prussian Eylau, 9th February, 1807

At a quarter of a league from Prussian Eylau, is an hillock, which defends the debouchure on the plain. Marshal Soult commanded the 46th and 18th regiments of the line. To carry it, three regiments which defended it were overwhelmed, but at the same moment a column of Russian cavalry charged the extremity of the left of the 18th, and threw one of the battalions into disorder. The dragoons of Klein, however, observed this affair in sufficient time. The troops were engaged in the town of Eylau. They had thrown some regiments into a church, and a church-yard, where they made an obstinate resistance, and from which they were not driven until ten at night, and after a great mutual slaughter. The division Legrand then bivouacked before the town, and the division St. Hilaire on its right. The corps of Marshal Davoust had in the evening marched to turn Eylau, and fall upon the left flank of the enemy if he did not quit his position. Marshal Ney was on march to turn his right flank. In this position the night was passed in each other's presence. On the following day, by the first dim ray of the morning, the Russians commenced the attack with a brisk cannonade. The Emperor visited the church which the Russians had defended with so much obstinacy on the day before. He made Marshal Augereau's corps advance, and the eminence upon which the church stood was cannonaded by 40 pieces of artillery belonging to his guard. The armies were now within half gun shot of each other. The thunder of the cannon was terrible. After the firing had continued for some time, the troops became impatient of suffering so much without any thing decisive happening. Some manoeuvres then commenced on both sides, in order to obtain advantages over each other, and in the mean time a thick fall of snow came on, in consequence of which the troops could not discern one another, at the distance of two paces. In this obscurity some of the corps lost their way, and the columns getting too much to the left wandered in uncertainty. This state of things lasted half an hour. When the weather cleared up, the Grand Duke, at the head of the cavalry, supported by Marshal Bessieres at the head of the guards, and the division of St. Hilaire, advanced and attacked the enemy. This bold manoeuvre, which covered the cavalry with glory, had become necessary in consequence of the circumstances in which our columns were placed. The enemy's cavalry, who endeavoured to oppose this manoeuvre, were completely routed. The slaughter was horrible. Two lines of Russian infantry were penetrated, and the third only maintained itself in consequence of having supported itself upon a wood. Some squadrons of the guards passed twice through the whole of the enemy's army. This brilliant attack, had it not been for the wood, and some other difficulties of the ground, would have decided the victory. General Hautpoult was wounded. General Dahlman perished gloriously in the attack.

For the 100 dragoons or cuirassiers of the guard which lay dead on the field, there were found beside them 1000 of their enemies. Marshal Davoust, who had been detached to fall upon the rear of the enemy, but whose progress was much impeded by the weather, was at last enabled to execute his orders, and decided the victory. The enemy, after several vain endeavours to repulse that General, retreated, leaving their wounded and 16 pieces of cannon on the field of battle. The number of killed and wounded in this action was on both sides very considerable, and it could not be otherwise when a constant fire was maintained from about 300 pieces of cannon for more than 12 hours, within a short distance of both armies. Marshal Augereau is wounded. General Desjardins, Heudalet, and Lochet, are also wounded. General Corbineau is killed, as are likewise Colonels Lacue, Lemarais, and Bouvieres. Our whole loss consists of exactly 1000 killed, and 5,700 wounded, including 1090, who are very badly wounded. But we have to set against this loss 7000 Russians, who have been counted dead on the field of battle. The plan of the enemy, which had for its object to extend themselves towards Thorn, and to turn our left wing, has completely miscarried, and their attempt to carry it into execution has proved exceedingly fatal to them. It has cost them from 13 to 15,000 prisoners, as many in killed and missing, 45 pieces of artillery, and 18 standards. The eagle of one of the battalions is lost, and has probably been taken by the enemy. The Emperor will give that battalion another standard, after it shall have taken one from the enemy. Having defeated this enterprise of the enemy, and driven them 100 miles from the Vistula, the army has returned to its cantonments and is going into winter quarters again.

Paris, February 21st, 1807
A courier which left Warsaw on the 6th, has brought the following intelligence to her Majesty the Empress, written on the 4th instant, on the field of battle at Liebstadt, by the Prince of Neufchatel, Minister at War:

We have fought the enemy at Altenstein, where he was attacked by the Emperor, while he suffered himself to be surrounded by another, column at Güttstadt. He was defeated at every point upon the whole of the line which formed his advanced guard.

We have taken a great number of prisoners, and some pieces of cannon. The enemy is completely broken, and in full retreat, in the utmost confusion, with the whole army in close pursuit of him. The Emperor commands the advanced guard, and was never in better health. The Grand Duke of Berg is quite recovered.

The Prince of Neufchatel writes to her Majesty from Great Glandau as follows:

> On the approach of his Majesty the Emperor, the Russian army fell back. On the 6th, in the evening, they were beyond Landsberg, with the view of continuing their retreat during the night. The Emperor commanding the advanced guard, ordered the enemy's rear, which had been reinforced, to be attacked. In vain they resisted; the violence of the attack, commanded by his Majesty in person, had the most complete effect. One division of cuirassiers maintained a most gallant contest with eight picked regiments of the Russian army, and cut them to pieces.
>
> The columns which formed the right and left wings have obtained similar advantages.
>
> We shall be at Koenigsberg to-morrow.
>
> Thus, since leaving winter-quarters, we have made about 10,000 prisoners, taken 27 pieces of cannon, and killed and wounded a great number, without taking into account the advantages which must result from the whole, and ultimately prove fatal to the enemy.

59TH BULLETIN OF THE FRENCH ARMY

Prussian Eylau, 14th February, 1807

The enemy has taken a position behind the Pregel. Our patrols are before Koenigsberg, but the Emperor has thought proper to concentrate his army, in winter-quarters, in such manner, that it may be in a condition to cover the line of the Vistula. The number of cannon which have been taken, since the battle of Bergfried, is about 60. The Grand Duke of Berg still has his head quarters at Wirtemberg, close upon the Pregel. General Hautpoult has died of his wounds; his loss is generally deplored;. but few warriors have terminated their career so gloriously. His division of cuirassiers has distinguished itself in all the battles. The Emperor has given orders for removing his body to Paris. On the 12th, Marshal Lefebvre advanced to Marienwerder, where he found seven Prussian squadrons; he defeated them and made 300 prisoners. Those who escaped fled towards Dantzic.

60TH BULLETIN OF THE FRENCH ARMY

Prussian Eylau, 17th February, 1807

The conquest of Silesia is prosecuted. The fortress of Schweidnitz has surrendered. The Prussian Governor of Silesia is shut up in Clatz, after having been driven by General Lefebvre out of the positions of Frankenstein and Neurohdo. In these affairs, the Wurtemberg troops behaved remarkably well. The enemy lost about 100 killed, and 300 prisoners. The siege of Cosel is conducted with vigor.—Since the battle of Eylau, the enemy have re-assembled behind the Pregel. We hoped to have driven them from that position, had the river remained frozen; but a thaw has commenced, and this river is a boundary, beyond which the French army has no interest to pursue them. About 3000 Russian prisoners, who were at Wellenberg, have been set at liberty by a troop of Cossacks, consisting of 1000 men. The cold has entirely ceased; the snow is every where melted, and the season exhibits a singular phenomenon of the mild weather of the last days of April, in the middle of the month of February. The army is entering into cantonments.

61ST BULLETIN OF THE FRENCH ARMY

Landsberg, 18th February, 1807

The battle of Eylau was at first considered as a victory by several of the enemy's officers. Such, indeed, was the belief at Koenigsberg, during the whole evening of the 9th; but the alarm was great when the Russian head quarters and the army arrived there. Soon after, our cannon was heard, and the French were seen in the possession of a height which flanked the whole of the Russian troops. The Russian General declared, that he would defend the town, which greatly increased the alarm of the inhabitants, who said, "We shall share the fate of Lubeck." It was fortunate, however, for this town, that it did not come within the plan of the French Generals to drive the Russians from this position. The number of dead in the Russian army, in generals, and other officers, is very remarkable. In consequence of the battle of Eylau, more than 5000 wounded Russians, found on the field of battle, or in the neighbouring hospitals, have fallen into the hands of the victors. It is reckoned that the Russians had 15,000 wounded, beside these 5000 which fell into the hands of the French.—The army has resumed its quarters. The districts of Elbing, Liebstadt, mid Osterode, are the finest in this country, and the Emperor has chosen them for the cantonments of his left wing. Marshal Mortier has gone back to Swedish Pomerania. Strallund is blockaded; and it is to be regretted that the enemy have, without any reason, burnt the line suburb of Kiuper. The fire presented a horrible spectacle, and more than 2000 persons are, in consequence of it, destitute of any home or shelter.

PROCLAMATION, DATED PRUSSIAN EYLAU

February 16th, 1807

Soldiers;—We had begun to enjoy a little repose in our winter quarters, when the enemy attacked the first corps, and showed themselves on the lower Vistula. We broke up and marched against him. We have pursued him, sword in hand, 80 miles. He has fled to his strong holds and retired beyond the Piegel. In the battles of Bergfried, Deppen, Hoff, and Eylau, we have taken from him 65 pieces of cannon and standards, besides his loss of more than 40,000 men in killed, wounded, and taken prisoners. The heroes who, on our side, remain in the bed of honour, have died a glorious death. It is the death of a true soldier.

Their relatives will always have a just claim to our care and beneficence.—Having thus defeated all the enterprises of the enemy, we shall return towards the Vistula and resume our winter quarters. Those who shall dare to disturb these quarters shall have reason to repent for, whether beyond the Vistula, or on the other side of the Danube; whether in the middle of winter, or in the beginning of autumn; we still will be found French soldiers, and soldier of the grand army.

Liebstadt, 21st February, 1807

The right of the grand army has been victorious, like the centre and the left. Genera Essen, at the head of 25,000 men, advanced to Ostrolenka on the 15th, along the two bank of the Narew; when arrived at the village of Flacis Lawowa, he met the advanced guard of General Savary, who commanded the 5th corps.—On the l6th, at break of day, General Gazan, with a part of his division, made an oblique movement upon the advanced guard. A nine in the morning he met the enemy, on the road to Novogorod, attacked, defeated, and put him to the route. But, at the same moment, the enemy attacked Ostrolenka by the left bank General Campana, with a brigade of the division of General Gazan, and General Ruffin with a brigade of the division of General Oudinot, defended that small town. General Savary sent thither the General of Division Redle, chief of the staff of the army. The Russian infantry, in several columns, endeavoured to carry the town. The enemy was suffered to advance half the length of the streets, when he was marched against and charged. He was three times cut down, and left the streets covered with the dead. The loss of the enemy was so great that he abandoned the town and took a position behind the sandhills which cover it—The divisions of General Suchet and Oudinot advanced: at noon the heads of their columns arrived at Ostrolenka. General Savary drew up his little army in the following manner:—General Oudinot commanded the left in two lines; General Suchet the centre; an General Reille, commanding a brigade of the division of Gazan, formed the right. He covered himself with all his artillery, and marched against the enemy. The intrepid General Oudinot put himself at the head of the cavalry, made a successful charge, and cut in piece the Cossacks of the rear guard of the enemy. The fire was very brisk; the enemy gave was on all sides, and was followed fighting during three leagues.—The next day the enemy was pursued several leagues, but without being perceived. His cavalry had retreated the whole night. General Suwarrow, and several other officers of the enemy are among the slain. The enemy has abandoned a great number of wounded, 1200 have been taken off the field, and more are bringing in every instant.

Seven pieces of cannon and two standards are the trophies of this victory. The enemy has left 1300 dead on the field of battle. On our side we have had 60 men killed, and from 4 to 500 wounded. But a loss most sensibly felt is that of the General of Brigade, Campana, who was an officer of great merit and promise: he was born in the department of Marengo. The Emperor has been much grieved at his loss. The 103rd regiment distinguished itself particularly in this affair. Among the wounded are Colonel Du Hamel, of the 21st regiment of light infantry; and the Colonel of artillery, Nourrist. The Emperor has ordered the 5th corps to go into winter quarters. The thaw is dreadful. The season will not permit any thing great to be achieved; it is that of repose. The enemy first broke up from his quarters; he has repented it.

63RD BULLETIN OF THE FRENCH ARMY

Osterode, 28th February, 1807

Captain Auzoni, of the Imperial Horse Guards, mortally wounded in the battle of Eylau, was lying upon the field of battle. His comrades came to take him up and carry him to the hospital. He recovered his senses only to say to them, "Let me alone, my friends; I die contented, since we have gained the day, and that I can die upon the bed of honour, surrounded by the cannons taken from the enemy, and the wrecks of their defeat. Tell the Emperor that I have but one regret, which is, that in a few moments I shall be no longer able to do any thing for his service, and the glory of our fine France—to her my last breath——."

The effort he made to utter these words exhausted the little strength he had remaining. All the reports we receive, agree in stating, that the enemy lost at the battle of Eylau 20 generals, and 900 officers killed and wounded, and upwards of 30,000 men disabled. At the engagement of Ostrolenka, of the 16th, two Russian generals were killed, and three wounded.

His Majesty has sent to Paris the sixteen stands of colours taken at the battle of Eylau. All the cannon are already sent off to Thorn. His Majesty has ordered that these cannon shall be melted down, and made into a brazen statue of General Hautpoult, commander of the second division of cuirassiers, in his uniform of cuirassier. The army is concentrated in its internments behind the Passarge, with its left supported by Marienwerder, the island of Nogat, and Elbing, countries which afford resources. Being informed that a Russian division had marched towards Braunsberg, at the head of our cantonments, the Emperor ordered it to be attacked. The Prince of Ponte Corvo assigned this expedition to General Dupont, an officer of great merit. On the 26th, at two o'clock in the afternoon, General Dupont presented himself before Braunsberg, attacked the enemy's division, 10,000 strong, overthrew it with fixed bayonets, drove it from the town, and made it re-cross the Passarge; took from it 16 pieces of cannon, two stands of colours, and made 2000 prisoners. We had very few men killed. On the side of Guttstadt, General Leger-Belair repaired to the village of Peterswalde, at daybreak on the 25th, upon receiving advice that a Russian column had arrived during the night, at that village, overthrew it, took the General Baron de Korff, who commanded it, his staff, several Lieutenant-Colonels and Officers, and 400 men. This brigade was composed of ten battalions, which had suffered so much, that they formed only 1,600) men under arms. The Emperor, in testimony of his satisfaction to General Savary for the engagement of Ostrolenka, has granted him the grand insignia of the Legion of Honour, and called him about his person. His Majesty has given the command of the 5th corps to Marshal Massena, Marshal Lannes continuing to be sick. At the battle of Eylau, Marshal Augereau, overrun with rheumatic pains, was sick and hardly in his senses; but the cannon awakes the brave: he flew in full gallop to the head of his corps, after getting himself tied upon his horse. He was constantly exposed to the greatest fire, and was even slightly wounded. The Emperor has just ordered him to return to France for the purpose of taking care of his health. The garrisons of Colberg and Dantzic, availing themselves of the little attention paid them, had encouraged themselves by different excursions. An advanced post! of the Italian division was attacked on the 16th at Stargard by a party of 800 men of the garrison of Colberg.

General Bosanti had with him only a few companies of the 1st Italian regiment of the line? which took to their arms in time, marched with resolution against the enemy, and routed him General Teuli, on his side, with the main body of the Italian division, the regiment of musketeers of the guards, and the first company of Gens d'Armes on duty, repaired to invest Colberg. On arriving at Naugarten, he found the enemy entrenched, occupying a fortress with pieces of cannon. Colonel Boyer, of the musketeers of the guards, gave an assault. Captain Montmorency, of the company of Gens d'Armes, made a successful charge. The fort was taken, 300 men made prisoners, arid six pieces of cannon carried off. The enemy left one hundred men upon the field of battle. General Dombrowski marched against the garrison of Dantzic: he fell in with it at Dirschau, overthrew it, made 600 prisoners, to seven pieces of cannon, and pursued it for several leagues. He was wounded with a musk ball. Marshal Lefebvre arrived in the meantime at the head of the 10th corps. He had been joined by the Saxons, and marched to invest Dantzic. The weather is still changeable. It froze yesterday; it thaws today. The whole winter has passed over in this manner. The thermometer has never been lower than five degrees.

64TH BULLETIN OF THE FRENCH ARMY

Osterode, 2nd March, 1807

The town of Elbing furnishes great resources to the army: a great quantity of wine and brandy was found there. This country of the Lower Vistula is very fertile. The ambassadors from Constantinople and Persia have entered Poland, and are on their way to Warsaw. After the battle of Kylau, the Emperor passed every day several hours upon the field of battle—a horrible spectacle, but which duty rendered necessary. It required great labour to bury all the dead. A great number of Russian slain were found with the insignia of their orders. It appears, that among them was a Prince Repnin. Forty-eight hours after the battle, there were still upwards of 500 wounded Russians whom we had not been able to carry off. Brandy and bread were carried to them, and they were successively conveyed to the hospital. Let any one imagine to himself, upon the space of a square league, 9 or 10,000 dead bodies, 4 or 5000 horses killed, whole lines of Russian knapsacks, broken pieces of muskets and sabres; the ground covered with cannon balls, howitzer shells and ammunition; twenty-four, pieces of cannon, near which were lying the bodies of their drivers, killed at the moment when they were striving to carry them off. All this was the more conspicuous upon a ground covered with snow: this spectacle is calculated to inspire princes with the love of peace, and an abhorrence of war. The 5000 wounded whom we had were all conveyed to Thorn, and to our hospitals on the left bank of the Vistula, in sledges. The surgeons observed with astonishment, that the fatigue of this conveyance did no harm to the wounded. The following are some details of the engagement of Braunsberg. General Dupont marched against the enemy in two columns. General Bruyere, who commanded the right column, fell in with the enemy at Ragarn, and drove him towards the river which runs before this village. The left column drove the enemy towards Villenberg, and the whole division shortly after stretched out of the wood. The enemy being driven from his first position, was obliged to fall back upon the river which covers the town of Braunsberg: he at first made a resolute stand, but General Dupont marched against him, overthrew him by a charge, and entered with him into the town, the streets of which were choked up with the Russian slain. The 9th of light infantry, the 32nd and the 96th of the line, which compose this division, distinguished themselves. Generals Barrois and Lahoussaye, Colonel Seinele, of the 84th of the line, Colonel Muenier, of the 9th light infantry, the chief of battalion, Rouge, of the 32nd of the line, and the chief of squadron, Hubinet, of the 9th hussars, are deserving of particular encomiums. Since the arrival of the French army upon the Vistula, we have taken from the Russians in the engagements of Pultusk and Golymin, 89 pieces of cannon; at the engagement of Bergfried, 4 pieces; in the retreat of Allenstein, 5 pieces; at the engagement of Deppen, 16 pieces; at the engagement of Holl, 12, pieces; at the battle of Kylau, 24 pieces; at the engagement of Braunsberg, 6 pieces; and at the engagement of Odtrolenka, 9 pieces; total, 175 pieces of cannon. It has been remarked upon this subject, that the Emperor never lost any cannon in the armies which he has commanded, either in the campaigns of Italy and Egypt, in that of the Army of Reserve, in that of Austria and Moravia, or in that of Russia and Poland.

Osterode, 10th March, 1807

The army army is gone into cantonments behind the Passarge. The Prince of Ponte Corvo is at Holland and Braunsberg; Marshal Soult at Liebstadt and Mohringen; Marshal Ney at Güttstadt; Marshal Davoust at Allenstein, Hohenstein, and Deppin; the headquarters are at Osterode; the parish corps of observation, under General Zayonscheck, is at Nieberberg; Marshal Lefebvre is before Dantzic; the 5th corps is upon the Omulew: a division of Bavarians, under the Crown Prince, is at Warsaw; the corps of Prince Jerome in Silesia; the 8th corps of observation is in Swedish Pomerania; the fortress of Breslau, Schweidnitz, and Brieg, are demolished; General Rapp, *aide-de-camp* to the Emperor, is governor of Thorn; bridges are thrown over the Vistula at Marienberg and Dirschau. On the 1st of March, the Emperor having been informed that the enemy, encouraged by the position of our army, had shown themselves on the right bank of the Passarge, ordered Marshals Ney and Soult to advance, reconnoitre, and drive the enemy back. Marshal Ney proceeded towards Guttstadt; Marshal Soult passed the Passarge at Wormditt. The enemy's posts, which retreated with precipitation, were pursued to the distance of eight leagues. The enemy, observing that the French were not inclined to pursue them any further, and that our force was merely an advanced guard that had left their main body in the rear, brought forward two regiments of grenadiers, and, in the course of the night, attacked our cantonments at Zecheno The 50th regiment received them upon the point of the bayonet. The 27th and 39th regiments also conducted themselves with great courage. In these trifling affairs the Russians had nearly 1000 men killed, wounded, and made prisoners. After having thus disturbed the enemy, the army returned again to its cantonments. The Grand Duke of Berg, being informed that a corps of cavalry had advanced to Willenberg, ordered the Prince of Borghese to attack that place, who, at the head of his regiment, charged eight Russian squadrons, overthrew, and put them to flight, making 100 prisoners, including three captains and eight officers. Marshal Lefebvre has completely invested Dantzic, and commenced the lines of circumvallation round that city.

66th Bulletin of the French Army

Osterode, 14th March, 1807

The grand army remains in its cantonments, where it takes repose. Frequent skirmishes have taken place between the advanced posts of the two armies. Two regiments of Russian cavalry came on the 12th instant to harass the 69th regiment of infantry of the line in its cantonments, at Lingour, before Guttstadt. A battalion of this regiment flew to arms from an ambuscade, attacked, and repulsed the enemy, who left 80 men on the field. General Guyot, who commands the advanced posts of Marshal Soult, has, on his side, had several affairs of outposts with the enemy, in which he has had the advantage. After the little battle of Willenberg, the. Grand Duke of Berg expelled the Cossacks, from the whole of the right bank of the Aller. In order to assure himself that the enemy was not making some movement, he went to Wirtemberg, Sedburgh, Meusguth, and Bischosburg. He had some engagements with the enemy's cavalry, and took 100 Cossacks prisoners. The Russian army appears to be concentrated on the side of the Bartenstein on the Aller; the Prussian division on the side of Creiltlbourg. The enemy's army made a retrograde movement, and have approached nearer to Koenigsberg. The whole of the French army is in cantonments; it is provisioned by the towns of Elbing, Braunsberg, and from the resources drawn from the Island of Nogat, which is extremely fertile. Two bridges have been erected over the Vistula, one at Marienwerder, the other at Marienberg. Marshal Lefebvre has completed the investment of Dantzic. General Lefebvre has invested Colberg. Each of these garrisons have been driven into these towns after a slight engagement. A division of twelve thousand Bavarians, commanded by the Prince Royal of Bavaria, has crossed the Vistula at Warsaw, and is coming to join the army.

67th Bulletin of the French Army

Osterode, 25th March, 1807

On the 14th instant, at three in the afternoon, the garrison of Stralsund, taking advantage of a fog, made a sortie with two thousand infantry, two squadrons of cavalry, and six pieces of cannon, in order to carry a redoubt thrown up by General Dupas. This redoubt, which was open, without palisades and without cannon, was defended by a company of voltigeurs, of the 58th regiment of the line. The immense superiority of the enemy had no effect upon these brave men; being reinforced by a company of voltigeurs of the 4th of the line (light infantry,) under Captain Barral, they resisted all the attempts of the Swedish brigade. Fifteen Swedish soldiers reached the parapet, but there found their death. All the enemy's attempts were equally fruitless. Sixty-two dead bodies of the Swedes were buried at the foot of the redoubt. It is supposed that 120 were wounded, and 50 were made prisoners, though there were not more than 150 men in the redoubt. Several Swedish officers were found among the dead, distinguished by their military decorations. This instance of bravery has attracted the Emperor's attention. His Majesty has sent three orders of the legion of honour for the companies engaged. Captain Drivet, who commanded on this weak redoubt, highly distinguished himself. On the 20th, Marshal Lefebvre ordered the brigade under General Schraam to cross over from the island of Nogat, in the Frisch Haff, in order to cut off the communication between Dantzic and the sea. These orders were carried into execution at three in the morning. The Prussians were routed, and 300 of them fell into our hands. At six in the evening, the garrison of Dantzic sent out a detachment of 4000 men to retake the post; but they were repulsed, with the loss of some hundreds of prisoners, and one piece of cannon. General Schraam had under his command the 2nd battalion of the 2nd regiment of infantry, and several Saxon battalions, who distinguished themselves. The Emperor has sent three orders of the legion of honour to be distributed among the Saxon officers; and three more for the privates, subalterns, and to the major who commanded them. In Silesia, the garrison of Niess has made a sortie, but fell into an ambuscade. A regiment of Wirtemberg cavalry took these troops in flank, killed 50, and made 60 prisoners. The winter in Poland seems to have resembled the winter at Paris, that is to say, variable. It freezes and thaws in alternate succession. However, we have the good fortune not to have any sick in the army. On the contrary, all accounts agree that the Russians have a great number of sick. The army remains tranquil in its cantonments. The works which compose, the *tête du pont* of Sierock, Modliu, Piaga, and Marienwerder, are every day becoming more formidable; and the magazines are organized, and are every where receiving provisions. Three hundred thousand bottles of Bordeaux wine were found at Elbing; and though each bottle cost four francs, the Emperor paid that price to the merchants, and ordered the wine to be distributed among the army. The Emperor has sent the Prince Borghese upon a mission to Warsaw.

<h2 style="text-align:center">68TH BULLETIN OF THE FRENCH ARMY</h2>

Osterode, 29th March, 1807

On the 17th of March, at three o'clock in the morning, the General of Brigade Lefebvre, *aid-de-camp* to Prince Jerome, passed near Glatz, in his way to Wunchelsbourg, with three squadrons of light horse, and the Taxis regiment of light infantry, when 1500 men, with two pieces of cannon, made a sortie from the place. Lieutenant-Colonel Gerrard immediately attacked and drove them back into Glatz, after having taken 100 soldiers, several officers, and two pieces of artillery. Marshal Massena is gone from Willenberg to Ortelsbourg, and forced an entrance there for the division of Becker's dragoons, which he has re-in-forced with a detachment of Polish horse. There were some Cossacks at Ortelsbourg, and several attacks were made, in which the enemy lost 20 men. General Becker, as he was coming to resume his position at Willenberg, was attacked by 2000 Cossacks. An ambuscade of infantry was formed, into which they fell, and lost 200 men. On the 26th, at five o'clock in the morning, the garrison of Dantzic. made a general sortie, which proved very fatal. It was repulsed on all sides. A colonel, named Cracaw, who had a command, was taken with 400 men, and two pieces of cannon, in an attack made by the 19th regiment of chasseurs. The Northern Polish Legion conducted itself in an excellent manner, and two Saxon battalions distinguished themselves. As for the rest, there is nothing new. The lakes are still frozen, though there is some appearance of the approach of spring.

Finckenstein, 4th April, 1807

The Gens d'armes of the ordnance have arrived at Marienwerder, and Marshal Bessieres has set out for that place, in order
to review them. They have behaved remarkably well, and have
displayed great courage in all the affairs in which they have been
engaged. General Teuli, who still superintends the blockade of
Colberg, has, in that command, exhibited great activity and skill.
The conducting of the siege is now entrusted to General Loison.
On the 19th of March, the redoubts of Selnow were attacked and
carried by the 1st regiment of Italian light infantry. On this occasion the garrison made a sortie; but the company of carabineers
of the 1st regiment of light infantry, and a company of dragoons,
drove them back. The voltigeurs of the 19th regiment of the line,
distinguished themselves greatly in the attack on the village of
Allstadt. In that affair the enemy lost three pieces of cannon and
200 prisoners. Marshal Lefebvre commands at the siege of Dantzic, and General Lariboisiere has the direction of the artillery.
The latter corps shows itself in all circumstances worthy of the
fame which it has so justly acquired. The French cannoniers will
merit the name of select troops. The manner in which the battalions of the train have performed their service has also afforded
perfect satisfaction. The Emperor has given audience at Finckenstein to a deputation from the chamber of Marienwerder. It consisted of Count Von Groeben, Counsellor Baron Von Schleinitz,
and Count Von Dolma, Director of the Chamber. The deputation
represented to his Majesty the great hardships which the inhabitants had suffered from the war. The Emperor answered, that he
entertained a lively feeling for their sufferings, and that he would
relieve Marienwerder, as well as Elbing, from the burthen of any
extraordinary contribution. He farther observed, that there were
evils belonging to the theatre of war which could not be avoided;
that he participated in the regret which those evils occasioned,
and would do every thing in his power to mitigate them. It is
believed that his Majesty will this day set out on a short journey
to Marienwerder and Elbing. The second Bavarian division has
arrived at Warsaw. The Crown Prince of Bavaria has gone to Pul-

tusk to take the command of the first division. The Hereditary Prince of Baden has marched at the head of his corps of troops to Dantzic. The contingent of Saxe-Weimar has arrived upon the Warta. There has not been a shot fired for a fortnight past at the advanced posts of the army. The heat of the sun begins to be felt, but it is not yet sufficiently powerful to penetrate and thaw the earth. All is still bound in frost. Spring approaches slowly in this country. A number of couriers arrive at the head-quarters from Constantinople and Persia.

The health of the Emperor continues excellent; it is even remarked that it appears better than formerly. Some days his Majesty makes excursions to the distance of forty miles on horseback. At Warsaw it was last week believed that the Emperor had arrived there about ten o'clock at night. The whole town was immediately and voluntarily illuminated. The fortresses of Praga, Sierock, Modlin, Thorn, and Marienberg, begin to be put into a state of defence. The works of Marienwerder are planned. All these fortresses form *tête du pont* on the Vistula. The Emperor praises the activity of Marshal Kellerman in forming the provisional regiments, many of which have arrived in good condition, and are incorporated in the army. His Majesty also bestows great praise on General Clarke, Governor of Berlin, who displays equal activity and zeal in the important post confided to him. Prince Jerome, who commands the troops in Silesia, has also given proofs of great activity, and has exhibited a degree of skill and penetration which is, in general, only the fruit of long experience.

70TH BULLETIN OF THE FRENCH ARMY

Finckenstein, 19th April, 1807

A Corps of 400 Prussians, who embarked at Koenigsberg, and landed on the peninsula opposite Pillau, advanced towards the village of Carlsberg. M. Mainguernaud, *aide-de-camp* of Marshal Lefebvre, marched towards that place with a few men: he manoeuvred so dexterously, that he took the 400 Prussians, among whom were 120 cavalry. Several Russian regiments have entered Dantzic by sea. The garrison has made several sorties. The

Polish legions of the north, and their commander Prince Michael Radzivil, have greatly distinguished themselves: they took about 40 Russians prisoners.. The siege is carried on with activity. The battering train begins to arrive. There is nothing new at the different posts of the army.

71ST BULLETIN OF THE FRENCH ARMY

Finckenstein, 19th April, 1807

The victory of Eylau having frustrated all the plans which the enemy had formed against the Lower Vistula, has enabled us to surround Dantzic, and to commence the siege of that fortress. But it was necessary to draw the battering train from the fortresses of Silesia and along the Oder, so that it had to come upwards of 100 leagues through a country in which there are no roads. This difficulty is now got over, and a part of that artillery is already arrived; 100 pieces of cannon are now on their way from Stettin, Custrin, Glogau, and Breslau, and in a few days we shall be provided with every thing necessary. The Prussian General Kalkreuth has the command at Dantzic. The garrison consists of 14,000 Prussians, and 6000 Russians. The inundations and marshes, several lines of fortifications, and the fort of Weixelmunde, have rendered it difficult to surround the fortress. The Saxon, the Polish, and the Baden troops, since the Hereditary Prince of Baden is at their head, are vieing with. each other in bravery. The enemy has not tried any other means of coming to the assistance of Dantzic, than by sending a few battalions and some provisions to the place by sea. In Silesia, Prince Jerome continues the siege of Neisse vigorously. Since the Prince of Pletz has declined to act, Baron Kleist, *aide-de-camp* to the King of Prussia, is arrived at Glatz, by way of Vienna, with the title of Governor General of Silesia. He is-accompanied by an English commissary, who must keep his eye upon the manner in which the £80,000 sterling are laid out, which were given by England to the King of Prussia. On the 13th instant, that Prussian officer advanced from Glatz with a corps of 4000 men, and attacked General Lefebvre (who commands the corps of observation which covers the siege of Neisse,) at Frankenstein. This operation has been ineffectual. Baron Kleist was repulsed with vigour. On the 14th, Prince Jerome fixed his head-quarters at Munsterberg. For these two months past, the grand army has been quiet in its cantonments. This time has been employed in recruiting the cavalry, and providing them with horses, repairing the arms, establishing large magazines of biscuits and brandy, and furnishing the soldiers with shoes. Independent of one pair in wear, each man has two more pairs in his knapsack. Silesia and the Island of Nogat have furnished a number of good horses to the cuirassiers, to the dragoons, and to the light cavalry. In the beginning of May, an army of observation, consisting of 50,000 French and Spanish troops, will be assembled on the Elbe: whilst Russia has assembled in Poland nearly the whole of her troops, there is only a part of the French military force in that country. This, however, is a consequence of the great difference which exists between the essential strength of the two countries. The 500,000 Russians, which the writers of newspapers made to march to the right and again to the left, only exist in their papers and in the imagination of some readers, who are the easier misled, by being shown the immense extent of the Russian territory, without the least mention of its extensive deserts and uncultivated districts. It is said that the guards of the Emperor of Russia have reached the army. They will see on the first meeting, whether the Imperial Guard is annihilated, as the enemy's generals have asserted. That guard is now more numerous than ever, and almost double the number it was at Austerlitz. Exclusive of the bridge thrown across the Narew, another is forming on piles between Warsaw and Prague: the work is in a very forward state. The bridges on piles are stronger and more serviceable than those of boats. Although it is very laborious to construct such bridges across a river of 400 rods in breadth, it is rendered easy through the skill and activity of the officers under whose direction it is performed, and from the abundance of timber. The Prince of Benevento is still at Warsaw, negotiating with the ambassadors of the Porte and of the Emperor of Persia. Independent of the services which he renders to the Emperor as a minister, some important operations are frequently entrusted to him relative to the wants of the army. The cold weather is again set in for these two days: the thaw is the only symptom we have of the spring; the earliest shrubs do not yet present the least sign of verdure.

72ND BULLETIN OF THE FRENCH ARMY

Finkenstein, 23rd April, 1807

The operations of Marshal Mortier have had the desired effect. The Swedes were so inconsiderate as to cross the river Peene, to advance upon Anclam and Demmin, and to move towards Passewalk. On the 16th, before break of day, Marshal Mortier assembled his troops, advanced from Passewalk on the road to Anclam, overthrew the posts at Belling and Ferdinandshoff, took 400 prisoners and two pieces of cannon, entered Anclam at the same time with the enemy, and made himself master of the bridge on the Peene. The column of the Swedish General Cardell was cut off. It remained at Uckermunde when we were already at Anclam. The Swedish General in Chief Armfeldt has been wounded by a grape shot. All the enemy's magazines are taken. The column of General Cardell, which has been cut off, was attacked on the 17th, by the General of Brigade Veau, near Uckermunde, when the enemy lost 3 pieces of cannon, and 500 men, which were taken. The rest escaped by getting on hoard the gun-boats in the Haff; 2 more pieces of cannon, and 100 men were taken near Demmin. Baron Von Essen, who commanded the Swedish army during the absence of General Armfeldt, proposed an armistice to General Mortier, informing him, that the King had granted him a special power to conclude the same. A peace or even an armistice, granted to Sweden, would accomplish the most sanguine wishes of the Emperor, who has always been very reluctant to carry on a war against a generous and brave nation, which, upon local and political grounds, is the friend of France. Must Swedish blood flow, either to protect or to subvert the Ottoman empire? Is it to flow for maintaining the balance, or for supporting the slavery of the seas? What has Sweden to fear from France? Nothing. What has she to fear from Russia? Everything. These reasons are too evident not to prompt an enlightened cabinet, and a nation which possesses clearness of mind, and independence of opinion, to put a speedy stop to the war. Immediately after the battle of Jena, the Emperor made known his desire to restore the ancient relations between Sweden and France. These first overtures were made to the Swedish minister at Hamburg, but rejected. The Emperor constantly directed his generals to treat the

Swedes as friends with whom we are at variance, and with whom we shall soon be reconciled, from the nature of things. Behold the true interests of both nations. If they did us any harm, they would regret it; and we, on our part, should wish to repair the wrong which we may have done them. The interest of the State will at last rise superior to all differences and petty quarrels. These were the Emperor's own words, in his orders. Animated by such sentiments, the Emperor ordered the military operations for the siege of Stralsund to be discontinued, and the mortars and cannon which were sent from Stettin for that purpose, to be sent back. He wrote to General Mortier in the following words: "I already regret what has been done. I am sorry that the fine suburb of Stralsund is burnt. Is it our business to hurt Sweden? This is a mere dream. It is our business to protect, not to do her any injury. In the latter, let us be as moderate as possible. Propose to the Governor of Stralsund an armistice, or a cessation of hostilities, in order to ease the burden, and lessen the calamities of war, which I consider as wicked, because it is impolitic." On the 8th, the armistice was concluded between Marshal Mortier and Baron Von Essen. On the 13th April, at eight in the evening, a detachment of 2000 men, from the garrison of Glatz, advanced with six pieces of cannon against the right wing of the post of Frankenstein. On the following day, the 17th, at break of day, another column of 800 men, marched from Silberberg. These troops, after their junction, advanced upon Frankenstein, and commenced an attack, at five in the morning, with an intent to attack General Lefebvre, who was posted there with a corps of observation. Prince Jerome set off from Munsterberg, when the first gun was fired, and arrived at Frankenstein at ten in the morning. The enemy was completely dispersed, and pursued to the covered way of Glatz: 600 of them were taken, together with three pieces of cannon. One major and eight officers are among the prisoners: 300 men were left dead on the field of battle: 400 men that had escaped in the -woods were attacked and taken at eleven in the forenoon. Colonel Beckers, commanding the 6th Bavarian regiment of the line, and Colonel Scharfenstein, of the Wirtemberg troops, have done wonders. The former would not quit the field of battle, although he was wounded in the shoulder; he showed himself every where at the head of his battalion, and every where he performed wonders. The Emperor has granted to each of these officers the eagle of the Legion of Honour. Captain Brocklield, who provisionally commands the Wirtemberg horse chasseurs, has likewise distinguished himself; and it was him that took the several pieces of cannon. The siege of Neisse is going on prosperously. One half of the town is already burnt, and the trenches are approaching very near the fortress.

73RD BULLETIN OF THE FRENCH ARMY

Elbing, 8th May, 1807

The Persian Ambassador has received his audience of leave. He brought some very fine presents to the Emperor, from his Master, and received in return the Emperor's portrait, enriched with very fine stones. He returns directly to Persia. He is a very considerable personage in his country, and a man of sense and great sagacity. His return to his country was necessary. It has been regulated that there shall henceforth be a numerous legation of Persians at Paris, and of Frenchmen at Teheran. The Journal of the siege of Dantzic will make known, that our troops have lodged themselves in the covert way, that the fire of the town is extinguished, and will give the details of the fine operation which General Drouet directed, and which was executed by Colonel Aime, the chief of battalion; Arnaud, of the 2nd light infantry; and Captain Avy. This operation puts us in possession of an island, which was defended by 1000 Russians, and five redoubts mounted with artillery, and which is very important for the siege, since it is in the back position which our troops are attacking. The Russians were surprised in their guard-house, 400 were slaughtered with the bayonet without having time to defend themselves, and 600 were made prisoners. Tins expedition, which look place in the night of the 6th, was in a great measure performed by the troops of Paris, who covered themselves with glory. The weather is growing milder; the roads are excellent; the buds appear upon the trees; the fields begin to be covered with grass, but it will require a month before they afford fodder to the cavalry. The Emperor has established at Magdeburgh, under the orders of Marshal Brune, a corps of observation, which will consist of nearly 80,000 men, half Frenchmen, and the other half Dutchmen and Confederates of the Rhine; the Dutch troops are to the number of 20,000 men. The French division of Molitor and Boudet, which also form a part of this corps of observation, arrived on the 13th of May at Magdeburgh. Thus we are able to receive the English expedition upon whatever point it may present itself. It is certain that it will disembark; it is not so that it will be able to re-embark.

74TH BULLETIN OF THE FRENCH ARMY

Finckenstein, 16th May, 1807

Prince Jerome, having discovered that three out-works of Neisse, alongside the Bielau, impeded the progress of the siege, ordered General Vandamme to occupy them. In the night from the 30th of April to the 1st of May, this General, at the head of the Wurtemberg troops, took the said works, put the enemy's troops by whom they were defended lo the sword, took 120 prisoners, and nine pieces of cannon. It seems, that a grand council of war was held at Bartenstein, since the arrival in the camp of the Emperor Alexander, at which the King of Prussia and the Grand Duke Constantine assisted; that the dangerous situation of the city of Dantzic was the subject of the deliberation of the said council, and that it was found Dantzic could only be relieved in two ways; first; by attacking the French army, to cross the Passarge, and to take the chance of a general engagement, the result of which (provided any advantage was obtained) would be, to compel the French army to raise the siege of Dantzic; the second, to throw succours into Dantzic from the sea-side. It seems that the first plan was deemed impracticable, unless the enemy would expose himself to be completely defeated and routed. It was therefore resolved to confine themselves to the other plan of relieving Dantzic by water. In consequence thereof, Lieut.-Gen. Kaminskoy; son of the Field Marshal, embarked at Pillau, with two Russian divisions, formed of twelve regiments, and several Prussian regiments. On the 12th, the troops were landed from 66; transports, under convoy of three frigates, in the port of Dantzic, under the protection of the fort of Weichselmunde. The Emperor immediately ordered Marshal Lasnes, who commands the reserve of the grand army, to advance from Marienberg (where he had his head quarters), with the division of General Oudinot, to reinforce the army of Marshal Lefebvre. He arrived, after an uninterrupted march, at the very moment when the enemy's troops were landing. On the 13th and 14th, the enemy made preparations for the attack. They were separated from the town by the distance of somewhat less than one league, but that part was occupied by French troops. On the 15th, the enemy advanced from the fort in three column with an intention to penetrate to the town along the right bank of the Vistula. The General of Brigade Schramm (who was at the advanced posts with the 2nd regiment of light infantry and one battalion of Saxons and Poles) received the first fire, and resisted the enemy at distance of a cannon-shot from Weichselmunde. Marshal Lefebvre had repaired to the bridge which is situated below on the Vistula, and ordered the 12th regiment of light infantry, together with the Saxons, to cross over that way, to support General Schramm. General Gardanne, who was charged with the defence of the right bank of the Vistula, also pressed that way with the rest of his troops. The enemy was superior in numbers, and the contest was continued with equal obstinacy. Marshal Lasnes, with the reserve of Oudinot, was placed on the left bank of the Vistula, where it was expected, the day before, that die enemy would make his appearance; but when Marshal Lasnes saw the movements of the enemy disclosed, he crossed die Vistula with four battalions of General Oudinot's reserve. The whole of the enemy's line and reserve were thrown into confusion, and pursued to the palisadoes and at nine in the morning the enemy were shut up in die fort of Weichselmunde. The field of battle was strewed with dead bodies. Our loss consists of 25 killed, and 200 wounded. The enemy's loss is 900 killed, 1500 wounded, and 200 taken. The enemy, from the height of his demolished and almost destroyed ramparts, was witness to die whole action. He was dejected, on seeing the hopes vanishing which he had formed of receiving succour. General Oudinot has killed three Russians with his own hand. It will appear, from the journal of the siege of Dantzic, that the works are carried on with equal activity, that the covered way is completed, and that we are occupied with preparations for crossing the ditch. As soon as the enemy knew that his maritime expedition had arrived before Dantzic, his light troops began to reconnoitre and alarm the whole line, from the position occupied by Marshal Soult, on the Passarge, to that of General Morand, upon the Aller. They were received at the mouth of the musket by the voltigeurs, lost a considerable number of men, and retired with more precipitation than they came. The Russians also presented themselves at Malga, before General Zyoncheck, the Commandant of the Polish corps of observation, and carried off one of his posts. The General of Brigade Fischer pursued, routed them, and killed 60 men, one colonel, and two captains. They likewise presented themselves before the 5th corps, and insulted General Gazan's advanced posts at Willenberg. This general pursued them several leagues. But they made a more serious attack upon the bridge of Omelew at Drengewo. The General of Brigade Girard marched against them with the 88th, and drove them into the Narew. General Suchet arrived, pursued the Russians closely, and defeated them at Ostrolenka, where he killed 60 men, and took 50 horses. On the same day, the 13th, the enemy attacked General Lemarrois, at the mouth of the Bug. This general had passed that river on the 10th, with a Bavarian brigade, and a Polish regiment, who, in the course of three days, had constructed several *tête-du-pont,* and had advanced to Wiskowo, with the intention of burning the rafts which the enemy had been at work upon during six weeks. This expedition completely succeeded, and the ridiculous work of six weeks was destroyed in a moment. At nine o'clock in the morning six thousand Russians arrived from Nur, and attacked him in his entrenched camp. They were received by musketry and grape: three hundred were killed. And when General Lemarrois saw them on the borders of the ditch, he made a sally and pursued them with the sword in their loins. The Bavarian colonel of the 4th regiment was killed; and the Bavarians lost 20 men killed, and about 60 wounded. All the army is encamped in divisions of square battalions, in very wholesome situations. These affairs of advanced posts have not occasioned any movements in the army. Every thing is quiet at the head quarters. This general attack upon our advanced posts seems to have had no other object than to occupy the French army, so as to prevent them from reinforcing the troops employed in the siege of Dantzic. The hope of succouring Dantzic, by means of a maritime expedition, appears very extraordinary to well-informed military men, acquainted with the ground and the position occupied by the French army. The leaves begin to appear; and the season resembles the month of April in France.

75th Bulletin of the French Army

Finckenstein, 18th May, 1807

The following are the particulars of the affair of the 15th. Marshal Lefebvre makes a very favourable report of General Schramm, to whom he, in a great measure, imputes the favourable issue of the affair at Weichselmunde. On the morning of the 15th, at two o'clock, General Schramm had formed in order of battle, covered by two redoubts, thrown up opposite the fort of Weichselmunde. He had the Poles on the left, the Saxons in the centre, mid the regiment of Paris in reserve. The Russian General Kaminskoy sallied from the fort at daybreak; and, after two hours hard fighting, the 12th regiment of light infantry, sent by Marshal Lefebvre from the left shore, and a battalion of Saxons, decided the victory. Scarcely a battalion belonging to Oudinot's corps had any occasion to take part in the action. Our loss is very trifling. M. Paris, a Polish colonel, was killed. The loss of the enemy is greater than we supposed. We have buried 900 Russians. We cannot reckon their loss at less than 2,500 men. We observed no more movements on the part of the enemy, who seemed to confine himself very prudently within the circuit of the works. The number of vessels sent off with the wounded was 14. The Emperor has issued a decree for making every person who distinguished himself on this occasion a member of the Legion of Honour they are about 30 in number. On the 14th, a division of 5,000 men, mostly Prussians from Koenigsberg, landed on the Nehrung, and advanced against our light cavalry as far as Karlsberg, who thought proper to fall back upon Furtenswerder. The enemy advanced to the extremity of the Frisch Haff. We ex-

196

pected they would have penetrated from thence Dantzic. A bridge thrown over the Vistula at Furtenswerder made the passage easy for our troops cantoned in the island of Nogat, so that the infantry might have attacked the enemy's rear; but the Prussians were too wary to proceed. The Emperor ordered General Beaumont, *aid-de-camp* to the Grand Duke of Berg, to attack them. On the morning of the 16th, at two o'clock, the General of Brigade Albert advanced, at the head of two battalions of grenadiers of the reserve, the 3rd and the 1st regiments of chasseurs, and a brigade of dragoons. He met the enemy about daybreak, between Passenwerder and Stege, attacked him, routed, and closely pursued him 11 leagues; made 1100 prisoners, killed and wounded a great number, and took four pieces of cannon. Thus the enemy has suffered considerably losses, at various points, since the 12th. On the 17th the Emperor caused the fusiliers of the guard to manoeuvre: they are encamped near the castle of Finckenstein in barracks, equally as handsome as those at Boulogne. On the 18th and 19th the imperial guard encamped upon the same spot. Prince Jerome is encamped in Silesia, with a corps of observation, covering the siege of Neisse. On the 12th the Prince learned that a column of 3000 men had left Glatz to surprise Breslau. He ordered General Lefebvre to advance with the 1st Bavarian regiment, and a detachment of 300 Saxons. In the morning of the 14th, the General came up with the enemy's rear near Cauth, which he immediately attacked, made himself master of the village with the bayonet, and took 150 prisoners: 100 of the Bavarian light cavalry fell upon those of the enemy, 500 in number, routed and dispersed them. The enemy again formed in order of battle, and offered resistance: 300 Saxons fled; this extraordinary conduct must have been the effects of dissatisfaction, as the Saxons have always behaved with valour ever since they joined the French. However, this unexpected event brought the 1st Bavarian regiment into a very critical situation. They lost 150 men, who were made prisoners, and they were compelled to beat a retreat, which they effected in good order. The enemy retook the village of Cauth. In the morning, at eleven o'clock, General Dumuy, who had advanced from Breslau with 1000 French dismounted dragoons, hussars and chasseurs, attacked the enemy in the rear: 150 of the hussars retook the village, after a charge with the bayonet, made 100 prisoners, and liberated all the Bavarians made prisoners by the Prussians. The enemy, in order to facilitate his retreat to Glatz, had separated in two columns. General Lefebvre, who left Schweidnitz on the 15th, fell in with one of these columns, killed 100, and made 400 prisoners, including 30 officers. A Polish regiment of lance-bearers had arrived on the preceding evening at Frankenstein, and a detachment of them being sent to join General Lefebvre, by Prince Jerome, distinguished themselves on this occasion. The second column endeavoured to regain Glatz, by passing the Silberberz. Lieutenant-General Ducoudrais, the Prince's *aid-de-camp*, fell in with them, and threw them in disorder. Thus a column of between 3000 and 4000 men, that left Glatz, was unable to return. They have been either killed, made prisoners, or dispersed.

76TH BULLETIN OF THE FRENCH ARMY

Finckenstein, 20th May, 1807

A fine English corvette, copper sheathed, having 120 English for her crew, and laden with powder and ball, presented herself off Dantzic, with an intention to enter that port. On approaching near our works, she was attacked from both the shores with a heavy shower of musketry, and forced to surrender. A picquet of the regiment of Paris was the first to leap on board. An *aid-de-camp* of General Kalkreuth, who was on his return from the Russian head quarters, and several English officers, were taken on board the vessel. She is called the undaunted, and had 60 Russians on board, besides the 120 English. The enemy's loss in the affair of Weichselmunde, on the 15th, was greater than was at first supposed. A Russian column, which held out to the last, was put to the bayonet to a man. There were 1300 Russians buried. On the 16th, a Russian division of 6000 men, under General Turkow, advanced from the Brock to the Bug, and towards Pultusk, with a view to prevent the execution of some new works for strengthening the *tête-du-pont*. These works were defended by six Bavarian battalions, under the command of the Crown Prince in person. The enemy advanced four times to the attack, and were four times repulsed by the Bavarians, and covered with grape shot from the batteries of the different works. Marshal Massena estimates the enemy's loss at 300 killed, and twice as many wounded. And what renders the conflict still more glorious is, that the Bavarians were not quite 400. The Royal Prince commends, in particular, the Bavarian General Baron Wrede, an officer of conspicuous merit. The loss of the Bavarians amounted to. 15 killed, and 150 wounded. The same mismanagement, as in the attack of the 16th at Pultusk, was displayed in that which the enemy made on the 13th, against the works of General Lemarrois; nor was their want of judgement less conspicuous in the preparation of a great number of rafts, which the enemy were preparing on the Bug for these six weeks past. The result was, that those rafts, which took them so long in preparation, were burnt in two hours time; and that those repeated attacks upon works well contrived, and defended by strong batteries, without a chance of success, have produced them a considerable loss. We are almost induced to think, that the purport of these attacks was to draw the attention of the French army to their right wing. But the position of the army was calculated, by anticipation, for every case, and for all operations of attack and defence. In the mean while, the important siege of Dantzic is continued. The loss of that important fortress, and of the 20,000 men shut up within the same, will be severely felt by the enemy. A mine which was contrived near the outer button, had the effect of blowing it up. A communication has been opened with the covered way by four entrances, and we employed in filling up the ditch. This day the Emperor reviewed the 9th provisional regiment. The first eight of those regiments have already been embodied. The Genoese conscripts among those regiments are much extolled for the readiness and zeal displayed by them.

77TH BULLETIN OF THE FRENCH ARMY

Finckenstein, 29th May, 1807

Dantzic has capitulated. That fine city is in our possession. Eight hundred pieces of artillery, magazines of every kind, more than 500,000 quintals of grain, well-stored cellars, immense collections of clothing and spices; great resources of every kind for the army lastly, a place of the first order for strength on our left wing, as Thorn supports our centre, and Prague our right; these are the advantages obtained during winter, and which have signalized the leisure hours of the grand army; this is, indeed, the first fruit of the victory of Eylau. The rigour of the season, the snow which has so often covered our trenches, the ice, which has added fresh difficulties, have afforded no obstacles to our operations. Marshal Lefebvre has braved all; he has animated with the same spirit the Saxons, the Poles, the troops of Baden, and has made them all conduce to his end. The difficulties which he artillery had to conquer were considerable. One hundred pieces of artillery, five or 6000 pounds weight of powder, and an immense quantity of bullets have been drawn from Stettin, and the strong places in Silesia. It was necessary to surmount many difficulties in removing the artillery, but the Vistula afforded easy and expeditious means. The marines of the guards have passed their boats under the fort of Graudentz with their accustomed skill and resolution. General Chasseloup, General Kirgener, Colonel Lacoste, and in general all the officers of the engineers, have served in the most distinguished manner. The sappers have shown an uncommon degree of intrepidity. The whole corps of artillery, under General Lariboissiere, has sustained its reputation. The second regiment of light infantry, the 12th, and the troops of Paris, with Generals Schramm and Puthod, have distinguished themselves. A detailed journal of this siege will soon be drawn up with care. It will consecrate a great number of acts of bravery, worthy of being exhibited as examples, and such as must excite enthusiasm and admiration. On the 17th, the mine blew up a block house, attached to the guard-house on the covered way. On the 19th, the descent and passage of the fosse were executed at seven o'clock in the evening. On the 21st, Marshal Lefebvre having prepared every thing for the assault, they were proceeding to the attack, when Colonel Lacoste, who had been sent in the morning into the place upon some business, signified that General Kalkreuth demanded to capitulate on the same conditions that he had formerly granted to the garrison of Mayence. This was agreed to. The Hackelsberg would have been stormed with very little loss, but the body of the place was yet entire. A large fosse, full of running water, presented such difficulties that the besieged might have held out for fifteen days longer. In this situation it appeared proper to grant them an honourable capitulation. On the 27th, the garrison marched put, with General Kalkreuth at its head. This strong garrison, which at first consisted 16,000 men, was reduced to 9000 men, of which number 4000 have deserted. Among the deserters there are even officers. "We will not," they say, "go to Siberia." Many thousands of artillery horses have been given up to us, but they are in very bad condition. They are now drawing up the inventory of the magazines. General Rapp is named Governor of Dantzic. The Russian Lieutenant-General Kaminskoy, after having been beat on the 15th, retired under the fortifications of Weichselmunde. He remained there without venturing to undertake anything; and he has been a spectator of the surrender of the place. When he perceived that they were erecting batteries, to burn his ships with red-hot balls, he embarked and retired. He has returned to Pillau. The fort of Weichselmunde still held out. Marshal Lefebvre summoned it on the 26th, and while they were regulating the terms of capitulation, the garrison advanced from the fort and surrendered. The commandant, thus abandoned by the garrison, saved himself by sea, and thus we are in possession of the town and port of Dantzic. These events are a happy presage of the campaign. The Emperor of Russia, and the King of Prussia, were at Heiligenbeil. They might have conjectured the surrender of the place from the cessation of the fire. They might have heard the cannon from that distance. The Emperor, to express his satisfaction to the besieging army has granted a present to each soldier. The siege of Graudentz is now commencing under the command of General Picton. General Lazowsky commands the engineers; and General Danthouard the artillery. Graudentz is strong from the number of its mines. The cavalry of the army is in fine order. The division of light cavalry, two divisions of cuirassiers, and one of dragoons, have been reviewed at Elbing, on the 26th, by the Grand Duke of Berg. On the same day, his Majesty arrived at Bishoverden and Stalsburgh, where he reviewed Hautpoult's division of cuirassiers, and the division of dragoons of General Grouchy. He has been satisfied with their appearance, and with the good condition of their horses. The Ambassador of the Porte, Seid Mohammed Emen Vahid, has been presented, on the 28th, at two o'clock, to the Emperor, by the Prince of Benevento. He delivered his credentials to his Majesty, and remained an hour in his cabinet. He is lodged at the Castle, and occupies the apartments of the Grand Duke of Berg, who is absent on account of the review. It is confidently said, that the Emperor told him that he and the Sultan Selim would be, for ever after, inseparably connected as the right hand and the left. All the good news respecting the success at Ismail and in Wallachia have just arrived. The Russians have been obliged to raise the siege of Ismail and evacuate Wallachia.

CAPITULATION OF DANTZIC

After a long resistance, and fifty-one days open trenches, circumstances having rendered it necessary to negotiate for the surrender of Dantzic to the troops of his Majesty the Emperor of the French and King of Italy, and his Allies, the following Capitulation has been agreed upon, between his Excellency General Kalkreuth, Knight of the Orders of the Black Eagle Of St Andrew; and the General of Division Drouet, Commandant of the: Legion of Honour, Grand Cross of the Royal Order of Bavaria, Chief of the General Staff of the 10th Corps of the Army, provided with full powers by the Marshal of the Empire Lefebvre, Commandant in Chief of the said Corps:

1. The garrison shall march out on the morning of the 27th, with arms and baggage, drums beating, colours flying, matches lighted, with two pieces of light artillery, pounders, and their ammunition wagons, each drawn by six horses.

2. The remainder of the artillery horses shall be delivered up to the French.

3. All the arms, of every kind, beyond what may be necessary for the officers and troops who leave the place, shall be delivered up to the Officers of Artillery nominated for that purpose.

4. The garrison shall be conducted to the advanced posts of the army of his Prussian Majesty, at Pillau, passing through the Nehrung; and night quarters shall be assigned the for a march of five days.

5. The garrison engages not to act against the French army

or its allies, during one year, reckoning from the day of signing the capitulation. General Count Kalkreuth, his Highness Prince Scherbatow, and the rest of the officers, engage, upon their honour, to observe, and cause the present article to be observed.

6. Hakelsberg, and the gates of Oliva, Jacob, and Naugarten, shall be delivered up to the troops of his Majesty the Emperor and King, and those of his allies, on the 26th, at noon.

7. The officers, subalterns, and privates, at present prisoners in Dantzic, whether belonging to his Majesty the Emperor, or his allies, shall be liberated without being exchanged.

8. In order to prevent confusion, the troops of his Majesty the Emperor, and those of his allies, shall not enter Dantzic till the Prussians and Russians have withdrawn. However a piquet shall be admitted into the place, and guards be posted at the gates.

9. As the means of conveying the whole baggage out of the place are not sufficient, a vessel shall be granted to sail directly for Pillau. The freighting of this vessel shall be made in the presence of a French Officer, nominated for this purpose.

10. Officers of the Engineers and Artillery shall be nominated on both sides, to take charge of what relates to the army, not forgetting the plans, charts, &c.

11. The magazines, regimental chests, and every thing in general, belonging to the King, shall be given up to the French Administration, and a Commissary shall be nominated to deliver them to the person provided with full powers to receive them by his Excellency Marshal Lefebvre.

12. The Prussian Officers, prisoners on parole, who were with their families in Dantzic. before the blockade commenced, may remain there, waiting for fresh orders from his Excellency the Prince of Neufchatel, Major-General; nevertheless, to enjoy this advantage, it will be necessary for them to produce a certificate, to attest that they have not taken any part in the defence of the place.

13. All the women belonging to the officers, and others, or persons in a civil employ, shall be free to leave the place, and shall have passports granted them.

14. The sick and wounded shall be left to the generosity of his Excellency Marshal Lefebvre; Officers and Surgeons shall be left to take care of them, to preserve good order and provide necessaries. As soon as they recover, they shall be sent to the advanced posts of the Prussian army, and enjoy the privileges of the capitulation.

15. An accurate list of the Officers, subalterns, and privates of each regiment, shall be delivered to his Excellency Marshal Lefebvre. The military remaining in the hospitals shall be inscribed in a separate list.

16. His Excellency Marshal Lefebvre has assured the inhabitants of Dantzic, that he will use every means to cause persons and property to be respected; and that the best order shall be maintained in the garrison.

17. A superior Officer shall be sent to the respective headquarters to guarantee the execution of the capitulation.

His Excellency the Governor has nominated Major Lestocq.

His Excellency Marshal Lefebvre has appointed the Adjutant Commandant Guichard,

18. The present capitulation shall be carried into execution, if, by the 26th at noon, the garrison shall not have been relieved. It is understood, that from the present time till then, the garrison of Dantzic shall not make any attack upon the besiegers, supposing any engagement should take place in the vicinity of the place.

Done at Dantzic, May 20, 1807

(Signed) *The General of Cavalry*

Kalkreuth, Governor.

78TH BULLETIN OF THE FRENCH ARMY

Battle of Spanden

On the 5th of June the Russian army put itself in motion. Its divisions on the right attacked the *tête-du-pont* of Spanden, which General Frere defended with the 27th regiment of light infantry. Twelve Russian and Prussian regiments made several ineffectual attempts. Seven times did they renew the attack, but were as often repulsed. The 17th regiment of dragoons charged the enemy immediately after the last assault, and forced them to abandon the field of battle. Thus, during a whole day, two divisions attacked without success a single regiment, which, it must be admitted, was entrenched. The Prince of Ponte Corvo, in visiting the entrenchments during the intervals of attack, received a slight wound, which will take him from his command fifteen days. Our loss in this affair was trifling. The enemy lost 1200 men, and a number of wounded.

Two Russian divisions belonging to the centre attacked at the same time the *tête-du-pont* of Lomitten. General Fetry's brigade (part of Marshal Soult's corps) defended the *tête-du-pont*. The Russian General was killed, along with 1100 men; 100 were taken, and a great many wounded. We had 120 men killed and wounded. During this period, the Russian Commander in Chief, with the Grand Duke Constantine, the Imperial Guard, and three divisions, attacked the positions of Marshal Ney, at Alizirzen, Güttstadt, and Volfsdorff. The enemy were every where repulsed; but when Marshal Ney perceived that the force opposed to him exceeded forty thousand men, he obeyed his orders, and conducted his corps to Ackendorff.

Battle of Deppen

On the following day, the enemy attacked the 6th corps in its position at Deppen, on the Passarge. They were repulsed. The manoeuvres of Marshal Soult, his intrepidity, which he imparted to all his troops, the abilities displayed in this situation by the General of Division Marchand, and his officers, merit the highest eulogiums. The enemy acknowledges having lost this day 2000 killed, and more than 3000 wounded. Our loss was 180 killed, 200 wounded, and 250 taken. The latter were for the most part taken by the Cossacks, who, on the morning of the attack, had got into the rear of the army.

Battle of June 8th

The Emperor arrived at Marshal Ney's camp, at Deppen, on the 8th He immediately gave the necessary orders. The 4th corps marched to Volfsdorff, where meeting the Russian division of Kaminskoy, which was on its way to rejoin the main body, the 4th corps attacked it, deprived it of between four and 500 men, made 150 prisoners, and in the evening took its position at Altzirken. At the same moment the Emperor advanced to Güttstadt with the corps of Marshal Ney and Lannes, his guard and the cavalry of reserve. Part of the rear-guard of the enemy, comprising 10,000 cavalry and 15,000 infantry, took a position at Glottau, and attempted to dispute the way. The Grand Duke of Berg, after some very skilful manoeuvres, drove the enemy from all their positions. The light brigades of cavalry under Generals Pagol, Bruyères, and Durosnel, and the division of the heavy cavalry under General Nansouty, triumphed over all the efforts of the enemy. In the evening at eight o'clock we entered Güttstadt by main force: 1000 prisoners, all the positions in advance of Güttstadt, and the redoubts of the infantry, were the results of this day. The regiments of cavalry and the Swiss guard suffered more than any of the rest.

BATTLE OF JUNE 10TH

On the 10th the army moved towards Heilsberg. It took several of the enemy's camps. About a quarter of a league beyond these camps, the enemy showed himself in a position. He had between 15 and 18,000 cavalry, and several lines of infantry. The cuirassiers of the division d'Espagne, the division of Latour Maubourg's dragoons, and the brigade of light cavalry, made several charges, and gained ground. At two o'clock the corps under Marshal Soult was formed. Two divisions marched to the right, while the division of Lagrande marched to the left, to seize on the extremity of a wood, the occupation of which was necessary, in order to support the left of the cavalry, and make various efforts to maintain themselves in the positions before Heilsberg. More than 60 pieces of cannon scattered death in supporting the enemy's columns, which our divisions nevertheless repulsed, with the most unexampled intrepidity and the characteristic impetuosity of the French. Several Russian divisions were routed, and at nine in the evening, we found ourselves under the enemy's entrenchments. The fusiliers of the guard commanded by General Savary were put in motion to sustain the division of Verdier; and some of the corps of infantry of the reserve, under Marshal Lannes, were engaged, it being already night fall; they attacked the enemy with the view of cutting off his communication with Lansberg, and succeeded completely, the ardour of the troops was such, that several companies of the infantry of the line insulted the entrenched works of the Russians. Some brave men met then death in the ditches of the redoubts at the foot of the palisades. The Emperor passed the 11th on the field of battle. He there arranged the corps of the army and the divisions, preparatory to a decisive action, such a one as should put an end to the war. The whole of the Russian army was collected. The Russian magazines were at Heilsberg. The Russians occupied a fine position, which nature had rendered very strong, and which they increased by the labour of four months. At four in the afternoon, the Emperor ordered Marshal Davoust to change his front, and push forward his left; this movement brought him upon the Lower Aller, and completely blocked up the road from Eylau. Every corps of the army had its post assigned to it; they were all re-assembled, the first corps excepted, which continued upon the Lower Passarge. Thus the Russians, who were the first to begin the battle, found themselves shut up in their entrenched camp, and were compelled to give battle in the position they had chosen themselves. It was for a long time believed they would make an attack on the 11th. At the moment when the French were making their dispositions, the Russians showed themselves, ranged in columns, in the midst of their entrenchments, fortified with numerous batteries. But whether those entrenchments did not appear sufficiently formidable, after viewing the preparations which they saw before them; or whether the impetuosity which the French army had shown on the 10th, had an effect upon them, they began to pass the Aller at ten o'clock at night, abandoning the whole country to the left, and leaving at the disposal of the conqueror, their wounded, their magazines, and their entrenchments, the result of long and painful labour. On the 12th, at day-break, all the corps of the army were in motion, and took different directions. The houses of Heilsberg and its neighbourhood are filled with wounded Russians. The result of the different affairs from the 5th to the 12th has deprived the Russian army of about 30,000 fighting men. They have left between three and 4000 prisoners in our hands; seven or eight pairs of colours, and nine pieces of cannon. According to the reports of the prisoners several of the most eminent Russian Generals have been killed or wounded. Our loss amounted to six or 700 killed, 2000, or 2,200 wounded, and 300 prisoners. The General of Division Espagne was wounded. General Roussol, chief of the staff of the guard, had his head carried away by a cannon ball. The Grand Duke of Berg had two horses killed under him. M. Segur, one of his *aides-de-camp*, lost an arm. M. Lameth, Marshal Soult's *aide-de-camp*, was wounded. M. Lagrange, Colonel of the 7th regiment of horse chasseurs, was killed. The detailed reports will communicate particular acts of bravery, and the names of those who were wounded in the memorable battle of June 10. Several thousand quintals of grain, and a great quantity of different kinds of provisions, have been found in the magazines of Heilsberg.

79TH BULLETIN OF THE. FRENCH ARMY

Wehlau, 17th June, 1807

The actions of Spanden and Lomitteu, the battles of Güttstadt and Heilsberg, were only the precursors of still more important events. On the 12th at four in the morning, the French army entered Heilsberg, General Latour Maubourg pursued the enemy with his division of dragoons, and Generals Durosnel and Wattiers' brigade of light cavalry, to the right bank of the Aller, near Bartenstein. In the mean time the light corps advanced in various directions, in order to pass the enemy to cut off his retreat to Koenigsberg, and get between him and his magazines. Fortune favoured the execution of this plan. On the 12th, at five o'clock, p.m. the Imperial Head-quarters arrived at Eylau. Here the fields were no longer covered with ice and snow; on the contrary, they presented one of the most beautiful scenes in nature. The country was every where adorned by beautiful woods, intersected by lakes, and animated by handsome villages. On the 13th, the Grand Duke of Berg advanced towards Koenigsberg with his cavalry, Marshal Davoust followed to support him. Marshal Soult advanced towards Creutzburg; Marshal Lannes towards Domnau; Marshals Ney and Mortier towards Lampasch. Meanwhile General Latour Maubourg wrote that he had pursued the enemy's rearguard; that the Russians had abandoned a great number of wounded in their flight; that they had evacuated Bartenstein, and that they bad directed their retreat on Schippenheil on the right bank of the Aller. The Emperor immediately proceeded towards Friedland. He ordered the Grand Duke of Berg, Marshals Soult and Davoust, to manoeuvre against Koenigsberg, while he advanced with the corps of Ney, Lannes, Mortier, the Imperial Guard, and the first corps, commanded by General Victor, on Friedland. On the 13th, the 9th regiment of hussars entered Friedland, but was driven out of that place by 3000 of the enemy's cavalry. On,the 14th the enemy advanced on the bridge of Friedland, and at three in the morning a cannonade was heard. "It is a fortunate day," said the Emperor; "it is the anniversary of the battle of Marengo." Marshals Lannes and Mortier were first engaged; they were supported by General Grouchy's dragoons, and by General Nansouty's cuirassiers. Several movements and actions took place. The enemy were stopped and could not pass the village of Postenheim. Imagining that they had only a corps of 15,000 men opposed to them, they followed the movements of our troops towards Koenigsberg; thus the French and Saxon dragoons and cuirassiers had the opportunity of making a brilliant attack, and of taking four pieces of cannon. By five in the evening the several corps were at their appointed stations. Marshal Ney was on the right wing, Marshal Lannes in the centre, Marshal Mortier on the left wing; the corps of General Victor and the guards formed the reserve. The cavalry under the command of General Grouchy supported the left wing. The division of dragoons of General Latour Maubourg was behind the right wing as a reserve. General Lahoussaye's' division of dragoons, and the Saxon cuirassiers, formed a reserve for the centre. Meanwhile the enemy deployed the whole of his army. His left wing extended to the town of Friedland, and his right wing a mile and a half in the other direction. The Emperor having reconnoitred the position, instantly determined to take the town of Friedland. Then suddenly changing his front, and advancing his right, he commenced the attack with the first part of that wing. About half past five Marshal Ney began to move forward. Some shots from a battery of 20 cannon were the signal. At the same moment the division of General Marchand advanced sword-in-hand upon the enemy, and proceeded towards the tower of the town; being supported on the left by the division of General Bison. When the enemy perceived that Marshal Ney had left the wood in which his right wing had been posted, they endeavoured to surround him with some regiments of cavalry, and a multitude of conquests; but General Latour Maubourg's division of dragoons rode up in full gallop to the right wing, and repelled the attack of the enemy. In the mean time General Victor erected a battery of 30 cannon in die front of his centre. General Senuarmont, who commanded this battery, pushed his works forward more than 400 paces, and greatly annoyed the enemy. The several manoeuvres they attempted, in order to produce a diversion, were all in vain. Marshal Ney was at the head of his troops directing the smallest manoeuvres with that coolness and intrepidity peculiar to himself, and maintained that example which has always distinguished his corps among the other corps of the grand army. Several columns of the enemy which attacked his right wing were received with the bayonet and driven into the Aller. Thousands found their graves in that river, and some escaped by swimming; meanwhile Marshal Ney's left wing reached the Raveline, which encircles the town of Friedland. The enemy who had posted the imperial horse and foot guards in ambush there, advanced with great intrepidity, and attacked Marshal Ney's left, which for a moment was in confusion: but Dupont's division, which formed the right wing of the reserve, fell upon the Russian imperial guards, defeated them, and made a most dreadful slaughter. The enemy sent forward several other corps from his centre, to defend Friedland: vain efforts! Friedland was forced, and its streets bestrewed with dead bodies. The centre, commanded by Marshal Lannes, was at the same time engaged. he attempts which the enemy had made upon the right wing; being frustrated, he wished to try the effect of similar efforts upon our centre; he was, however, suitably received by the brave divisions of Oudinot and Verdier, and the commanding Marshal. The repeated attacks of the enemy's infantry and cavalry were incapable of obstructing the march of our columns, all the powers and all the courage of the Russians were exerted in vain. Marshal Mortier, who, during the whole day, had given great proofs of coolness and intrepidity, in supporting the left wing, now advanced, and was in his turn supported by the fusiliers of the guard under the command of General Savary. The cavalry, infantry, and artillery—all, on this occasion, generally distinguished themselves. The imperial horse and foot guards, and two divisions of the first corps, were not in the action. The victory was never for a moment doubtful. The field of battle is horrible to behold. It is not too much to estimate the number of the dead on the side of the Russians, at from 15 to 18,000. The number of the dead on the French side was not 500, but we have 3000 wounded. We have taken 80 cannons, and a great number of caissons. A great number of standards have also fallen into our hands. There are 25 of the Russian Generals either killed, wounded, or taken. Their cavalry has suffered an incalculable loss. General Drouet, Chief of Marshal Lannes' corps; General Cohorn; Colonel Regnaud of the 15th of the line; Colonel Lajonquire of the 60th; Colonel Lamotte, of the 4th dragoons; and Brigadier General Brunryn, are wounded. General Latour Maubourg is wounded in the hand. Deffourneux, Colonel of the Artillery; Hutin, Chef d'Escadron, and first aide-de-camp of General Oudinot, are killed: Two of the Emperor's aides-de-camp, Mouton and Lacoste, are slightly wounded. Night prevented us from pursuing the enemy; they were followed until 11 o'clock. During the remainder of the night, the cut-off columns tried to pass the Aller at several fordable places, and next day, we saw caissons, cannon, and harness, everywhere in the river. The battle of Friedland is worthy to be numbered with those of Marengo, Austerlitz and Jena. The enemy were numerous, had fine cavalry, and fought bravely. Next day the enemy endeavoured to assemble on the right bank of the Aller, and the French army made manoeuvres on the left bank to cut them off from Koenigsberg. The heads of the columns arrived at the same time at Wehlau, a town situated at the confluence of the Aller and the Pregel. The Emperor had his headquarters in the village of Peterswalde. The enemy having destroyed all the bridges, took advantage of that obstacle, at day-break, on the l6th, to proceed on their retreat towards Russia. At eight in the morning, the Emperor threw a bridge over the Pregel and took a position there with the army. Almost all the magazines which the enemy had on the Aller have been thrown into the river, or burnt. Some idea may be formed of the great extent of their loss by what yet remains to us. The Russians had magazines in all the villages, which, in their passage, they every where burnt. We have, however, found more than 6000 quintals of corn in Wehlau. Koenigsberg was abandoned on the arrival of the intelligence of the battle of Friedland. Marshal Soult has entered that place, where much wealth has been found. We have taken there some hundred thousand quintals of corn, more than 20,000 wounded Russians and Prussians, all the ammunition which England had sent to the Russians, including 160,000 muskets which had not been lauded. Thus has Providence punished those, who instead of negotiating with good faith to bring about a salutary peace, treated that object with derision, and regarded the repose taken by the conquerors, as a proof of timidity and weakness. The army is now in a delightful country. The banks of the Pregel are rich. In a short time the magazines and cellars of Dantzic and Koenigsberg will afford us new resources of superfluity and health. The names of the brave men who have distinguished themselves, cannot be contained within the limits of one bulletin. The staff is employed in collecting their deeds. The Prince of Neufchatel gave extraordinary proofs of his zeal and knowledge in the battle of Friedland. He was frequently in the hottest part of the action, and made arrangements which were of great advantage. It was on the 5th the enemy renewed hostilities. Their loss in the ten days which followed their first operations may be reckoned at 60,000 men, killed, wounded, taken, or otherwise put *hors de combat*. A part of their artillery, the necessary supply of military stores, and all their magazines, on a line of more than 40 miles, are lost to them. The French army has seldom obtained such great advantages with so little loss.

80TH BULLETIN OF THE FRENCH ARMY

During the time that the French arms signalize themselves on the field of battle at Friedland, the Grand Duke of Berg arrives before Koenigsberg, and takes in flank the corps of the army commanded by General Lestocq. On the 13th, Marshal Soult found at Creutzburg the Prussian rearguard. The division of Milhaud's dragoons makes a fine charge, defeats the Prussian cavalry, and takes several pieces of cannon. On the 14th, the enemy was compelled to shut himself up in Koenigsberg. About noon, two of the enemy's columns, which had been cut off before that place, attempted the bold effort of forcing their way, with a view of entering it. Six pieces of cannon, and from three to four thousand men, who composed this troop were taken. All the suburbs of Koenigsberg were rased, and a considerable number of prisoners were made. The result of all these affairs is between four and five thousand prisoners, and fifteen pieces of cannon. On the 10th and 16th, Marshal Soult's corps was occupied before the entrenchments of Koenigsberg, but the advance of the main body towards Wehlau obliged the enemy to evacuate Koenigsberg, and this place fell into our hands. The stores found at Koenigsberg are immense: two hundred large vessels from Russia are still all loaded in the port. There was much more wine and brandy than we had any reason, to expect. A brigade of the division of St. Hilaire advanced before Pillau, to form the siege of that place; and General Rapp has sent off to Dantzic for a column, ordered to go by the Nehrung, to raise before Pillau a battery which may shut the Haff. Vessels manned by marines of the guard render us masters of this small sea. On the 17th, the Emperor transferred his head quarters to the farm of Drucken, near Klein Sehirau. On the 18th he advanced them to Sgaisgirren; and on the 19th, at two in the afternoon, he entered Tilsitz. The Grand Duke of Berg, at the head of the greater part of the light cavalry, some divisions of dragoons and cuirassiers, has followed the enemy in his retreat these three last days, and did him much injury. The 5th regiment of hussars distinguished itself. The Cossacks were repeatedly routed, and suffered considerably in these different charges. We had a few killed and wounded: among the latter is the Chef d'Escadre Picton, *aide-de-camp* to the Grand Duke of Berg. After the passage of the Pregel, opposite to Wehlau, a drummer was charged by a Cossack at full gallop; the Cossack takes his lance to pierce the drummer; but the latter preserved his presence of mind, takes his lance from him, disarms the Cossack, and pursues him. A singular circumstance, which excited the laughter of the soldiers, occurred for the first time near Tilsitz, where a cloud of Cossacks were seen fighting with arrows. We were sorry for those who gave the preference to the ancient arms, over those of the modern; but nothing is more laughable than the effect of those arms against our muskets. Marshal Davoust, at the head of the third corps, defiled by Labian, fell upon the enemy's rear-guard, and made 2500 prisoners. Marshal Ney arrived on the 17th at Insterbourg, and there took 1000 wounded, and the enemy's magazines, which were considerable. The woods, the villages, are full of straggling Russians, sick or wounded. The loss of the Russian army is enormous. It has not with it more than 60 pieces of cannon. The rapidity of our marches prevent us from being able as yet to ascertain how many pieces we have taken; but it is supposed that the number exceeds 120. Near Tilsitz, notes were transmitted to the Grand Duke of Berg; and afterwards the Russian Prince, Lieut-General Labanoff, passed the Niemen, and had a conference for an hour with the Prince of Neufchatel. The enemy burned in great haste the bridge of Tilsitz over the Niemen, and appeared to be continuing his retreat into Russia. We are on the confines of that empire. The Niemen, opposite Tilsitz, is somewhat broader than the Seine. From the left bank we see a cloud of Cossacks, who form the rearguard of the enemy on the right bank. Hostilities have already ceased. What remained to the King of Prussia is conquered. That unfortunate prince has only in his power the country situate between the Niemen and Memel. The greater part of his army, or rather of the division of his troops, is deserting, being unwilling to go into Russia. The Emperor of Russia remained three weeks at Tilsitz with the King of Prussia. On receiving advice of the battle of Friedland, they both left the place with the utmost haste.

81st Bulletin of the French Army

Tilsitz, 21st June, 1807

At the affair at Heilsberg, the Grand Duke of Berg passed along the line of the 3rd division of cuirassiers, at the moment when the 6th regiment had just made a charge. Colonel d'Avary, commander of the regiment, his sabre dyed in blood, said, "Prince, review my regiment, and you will find that there is not a soldier whose sword is not like mine." Colonel Borde Soult was wounded; Guihenene, *aide-de-camp* to Marshal Lasnes, was wounded, &c. &c. &c. The sons of the senators Perignon, Clement de Ris, and Grattan Coulon, died with honour on the field of battle. Marshal Ney proceeded to Gumbinnin, secured some of the enemy's parks of artillery, many wounded Russians, and took a great number of prisoners.

82nd Bulletin of the French Army

Tilsitz, 22nd June, 1807

An armistice has been concluded upon the proposition of the Russian General. The French army occupies all the Thalweg of the Niemen, so that there only remains to the King of Prussia the town and territories of Memel.

Proclamation of the Emperor and King
to the Army

Soldiers!—On the 5th of June we were attacked in our cantonments by the Russian army. The enemy mistook the causes of our inactivity. He found too late that our repose was that of the lion—he regrets having disturbed it. In the affairs of Guttstadt, Heilsberg, and the ever memorable one of Friedland, in a ten days campaign, in short, we took 120 pieces of cannon, seven standards; killed, wounded, or took 60,000 Russians, carried off all the enemy's magazines and hospitals; and remain masters of Koenigsberg, the 300 vessels that were there, laden with all sorts of ammunition, and 160,000 fusils sent by England to arm our enemies. From the banks of the Vistula we have reached the borders of the Niemen with the rapidity of the eagle. You celebrated at Austerlitz the anniversary of the coronation; you celebrated this year, in an appropriate manner, the battle of Marengo, which put a period to the second coalition. Frenchmen, you have been worthy of yourselves and of me. You will return to France covered with laurels; after having obtained a glorious peace, which carries with it the guarantee of its duration. It is time that our country should live at rest, secure from the malignant influence of England. My benefits shall prove to you my gratitude, and the full extent of the love I bear you.—At the Imperial Camp at Tilsit, June 22.

83rd Bulletin of the French Army

Tilsit, 23rd June, 1807

Annexed is the capitulation of Neisse.—The garrison, 6000 strong in infantry, and 500 in cavalry, defiled on the 16th before Prince Jerome. We found in the place 300,000 pounds of powder, and 300 pieces of cannon.

84th Bulletin of the French Army

Tilsit, 24th June, 1807

The Marshal of the Palace, Duroc, went on the 24th to the head-quarters of the Russian army, on the other side of the Niemen, to exchange the ratifications of the armistice, which had been ratified by the Emperor Alexander. On the 24th, Prince Labanoff having demanded an audience of the Emperor, was admitted on the same day at two in the afternoon; he remained a long time in the cabinet with his Majesty. General Kalkreuth is expected at the head-quarters to sign the armistice with the King of Prussia. On the 11th of June, at four o'clock in the morning, the Russians attacked Druezewo in great force; General Claparede sustained the enemy's fire; Marshal Massena rushed along the line, repulsed the enemy, and disconcerted their projects; the 17th regiment of light infantry maintained its regulation; General Montbrun distinguished himself; a detachment of the 28th light infantry, and a piquet of the 25th dragoons, put the Cossacks to flight. All the enterprizes of the enemy against our posts, on the 11th and 12th instant, turned to their own confusion. It is already seen by the armistice, that the left wing of the French army supports itself on the Curisch Haff, at the mouth of the Niemen, whence our line extends itself towards Grodno; the right, commanded by Marshal Massena, reaches to the confines of Russia, between the sources of the Narew and the Bug. The head-quarters are about to be removed to Koenigsberg, where every day new discoveries are made of provisions, ammunition, and other effects, belonging to the enemy. A position so formidable is. the result of successes the most brilliant; and while the enemy's army flies routed and destroyed, more than half the French army has not fired a musket.

Vienna, 17th June, 1807
The Governor General Gouvion has published the following particulars of the affairs of the 11th and 12th on the right bank of the Omelew:

On the 11th, the Russians made some movements as if they intended to cross the Narew near Rozan; at the same time they attacked the camp of Boski, with a column of 6000 men, 2000 cavalry, and some pulks of Cossacks. The enemy's superior numbers, and the numerous batteries which he opened on the other side of the river, obliged General Claparede, after an obstinate resistance, to evacuate the camp, and retire with his twelve companies of the 17th regiment of infantry, in good order, to Norzewo.

On the 12th, all the Russian troops were again in motion. General Gazan was attacked upon his whole line, but in vain. By the various motions of the enemy, the Marshal was convinced that it was necessary to turn his principal attention to Dronzewo and Boski. His Excellency, therefore, gave orders to march against the Russians, and, notwithstanding the entrenchments which they had hastily thrown up, the camp of Boski was carried by the bayonets of the 17th regiment, while the enemy was pushed and driven on the other side of the Omelew, where he was only enabled to form again under his numerous batteries.

85th Bulletin of the French Army

Tilsitz, 24th June, 1807

Tomorrow the two Emperors of France and Russia are to have an interview. For this purpose a pavilion has been erected in the middle of the Niemen, to which the two monarchs will repair from each of its banks. Few sights will be more interesting. The two sides of the river will be lined by the two armies, while their chiefs confer on the means of re-establishing order, and giving repose to the existing generation. The Grand Marshal of the Palace, Duroc, went yesterday, at three in the afternoon, to compliment the Emperor Alexander. Marshal Count Kalkreuth was presented this day to the Emperor: he remained an hour in his Majesty's cabinet. The corps of Marshal Lannes was reviewed this morning by the Emperor. He made several promotions, gave rewards to those who distinguished themselves by their bravery, and expressed his satisfaction to the Saxon cuirassiers.

86th Bulletin of the French Army

Tilsitz, 25th June, 1807

This day, at one, the Emperor, accompanied by the Duke of Berg, Prince Neufchatel, Marshal Bessieres, the Marshal of the Palace, Duroc, and the Grand Equerry, Caulaincourt, embarked on the banks of the Niemen, in a boat prepared for the purpose. They proceeded to the middle of the river, where General Lariboissiere, commanding the artillery of the guard, had caused a raft to be placed, and a pavilion erected upon it. Close by it was another raft and pavilion for their Majesties' suite. At the same moment the Emperor Alexander set out from the right bank, accompanied by the Grand Duke Constantine, General Bennigsen, General Ouwaroff, Prince Labanoff, and his principal *Aide-de-Camp* Count Lieven. The two boats arrived at the same instant, and the two Emperors embraced each other as soon as they sat foot on the raft. They entered together the saloon which was prepared for them, and remained there two hours. The conference having been concluded, (he persons composing the suite of the two Emperors were introduced. The Emperor Alexander paid the handsomest compliments to the officers who accompanied the Emperor, who, on his part, had a long conversation with the Grand Duke Constantine and General Bennigsen. The conference having terminated, the two Emperors embarked each in his boat. It is supposed that the conference has had the happiest result. Shortly after, Prince Labanoff went to the French head-quarters. An agreement has taken place that one half of the town of Tilsitz is to be rendered neutral. The apartments appointed there for the residence of the Emperor of Russia and his court have been fixed upon. The imperial Russian guard will pass the river, and be quartered in that part of the city destined to that purpose. The vast number of persons belonging to each army, who flocked to both banks of the river to view this scene, rendered it the more interesting; as the spectators were brave men, who came from the extremities of the world.

GENERAL ORDERS

Headquarters at Stettin, 10th July, 1807

The corps of observation of the grand army must return an attack, and advance into Swedish Pomerania. On the 18th of April an armistice was concluded at Schlatkow, which was to have continued until ten days should have expired after notice had been given of the intention to resume hostilities. In consequence of some subsequent conferences between the commanding Generals, the term of ten days was extended to thirty days by an additional article, signed the

29th of the same month. The latter arrangement experienced no kind of difficulties: but his Majesty the King of Sweden appeared in Pomerania, assumed the command of his army, and immediately declared his intention to acknowledge merely the first stipulation of a term of ten days. At the same time the Swedish navy, in spite of the armistice, committed hostilities before Colberg against the corps of French troops and their allies which besieged that place. In this state of affairs, an explanatory correspondence arose between the commanding General, and the King of Sweden proposed a conference to me, in order to put an end to the subsisting differences, which conference was to be held at Schlatkow, in the Swedish territory. Hopes were then entertained, that the opposition his Majesty experienced, arose merely from his wish to conduct the affairs himself; and that the conference proposed might perhaps lead to peaceful overtures, and some permanent arrangement. On the 4th of June, I accordingly proceeded to Schlatkow, attended by five or six officers of the staff, and by as many orderly gens d'armes. The *aides-de-camp* of his Swedish Majesty had declared to me, that the King was at Schlatkow, almost without an escort, attended merely by a retinue by no means numerous. On my arrival I found the house where the King was, without guards, but in the court a squadron of horse was drawn up in order of battle. Being alone admitted to the Prince, I represented to him the object of the conference, but he interrupted me almost immediately, and declared, that his determination in favour of the term of the first armistice was unalterable, and thus cut off all questions, which were to form the object of the conference. Europe will learn it with indignation, because the laws of nations, mid the laws of honour, were violated; he dared to propose to the French General, to one of the first subjects of the Emperor Napoleon, to betray his sovereign and his country; to espouse the cause of the English under the disgraceful banner of a band of deserters, who feel neither for the happiness of their native country, nor share in its glory. Since that conference, the King, caused the above hostilities before Colberg to be continued, and others to be continued at the mouth of the Trave. He has drawn from England both money and soldiers; he has collected as many fugitives and deserters as came within his reach, and full of confidence in his force, he gave on the 30th of this month notice, that at the expiration of ten days the armistice would be at an end; he gave that notice at the very moment when he could be informed of the change of dispositions on the part of Russia and Prussia. The hostilities with Sweden recommence therefore on the 13th of this month. We might begin them sooner, because the king's conduct has been nothing but a series of violations and infringements; but it is a prominent feature in the character of our sovereign to be as great in magnanimity and moderation, as he is through his genius and heroic exploits. Europe will know how to appreciate such conduct, and discern those who wish to prolong the scourge of war. The French troops will vie with those of the allies in discipline and valour; they will not forget that the Emperor Napoleon has his regards fixed on them, and feel confident that we shall all deserve his approbation by our attachment.

Marshal Brune

87TH BULLETIN OF THE FRENCH ARMY

Koenigsberg, 12th July, 1807

The Emperors of France and Russia, after 20 days residence at Tilsitz, where the Imperial Palaces were in the same street, and at no great distance, took leave of each other with the greatest cordiality, at three o'clock in the afternoon of the 9th. The Journal which contains an account of what passed between them will be very interesting to both nations. At half past four, the Emperor Napoleon having received a visit from the King of Prussia, who came to take his leave, set out for Koenigsberg, where he arrived at ten at night. The King of Prussia went to Memel. Yesterday the Emperor Napoleon inspected the port of Koenigsberg, in a boat manned by the Imperial Guard. Today his Majesty will review Marshal Soult's corps, and at two o'clock to-morrow he will set out for Dresden. The number of Russians killed in the battle of Friedland amounts to 17,500, the prisoners to 40,000; 18,000 of whom have already passed through Koenigsberg, 7000 remain sick in the hospitals, and the rest have been conducted to Thorn and Warsaw. Orders have been issued to send them home to Russia, without delay; 7000 have already returned again to Koenigsberg. Those in France are to be formed into provisional regiments. The Emperor has ordered them to be clothed and armed. The ratifications of the treaty of peace between France and Russia were exchanged at Tilsitz, on the 9th. The ratification of the treaty of peace between France and Prussia will be exchanged here this day. The plenipotentiaries charged with these negotiations were, on the part of France, the Prince of Benevento; Princes Kurakin and Labanoff, on the part of Russia; on the part of Prussia, Field Marshal Count Kalkreuth, and the Count de Goltz. After such events as these, one cannot but smile when the great English expedition is mentioned, and at the new frenzy which animates the King of Sweden. Besides, we may remark that the army of observation, between the Elbe and the Oder is 70,000 strong, exclusive of the grand army, without including the Spanish divisions, which are now upon the Oder also. It was, therefore, necessary for England to have brought her whole force together, her soldiers, her volunteers, fencibles, &c. in order to have made a diversion of any interest. But when we take into our account, that England, under the present circumstances, has sent 6000 men to Egypt only to be slaughtered by the Arabians, and 7000 men to the Spanish West Indies, we can alone feel sentiments of pity for the extravagant avarice with which that cabinet is tormented. The peace of Tilsitz puts an end to the operations of the army; notwithstanding this, all the Prussian coasts and ports will be shut against the English; and it is probable that the continental blockade will not prove a mere sound. The Porte is included in the treaty. The revolution which lately occurred at Constantinople, was an anti-Christian revolution, which has nothing in common with the policy of Europe. The Adjutant-Commandant Guilleminot is gone to Bessarabia, where he will communicate to the Grand Vizier the intelligence of the peace, and the liberty given to the Porte to take part in it,.as well as of the conditions of the treaty in which the Porte is interested.

Appendix 3

Russian Documents

Declaration of the Court of St. Petersburg

The events which have extended in Europe the horrors of war, and the overwhelming calamities produced by the insatiable ambition of the French Government, are known to all the world. All our efforts to arrest the progress of these misfortunes, and to preserve, by pacific measures, the tranquillity and integrity of the powers which are our allies, have proved ineffectual. The perfidy with which the common enemy tramples under foot the most sacred treaties, and the rights of nations—in threatening Europe with universal devastation, has engaged us to take up arms to support the neighbouring kingdoms.

The continued disasters which the arms of Austria have experienced, have obliged this Power to conclude a disadvantageous peace, dictated by the ambition of the conqueror, and submitted to by the hard necessity of circumstances. Prussia, who has again vainly endeavoured to resist the progress of the evil, by a negotiation for a solid and general peace, has not been able to exempt herself any longer from the calamities of war, in spite of all the sacrifices she has made to preserve her alliance with France; in spite of all the condescension with which she conformed to all the demands of the enemy. Plunged in a deceitful security by the hope of a peace which she vainly flattered herself to enjoy, and the false confidence she had placed in a perfidious ally, she has suddenly been precipitated in an abyss of misfortunes. The armies of Napoleon, lancing upon the Prussian troops before they had time to reunite, defeated them, and the Capital unprotected, became for the French an easy conquest, and, finally, they have made themselves masters of the greatest part of the provinces of the kingdom.

In this state of affairs, seeing that the neighbouring Power which separated France from the western provinces of our Empire was deprived of all means of defence, it has become indispensably necessary for us to advance our army under the conduct of Field-Marshal Count Kaminskoy, for the defence of our territory, menaced on this side by an hostile invasion, and after having implored the assistance of the All-powerful, who always espouses the just cause, we have ordered every possible effort to defeat this dangerous assailant, who, in the proclamations that he has published, has the audacity to menace openly his intentions of pursuing his conquests even into our states. At the commencement of this inevitable war, of which, after the total defeat of our allies, all the weight falls upon us, we consider it is our duty to redouble efforts for the maintenance of the tranquillity and integrity of our Empire, by augmenting and concentrating the armed force of the brave, faithful, and magnanimous, that Providence has entrusted to our care.

The calamities which have fallen upon the neighbouring powers with so much rapidity, prove the necessity of recurring to extraordinary means—to measures great and vigorous, which cannot be put into execution but by the most zealous love for the country, by a courageous firmness, and by a just conception of the national honour.

A people really animated, and conducted by such sentiments, and generally armed, can oppose an invincible rampart to every attack however formidable. Nations in the present war have neglected to oppose to the French system of pillage and rapine, such a system of interior defence; and, for want of this precaution, Austria has suffered the greatest disasters, and been prevented from contributing to the aid of Prussia. Their fate has been decided by the loss of several battles, after which, the enemy, meeting with no obstacle, and fearing no opposition on the part of a disarmed multitude, has rapidly penetrated into the interior of the country, spread terror "and desolation by its prompt and fleet depredations, and destroying the dispersed wrecks of the army, has completed the total subversion of their states. The bravery of the Russian hoops, and the victories that their undaunted valour has gained, during the last age, over their enemies in the most distant countries; the trophies yet existing in different parts of this Empire, which they have aggrandized by their exploits; and, finally, the memory of that glory which they have thus acquired, authorize us to hope, on the present occasion, that, with the blessing of Providence, which always protects the arms of the just, that the machinations of our enemies will be confounded, and the only traces that they will leave upon our territory, will be the tombs that they come to find. The immense extent of the territory upon which their armies must act, occasioning various obstacles to a prompt co-operation to a defence of an extensive frontier; the danger which would result from the event which, God forbid, of an enemy penetrating into the interior of our Empire, obliges us to oppose the most efficacious measure, by the establishment of a temporary general militia, which shall be ready at the first order to sustain the regular troops, and to oppose to the enemy the invincible force of true sons of their country, armed for the preservation of their dearest interests.

In circumstances so difficult, we revert, with the most entire confidence, to the order of the hereditary nobility of the Empire, to whose faithful services and sacrifices Russia owes her actual greatness ; to an order which has always been ready to offer to the state its blood and its fortunes;—to this order, which by heroic examples has, in all circumstances, sustained the courage of the lower classes, and induced them to contribute to the defence, the safety, and glory of the Empire. The memorable proofs of patriotism and loyalty that the nobility of Russia, in all ancient as well as modern times, have given, and the zeal with which it obeys the orders of its Sovereign, when the public good requires, and which braves all fatigues and dangers for the safety of the Empire, is a guarantee to us that it will efficaciously second the formation of a provisional armament, which is indispensably necessary, and which is ordered for the safety of the state. We are equally convinced, that all our faithful corporations, and all classes of citizens, as well as the peasants of the Crown, and the free cultivators, will unite their efforts to support the common burthen of this armament, of which the object is the defence of our holy faith and individual security—the formation of national troops or militia to exist during the time the country is menaced. It should be made on the following plan.

(Then follows the detail of arrangements, the organization, equipment, and armament of 400,000 men.)

When, with the aid of the Almighty, our efforts, and those of our faithful subjects, for the defence of the Empire and the defeat of the arrogant enemy, shall have the desired effect, and the dangers which menaced shall have ceased, then, with a heart full of gratitude towards that Providence who protects us, the troops shall deposit their arms, and return to the bosom of those families, that their courage has protected, to enjoy a peace so gloriously acquired. We give solemnly our imperial word, and we sacredly engage, as the representative of a grateful country, to confer marks of grace and favour, and recompenses of distinction, due to merit and eminent services, to all the true children of Russia, who, on the present occasion, shall manifest their zeal by acts of courage, by the sacrifice of their property, or by actions useful to the public; and the names of these men, who have thus rendered service to their country, shall be celebrated with the admiration of posterity, and consecrated in the pages of history.

(Signed) *Alexander.*

Petersburg

30th of November, 1806

FROM BRITISH MERCHANTS TO COUNT KOTCHUBEY

St. Petersburg, 11th January, 1807

The British merchants, residing in St. Petersburg, participating in the general loyalty and public spirit so happily and conspicuously manifested at present in this country, and anxious to give a proof of their sentiments, avail themselves of his Imperial Majesty's most gracious permission to present the sum of 135,000 roubles, towards the expenses of the measures which his wisdom has adopted against the general enemy of Europe. They are perfectly sensible of the small importance of such a sum, from a few foreign individuals, in the expenditure of this great empire; but they venture to hope, that his Imperial Majesty will, in his goodness, be most graciously pleased to regard it as a testimony of their attachment to his person and Government, and of their sincere wishes for the prosperity of those extensive dominions over which he reigns, and of which they pray that Divine Providence may long, preserve him the happy and beloved Sovereign.

Answer to the Above

21st January, 1807

The Minister of the Interior has esteemed it as a duty imposed upon him, to lay before his Imperial Majesty the communication, by which the Body of British Merchants trading in Russia, in expressing their feelings of attachment and zeal towards the person of his Imperial Majesty, have offered to contribute, on their part, a sum of 135,000 roubles towards the defraying of the expenses incurred at present by all ranks and stations in the Empire, in arming the Militia.

His Majesty the Emperor, being always most graciously disposed towards the English Merchants, as one of the most ancient commercial bodies established in this metropolis, has been pleased to permit their participating in the general contributions above-mentioned, according to their wishes ; and to order that, on this occasion, his Majesty's especial satisfaction shall be made known to such of his Britannic Majesty's subjects as have made this gratuitous donation.

The Minister of the interior, in fulfilling these his Majesty's commands, has the honour of communicating them to the Gentlemen deputed to him from the English Merchants; at the same time informing them, that the money, destined by them in aid of the present extraordinary military preparations, can be paid, at their own convenience, into the Imperial Treasury.

(Originally signed) *Count V. Kotchubey*

Official report of the Battle of Pultusk
copy of a dispatch of General Bennigsen

Rozan, 15-26th December, 1806

I have the happiness to inform Your Imperial Majesty, that the enemy attacked me yesterday, before 12 o'clock, close to Pultusk, and that I succeeded in checking him at all points. General Suchet, with 15,000 men, commanded the first attack, which was directed on my left against the advanced works of Gurka, in order that they might render themselves masters of that city. I had to oppose them; 5,000 men, under the orders of General Baggavout, who defended himself with the utmost bravery, until I could send to his assistance three battalions of reserve to the same point. I also at last detached General Ostermann Tolstoy with three other battalions, which caused the enemy to be totally beaten on his right wing. The second attack of the enemy (which proved a very sharp one) was directed against my right flank. General Barkley de Tolly was with the advanced guard in this wing, on its route to Stegoezin, was sheltered by a hedge, in which I had placed masked battery. Notwithstanding this disposition, the enemy made a feint of turning my flank, which determined me to change my front to the rear on the right: this movement completely succeeded. After having reinforced General Barkley de Tolly with three battalions, ten squadrons, and a train of artillery, the enemy were dislodged from the wood and defeated in every direction; after which they began their retreat.

The attack commenced at 11 o'clock in the morning, and continued until the close of evening. From the report of the prisoners, the Prince Murat, Davoust, and Lannes, commanded against me 50,000 men. All my troops fought with the greatest bravery. The following Generals particularly distinguished themselves: Generals Ostermann, Tolstoy, Barkley de Tolly; Prince Dolgorucky, Baggavout, Summow, and Gondorff, of the cavalry. The General Koxin, Colonel de Zeguelin, charged the left wing of the enemy with the regiment of Polish Tartars of Kochawski, and did them considerable mischief. Colonel Knoring, with his regiment of Tartars, almost entirely destroyed a regiment of light horse: and a regiment of cuirassiers, belonging to the Emperor, attacked a column of infantry and threw them into the greatest disorder.

Marshal Kaminskoy departed on the 14—26th, the morning previous to the attack of Pultusk, for Ostrolenka. He appointed me to the chief command. I was fortunate enough to act singly throughout the whole affair, and to defeat the enemy.

I regret that the succours, so much desired by General Buxhowden, did not arrive in time, although it was scarcely distant from me two miles in the neighbourhood of Makow, and that it had halted half way to afford me all the advantages of my victory. I also regret that the absolute want of provisions and forage obliged me to retrograde the whole of my forces towards Rozan, in order to resume them in my rear: what proves how much the enemy must have suffered, is that they made not the slightest attempt to interrupt my rear guard during this, movement. I transmit this report to Your Imperial Majesty through Captain Wrangen, who was at my side during the whole transaction, and who will acquaint you with every other detail relative to this affair.

Bennigsen

EXTRACT OF THE REPORTS RECEIVED
FROM GENERAL BENNIGSEN

St. Petersburg, February 7th, 1807

January 7.—Lieutenant-Colonel Vlastoff was detached with two companies of chasseurs and 200 Cossacks, who surrounded a party of the enemy, killed about 200, and made eighteen prisoners.

January 8.—General Galitzin having learnt that the enemy was near Langheim, detached a party of Cossacks, who surrounded a whole squadron of the 3rd regiment of French Hussars, killed a part, and look Captain St. Obain Lebrun, two officers, and 59 men, prisoners.

On the 9th, our army took possession of those quarters which the enemy had evacuated on the 4th. That day one French officer and seven men were taken prisoners.

On the 11th, Generals Markoff and Ostermann were ordered by the Commander in Chief to move forward, the former with his van-guard from the side of Heilsburg and Güttstadt, and the latter, with the second division and the detachment of General Baggofut, towards Seburg, to harass the enemy in the night. They report, that the enemy retreated speedily from those places.

January 12.—General de Tolly reports, that he had detached a squadron of Hussars and 60 Cossacks, who fell in with two squadrons of French cavalry, of which they killed a part, took two captains and 25 men prisoners. General Markoff reports, that on his arrival at Elditten, he learnt that the enemy was at Liebstadt, with two regiments of dragoons, one of hussars, and several hundred infantry; and that having received information of our troops advancing, was preparing to retreat. General Markoff immediately collected those of his men who were the least fatigued, advanced speedily towards Liebstadt; before reaching it, however, he fell in with the out-posts of the enemy, supported strongly by infantry, which he repulsed, and forced out of the said place: 18 officers, amongst them one Lieutenant-Colonel, and 291 men, were taken prisoners, and about 300 killed; our loss, which was very inconsiderable, is not exactly ascertained yet.

January 13.—Major-General Markoff having proceeded from Liebstadt to pursue the enemy, who had retreated with 4000 men to Mohrungen, fell in with the rear guard of the same, and commenced an engagement. The enemy then received succour from all his corps de reserve, under the personal command of Bernadotte. Notwithstanding this, the enemy was twice repulsed. Two regiments of French advanced with the bayonet against our regiment of Ekaterinoslau, who faced them with such firmness, that both regiments stopped short within twenty paces of it. On account of the great increase of the enemy, our van-guard retreated somewhat, which was done with the greatest order; but having been joined shortly by part of the cavalry under General d'Anrep, who having heard the report of cannon, had hastened to its assistance, the enemy was again attacked and defeated. On this occasion, one French standard was taken, two officers and 53 men made prisoners. In this engagement, the particulars of which have not as yet been received, the loss in killed and wounded on our part is not above 500 men, but the loss of the enemy is at least 1500 men. The great loss of the enemy has been effected by the skilful management of our artillery, and the brave onset of our battalions with the bayonet. To the general regret of all the army, we have, on this occasion, lost the brave and ingenious General d'Anrep, who was shot in the head by French tirailleurs, as he was reconnoitring with General Markoff and two other officers. General Galitzin reports, that Colonel Dolgorucky, who commanded three squadrons of dragoons, having been informed that the greatest part of the troops under Bernadotte at Mohrungen were moving towards our van-guard, on the road to Liebstadt, had attacked the enemy at Mohrungen, in order to cause a diversion, had killed and taken about 100 men, and seized the baggage of General Bernadotte, consisting of some carriages, wagons, and riding horses. The Commander-in-Chief, Bennigsen, particularly recommends the courageous conduct of Colonel Dolgorucky.

COPY OF GENERAL BENNIGSEN'S DISPATCH

FROM THE FIELD OF BATTLE

Eylau, 8th February, 1807

I am very happy to be able to acquaint your Majesty, that the army which has been entrusted to my command, has been again victorious. The sanguinary and murderous battle, which we have just fought, commenced on the 7th, at 2 o'clock, p.m. and only terminated on the 8th, at 8 o'clock at night. The enemy has been completely beaten, near 2000 prisoners are made, and twelve standards, which I lay at the feet of your Majesty, have fallen into the hands of the conquerors. Buonaparte this day attacked me with the elite of his troops upon the centre and two wings; but every where he was repulsed and beaten. His guards made several attempts to pierce my centre, but without the least success, and they were repelled after a very vigorous fire, by charges of the bayonet, and of the cavalry. Several columns of infantry, and regiments of chosen cuirassiers, were destroyed. I shall not fail to lay at the feet of your Majesty, as soon as possible, a detailed relation of the memorable battle of Eylau. I believe our loss exceeds 6,000 men killed, and I certainly do not exaggerate that of the enemy when I estimate it as having greatly exceeded altogether twenty thousand men.

RUSSIAN OFFICIAL ACCOUNT OF THE BATTLE OF EYLAU

I marched out of Landsberg the 25th of January, my army only consisting of 70,000 men, different detachments of it having been separated; that of Buonaparte amounted to 90,000, and was composed of the five corps of the Marshals Augereau, Soult, Murat, Davoust, Ney, and afterwards, towards evening, Bernadotte. They marched upon our footsteps, and fought without

ceasing against my rear-guard, commanded by the Prince Bagration, and formed the brigades of the Generals Markoff, Bagovoust, and Barkley de Tolly.

On arriving at Preussisch-Eylau, I disposed of my army at some
distance on this side of the town, and I ordered my rear-guard to
stand firm before the enemy to protect the march of my heavy
artillery, of which, from Wolsdorf, I found it expedient to take a
circuitous route, as much to avoid the roads almost impassable, as
to facilitate the march of my columns. At the same time, I made
General Barkley occupy the town of Preussisch-Eylau, I sent to the
assistance of the rear-guard some regiments of the eighth division,
and General Markoff, strengthened by these last, took a strong position, and established a battery there. Meanwhile, the enemy lost
no time in coming up with them, and preceded by their flanks,
they directed three strong columns against the elevation occupied
by General Markoff. He (the General) sent some tirailleurs (sharpshooters) to meet them, and discharged grape from his battery; the
enemy, however, did not stop, when the two regiments of Pskoff and
Sophie charged them at the point of the bayonet, and immediately
dispersed one of then columns another was overthrown and almost
entirely destroyed by the dragoons of Petersburg, and the third annihilated by our batteries, commanded by the brave Colonel Yermoloff. Then, the enemy advancing his army, marched against our
line in four columns, and directed a fifth upon our left, in order to
turn the flank of it. The regiments of Sophie and Pskoff, too weak
to oppose them, received orders to wheel about; the grenadiers
of Moscow, and the 12th chasseurs then came forward, and were
seconded by the cuirassiers du corps, body dragoon guards, the dragoons of Kargopol, Ingria, and the hussars of Elizabethgrad. These
four regiments charged the French cavalry, who were advancing to
turn our right wing, and killed a great many of them. The batteries
of the 8th division stopped the enemy on the left, and the hussars
of Izum charged them with the greatest success.

Although repulsed at all points, the enemy still gathering
strength, threatened to cut in pieces our advanced troops, which
I ordered to retreat, and immediately the 8th division, and then
all the rear-guard, crossed Preussisch-Eylau, and came and joined
the whole body of the army ranged in order of battle in the fol-

lowing order:—5th, 7th, 8th, 3rd, and 21st divisions were ranged in two lines, of which the second formed one column, the—4th and 14th formed my reserve. The right wing was commanded by Lieutenant-General Toutschkoff; the centre by Lieutenant-General Baron de Zachen; the left wing by Lieutenant-General Count Ostermann; and all the advanced guard by the Prince Bagration. The cavalry of the whole army was under the command of the Lieutenant-General Prince Gallitzin; it covered the two wings, and was partly ranged in the line. Some heights, situated in my front, were surmounted by our batteries. General Barkley still occupied the town of Preussisch-Eylau: with the flying artillery of Colonel Yermoloff, who had protected the retreat of the rearguard; but the enemy soon came from all sides and besieged the town, and General Barkley notwithstanding he had performed prodigies of valour, was obliged to yield to numbers and to-retire. I then sent the 4th division to his succour; it marched in three columns, overthrowing every thing before it, retook the town by assault, in which a prodigious number of French perished, who had planted cannon even in the very streets, and who fired upon us from the windows, and from all sides. General Barkley there received from them a bad wound in the arm.

When the night came on, and the enemy had entirely ceased firing, I evacuated the town with the design to assemble all my forces on the other side, preparing myself for a general attack on the morrow, and, in order to secure myself from all alarm during the night, I joined to the 4th division the regiment of Archangel, which I placed between the army and the town; and I sent the detached corps of General Barkley to strengthen the left wing of General Bagovoust. The 27th, at five o'clock in the morning, I formed in my centre two columns of reserve, composed of the seventh and fourth division, of which I confided the command to Lieutenant-General Doctoroff; and I placed a third on the left wing formed by the division of General the Count de Kaminskoy. The brigade of General Markoff came and filled the interval that the seventh, in quitting the line, had made.

The enemy began to file out of the town at daybreak; I sent some regiments of chasseurs to meet them, and I distinguished, at the same time, some strong columns of French, placed between the town and some heights on the right, and upon which their batteries were placed, which, with the columns, menaced my centre. I immediately directed my batteries against theirs, and against the troops that were marching out of the town; the columns were forced to stop.

On another side, General Toutschkoff having been attacked on the right wing by the French cavalry, he overthrew them by the fire of the battery of the Count de Sievers. The enemy had just possessed themselves of a village situated in front of our right wings, and seemed as if they intended to open from thence a considerable force to take us in our flank. I, however, dislodged them directly, by the means of the 24th regiment of chasseurs and other *tirailleurs,* when several columns of the French guard marched out of Preussisch-Eylau and attacked my right wing and centre. General Toutschkoff detached directly Major General Fock, who, supported by two regiments of dragoons, charged the enemy with bayonets, put them to the route, and destroyed a great part of them; they retired in disorder, and abandoned eight cannons. General Zapolskoy, who was in the centre, deployed, by the orders of General Doctoroff, one of the columns of the reserve, and commenced firing upon those who came to attack them. His musketry soon put the enemy to the route, and, without giving them time to rally, he charged them with the bayonet, overthrew them, and took an eagle and 130 prisoners. At this moment, some French squadrons, supported by the infantry, arrived near the left of our centre, and finding an interval, they passed behind our first line. The Cossacks and some cavalry fell upon them, and only 18 men of them escaped. The infantry that supported these squadrons were, on their side, overthrown by the grenadiers of Moscow, commanded by Prince Charles of Mecklenburgh, and the *musketeers* of Schlüsselburg, which General Essen had sent against them. They fell back and joined the column that General Zapolskoy had just repulsed. This last, reinforced at the same moment by two other columns of cavalry, made a new attack. Immediately General Somoff and Zapolskoy, and two regiments of cavalry that were behind our front, fell upon them, and repulsed them with great impetuosity.

The Count Orourke, with three squadrons of Pavlograd hussars, made a charge upon the right flank of this troop, and pursued them to the very mouth of the French cannon. The dragoons of Petersburg, and the *musketeers* of Wladimir, took from them two eagles. The enemy retiring, abandoned 20 more pieces of cannon. The attack directed upon our right was stopped by the *tirailleurs* of General Zachen. General Bagovoust, that occupied, with a detachment of the advanced guard, the village of Serpaler, was likewise attacked at break of day; he defended himself directly with his *tirailleurs,* but, as the column which was before him endeavoured *to turn* him, General Kochoffsky, chief of the *Hulans* of Lithuania and Little Russia cuirassiers, came to his assistance, forced the enemy to retire in the greatest disorder, and drove them into a wood. These same regiments obtained afterwards a success no less decisive against other French columns, who, supported by the cavalry, were directing their course towards our line. They threw them into the greatest disorder, killed more than 300 men, and made 67 prisoners, four of which were officers. The Count Pahlen, with General Korff's brigade of cavalry on their side, attacked other French columns that were marching against General Zachen's division; he overthrew them, and took from them a pair of colours. The regiment of Izum hussars, and the dragoons of Courland, made also several charges with the happiest success.

Repulsed on all sides, with as much impetuosity on our side as loss on theirs, the enemy assembled a great part of their force, formed them in very thick columns, and directed them against our left with the intention of turning it. General Bagovoust finding it impossible to resist such superior forces, burned the village of Serpallen that he occupied till this time, and went and took another position. The cavalry which was before him, again made some charges, and placed themselves behind our left wing; notwithstanding, the enemy reinforced continually, and pursued their project of turning, our flank. General Kaminskoy, who had just sent a reinforcement to General Bagovoust, placed the regiments of Ouglitz and Ostermann on his left, and made that of Rézan occupy Sausgarten.

The Count Ostermann, seeing very superior forces advancing towards him, judged it proper to make his left wing fall back, and was soon joined by General Bagovoust, who was already forced to retire by several strong French columns preceded by artillery, tirailleurs, and flanking detachments, who advanced rapidly, and had already reached our flank. The Count Ostermann had opened a very brisk fire of musketry, which, however, could not hinder the enemy from advancing upon him. The Count made several more charges of the bayonet, but, notwithstanding his redoubled efforts, he was obliged to give ground.

Already the enemy had turned our left wing, and forced the divisions of General Zachen and Count Ostermann to take a more retired position. He directed all his attacks upon this point, and briskly repulsed us. I then made my flying artillery advance. General Koutagzoff and Colonel Yermoloff established their batteries upon an elevated position, and opened such a terrible fire, that in a moment the enemy stopped, precipitately abandoned the strong hold of Anglapen, which they had occupied, and finished by flying in extreme disorder. At the same lime, General Tchaplitz, commanding a detachment of cavalry, drove the French from the village of Kouchitten, and fell on a column that defended it, destroying it almost entirely.

General Lestocq now arriving at the head of the Prussian corps, and of two regiments of Russian infantry, reinforced our left wing; and having united to Count Kaminskoy's division mill the detachment of General Tchaplitz, he marched against the enemy with all his batteries firing. He directly made a rapid movement towards the enemy's left wing to turn it himself, and pursued them till night-fall, which obliged him to stop. The arrival of this Gene-mi, and the activity of his operations, contributed much to obtain us the gain of this battle.—Whilst the batteries belonging to the left wing overwhelmed the enemy, and General Lestocq began to pursue him, the right wing, in which now only remained the division of General Toutschkoff, was not attacked by the French, who, although masters of the village of Schloditten, did not dare to hazard any thing upon this point, which was defended by a strong Prussian battery, established by General Fock upon an elevation. When night came on, I drove the enemy from the village of Schloditten, where they lost a great many men. The Cossacks particularly distinguished themselves during the whole affair, and made 470 prisoners.

This bloody battle lasted from three o'clock in the afternoon of the 26th of January, till midnight. The loss of the enemy, by their own confession, amounted to 20,000 men killed, 30,000 wounded, near 2,000 prisoners, and 12 pair of colours. Ours is 12,000 killed, and 7900 wounded. 14 French Generals were killed or wounded; nine of ours were slightly wounded, and the greatest part of these Generals returned to the army.

I should think I was wanting in my first duty, if I did not place at the feet of your Imperial Majesty, the homage due to the bravery of your troops. In covering themselves with an immortal glory, they give a memorable example to the world of what a nation can do when armed to defend their country, and to serve the generous designs of the most cherished of Sovereigns. In vain Buonaparte lavishes all his resources; in vain he tries to animate his soldiers; in vain he sacrifices an immense number; the valour and intrepidity of the Russians opposes itself to all his efforts, and wrests from him a long disputed victory. Master of the field of battle I remained on it all the night, then meditated upon the part I ought to take, and I cannot but felicitate myself of having moved on Koenigsberg. It is there, that my army, abundantly provided with every thing necessary, reposed themselves from their honourable fatigues; whilst the French army, enfeebled and discouraged, remained constantly upon their arms.—I hoped, by my retrograde movement, to have drawn them towards us, but a dozen regiments of cavalry, conducted by Marshal Murat, only dared to appear: they were entirely destroyed near Mahnsfield. It is since this new check that the enemy was obliged to retreat.

(Signed) *Baron de Bennigsen*

EXTRACT OF A DISPATCH FROM
GENERAL BARON DE BENNIGSEN

Headquarters, Landsberg, 27th February, 1807

I left Koenigsberg on the 25th, and am at the enemy's heels. They continue their retreat in extreme disorder. The cannon, wagons, caissons, and baggage, which they abandon on-the roads, are the only obstacles which they seem anxious to oppose to us. My advanced guard, which has been considerably reinforced by the Cossacks of the Don, harass them incessantly, and always with considerable success. According to the most accurate reports, we have take prisoners, since the battle of Eylau, 48 officers, 70 subalterns, and 3205 soldiers, not including 300 others, who have died of their wounds. The reinforcements which I expect from Russia are already on their march; and their early arrival will enable me to follow with as much precision as confidence, the plan of operations which I have laid down. The garrison of Dantzic has made another sortie against the Polish Insurgents, and has completely beaten them near Dirsthau.

BULLETIN OF THE OPERATIONS OF THE IMPERIAL RUSSIAN ARMY

(14th) 26th December to (4th) 16th March, 1807

Baron de Bennigsen, having,after the battle of Pultusk,effected his junction with the troops under orders of Count Buxhowden, obtained a short time afterwards the command in chief.The whole army then made a movement on the right; the object of which was to protect Regal Prussia, and to stop the corps of Marshals Ney and Bernadotte, which threatened Koenigsberg. Although this march lay through a country intersected with morasses and small rivers, the passage of which became more difficult on account of the cold, and of the thaws which often separated the different divisions of the army to a considerable distance from each other; nevertheless, the defeat which the French experienced at Pultusk, did not allow them to profit by those circumstances, and the army, after having concentrated itself, recommenced its operations. In the mean time, the corps of Lieutenant-General Essen took a position in the environs of Brok, from whence, according to circumstances, it could cover the left wing of the Grand army, and the frontiers of the empire towards Grodno and the Bug, if the enemy attempted to approach them. The 19th of January, the headquarters of Baron De Bennigsen were at Rhein, and the next day he advanced to Heiligen Linden. A corps of 30,000 men, under the orders of Marshal Ney, comprising the Guards of Buonaparte, commanded by Marshal Bessieres, posted behind the Aller, endeavoured to entrench themselves there, but were obliged to fall back. Another corps, under the command of Bernadotte, had penetrated as far as Preussisch-Holland to rejoin the former; but being pressed by the Russian van-guard, this body fled with so much precipitation, that it was impossible to attack the two corps separately.

The 23rd of January, the head-quarters were at Bischoffstein. Ney and Bernadotte effected their junction, and continued their retreat in disorder, and our troops took many prisoners, who all agreed that our unexpected march to Regal Prussia, had spread the greatest alarm throughout the French army, to whom their officers had promised winter quarters, giving them to understand at the same time, that an armistice had been concluded with our Generals.

The 26th of January, General Bennigsen was at Liebstadt. Very brisk actions took place in the neighbourhood of Mohrungen. Our advanced guard under General Markoff, attacked by the whole corps of Marshal Bernadotte, at first fell back; but being reinforced by the division of Lieutenant-General d'Anrep, the enemy was repulsed with loss. He lost a great number killed, and some hundreds taken prisoners. Nineteen officers, and a standard, fell into our power. Marshal Bernadotte lost all his carriages, plate, horses, &c. and only owed his safety to flight, by saving himself in a peasant's little sledge. The inhabitants of Mohrungen cannot conceive how he escaped the Cossacks.

The brave General d'Anrep was wounded in the head by a musket ball, as he was reconnoitering after the affair was over. Some sharpshooters, concealed in the bushes, singled him out; and a few hours after, this distinguished officer died, to the great regret of the whole army.

The 27th of January, the head-quarters were transferred to Mohrungen. Many skirmishes among the advanced posts were decided to our advantage, and gained us prisoners. The Prussian corps, under General Lestocq, also gained some advantages. It took prisoners General Poultrier and Lasseur. General Victor had been taken prisoner near Colberg. The garrison of Dantzic, having made a sortie, routed the Polish insurgents, commanded by Dombrowski, and took from them many pieces of cannon, and a military chest.

Buonaparte, after receiving reinforcements from the Vistula, and assembled the different corps, which were falling back upon his army, concentrated himself, and marched against General Bennigsen. The latter, not thinking his position sufficiently good to risk a battle, retreated in two columns upon Wolsdorf, where he arrived on the 4th of February.

The two rear-guards, commanded by Generals Prince Bagration and Barklay de Tolly, covered the retreat, and repulsed the repeated attack of the enemy. The next day they followed us close to Burgerswald. The rearguard had new attacks to support; but the next day, at the gates of the town of Landsberg, at one o'clock in the afternoon, a very brisk affair took place between the enemy and the corps of Barclay de Tolly, which lasted till six o'clock in the evening. The rear-guard had succeeded in repulsing the enemy; but not being content with that achievement, it engaged in a pursuit which drew upon it three columns, and obliged the General in Chief to send a reinforcement of three regiments, commanded by Prince Basil Dolgorucky. This corps of 10,000 men fought for many hours against near 40,000 French, men, and maintained the field of battle.

Lieutenant-General Essen, who, in consequence of the movements of General Bennigsen, had repaired to Wyoki Maziowechi, at first judged it prudent to watch only that corps of the enemy which was opposed to him, but although that corps was at least equal to his in number, and occupied a very advantageous position intersected by morasses and woods, he nevertheless frequently harassed it, by sending out large detachments to attack, and who, in all the engagements, obtained important advantages, and took many prisoners. When it was known that Buonaparte had quitted Warsaw, and that he was advancing with a superior force against the army of General Bennigsen, Lieutenant-General Essen, in order to make a diversion in favour of the Grand Army, attacked the enemy on the 22nd of January, on the whole length of his line, overthrew him at all points, and repulsed Generals Savary, Suchet, and Becker, as far as the Narew. This battle, however, did not prevent Buonaparte from following General Bennigsen, who having chosen behind Prussian Eylau a position which he judged proper to allow all his troops to act to advantage, and particularly his cavalry, had taken post there, in order to wait the arrival of the French army, whose advanced guard attacked incessantly and impetuously the corps of Major-General Barclay de Tolly. The ever-memorable day of the 7th of February put an end to the enemy's progress. At three in the afternoon, the battle began through the whole line of the main army. It was bloody, and the night came on without the enemy being able to gain any ground. Early on the morning of the 8th the attack was renewed by the French. Both sides fought with fury; but in the evening the enemy was repulsed on all sides, and the Russian army remained in possession of the field of battle. Buonaparte commanded in person, and under him Marshals Augereau, Davoust, Soult, Ney, and Bessieres at the head of the guards, who particularly suffered. We took on this day 1500 prisoners, among whom are 30 officers, besides 18 standards, and 20 pieces of cannon. The French Generals Corbineau, Desjardins, Duhesma, and Gudin, were killed; Augereau wounded; Vial lost an arm; Suchet had his thigh broken; and Generals Hautpoult, Piccard, Friand, St. Sulpice, Despagne, Second, and Martin, were wounded.

As the occupation of the town of Preussisch Eylau, in front of the field of battle, formed no part of General Bennigsen's plan, and as the army, after so much fatigue, had need of rest, and was also in want of warlike stores, the Commander in Chief entrenched himself in the environs of Mulhausen, established his headquarters at Koenigsberg, and left Lieutenant-General Platow, who arrived two days after the battle, with 15,000 Cossacks, to harass the French in their retreat. The enemy, on quitting the positions which he occupied, abandoned his sick and wounded.

On the 21st of February, the Cossacks advanced towards the environs of Liebstadt, took several hundred prisoners, four officers, and a number of baggage wagons, and even forage and provisions. A detachment of nearly two thousand Russian and Prussian prisoners, who were on their route to Warsaw, were delivered; and some hundreds of horse chasseurs, who escorted them, were either killed or taken.

On the 27th of February, the Russian headquarters were at Landsberg. In various petty encounters, the Cossacks took some hundreds of prisoners. The garrison of Dantzic defeated the insurgents under Dombrowsky. General Platow, who was constantly in pursuit of the enemy, took from him a piece of cannon, some wagons, and a good deal of baggage. On this day, the number of prisoners taken from the French army, after the battle, and during its retreat from Preussisch Eylau, amounted to 2000 soldiers, and 48 officers.

The head-quarters remained at Landsberg on the 28th of February. General Lestocq's corps of Prussians found itself opposed to that of Bernadotte, between Muhlsack and Heiligenbeil. The enemy retired behind the Parsarge, and for a time evacuated Guttstadt. The Cossacks drove them to the environs of Allenstein; and the engagements on this occasion cost them 400 men, who remained on the field, and 55 prisoners. One hundred Russian prisoners were also recovered.

On the 1st of March Major General Knoring attacked the enemy at Allenstein, beat them, killed a great number, took 50, and delivered 200 Russians.

The army remained in the same position on the two following days. Count Tolstoy's corps formed the left flank at Bishoffstein.

On the 4th of March there were some affairs of out-posts. Two officers, a secretary, mid seventy-four soldiers were taken. The army kept the same position till the (10th of March) during which time there were only affairs of out-posts.

On the 8th of March the demonstrations of the French army had obliged the. Commander in Chief to concentrate all his forces before Heilsberg. There was an affair between the advanced posts, at the close of which the enemy were repulsed, and pursued by die Cossacks. The head-quarters were removed to Bartenstein, and Buonaparte was still at Osterode.

On the 13th of March, General De Wittgenstein, having advanced with a detachment to the environs of Neidenburg and Ortelsbourg, carried off from thence the enemy's patrols, and took prisoners Lieutenant-Colonel Le Grange, *aide-de-camp* to General Ney, and a Major, commander of a regiment of chasseurs. These advantages having attracted the attention of the French, they advanced in force to these points; and General Platow was detached, with eight regiments of Cossacks, to support General Wittgenstein, which induced the enemy to retreat.

The army remained in the same position on the 16th March. Murat advanced, with 12 regiments of infantry and cavalry, to Bishoffsburg, whence he dislodged a detachment of one hundred Cossacks, who, nevertheless, in their retreat, made fifty prisoners. In consequence General Platow received orders to repair to the spot, with 5000 Cossacks, but the French did not wait his arrival.

March 18th. According to the latest advices, Buonaparte is still at Osterode; Davoust at Allenstein; Ney at Guttstadt; Soult at Liebstadt; and Bernadotte in the neighbourhood of Wormditt. Murat makes incursions in the neighbourhood of Wartenberg, Bishoffsburg, Passenheim, Ortelsburg, and Willenberg. According to the best information we have of the French cavalry, it is supposed that Murat makes his incursions for the purpose of procuring forage. General Platow, with a considerable corps, is on the point of cutting of all the French detachments which are beyond this little town.

****

According to advices received from the army, down to the 8th instant, the enemy remained in their position behind the Passarge. On the 26th ult. the Prussian corps, under Lieutenant-General Plotz, had passed over the Parsarge, through Braunsberg, to repulse the enemy's left wing, and facilitate the passage over the river to General Lestocq's corps. The latter was immediately attacked, with great superiority of numbers, by Bernadotte's corps. The Prussians actually succeeded in repelling the enemy on every point; but the enemy receiving constant reinforcements, the Prussians were obliged to retreat at night into Braunsberg, where the infantry sustained a most obstinate engagement. The Prussian force, now compelled to give way to superior numbers, retreated to Heiligenbeil, without being pursued by the enemy, who were satisfied with having taken the town. The loamy ground had become so slippery, from the thaw, that neither the artillery nor cavalry could take a decisive part in the action, on which account the infantry sustained no inconsiderable loss; it may amount to 500 men, in killed, wounded, and missing. In the following days, the two corps formed a junction under General Lestocq, and took a position near Heiligenbeil and Muhlsack, the van in Wormditt and Güttstadt, and the advanced posts along the Passarge. The corps under General Tolstoy advanced by Bischoffstein and Seeburg, to the neighbourhood of Wartenberg. His out-posts drove the enemy from Allenstein, while the Cossacks occupied Passenheim. In Lansberg were found 264 Frenchmen, left behind. Skirmishes are daily fought between the advanced posts. At the end of February, the Attaman Platow brought in 400 prisoners; and General Tolstoy 60 prisoners and 80 horses, on the 27th of February. On the 3rd instant, Platow brought in again three officers and 60 privates. On the 3rd instant the enemy attacked the whole front line of the Russian advanced posts, crossing the Passarge at different parts, and masking his main attack on Güttstadt and Allenstein, which were occupied by the enemy. After a smart engagement, and a violent cannonade, the Russians, after a brave resistance, fell back to their main position. The enemy appearing at the same time near Braunsberg, against the corps of Lestocq, seemed seriously prepared for offensive movement, but the brave resistance of the Russians, and the skilful movements of General Lestocq prevented them, and the position of both armies remained as before.

By reports-from General Essen, of the 15th of February, he had that day an engagement with the enemy near Ostrolenka; the issue of which, though not altogether such as he intended, obliged the enemy to retreat upon Pultusk, upon which the Russian corps advanced beyond Ostrolenka, and has already established a communication with the corps of Tolstoy, which forms the left wing of the Russian Grand Army.

Russian Official Report—
Extract from the Journals of the
Military Operations of the Russian Army

From the 7th March to 14th April, 1807

On the 7th of March, three garrison battalions which arrived on the frontiers, under the-orders of Major-General Tcherbatoff, were detached to reinforce the garrison of Dantzic. According to the account given Lieutenant-General Platow, of the date of the 7th of March, Major-General Ilavoisky attacked the enemy with four regiments of Cossacks, close to the-village of Klein-Schemtuer, killed 200 men, and made prisoners one officer and 87 soldiers. During this time, Lieutenant-Colonel Karpoff had attacked a brigade of confederates under the orders of General Zayontscheck, completely defeated them, killed 700 men, and took nine officers, and 208 soldiers prisoners—our loss was very inconsiderable. Major-General Tchapliz, detached by General Platow, with a party of his own regiment, encountered close to the village of Kurken, a party of Marshal Davoust's corps, killed a considerable number, and took prisoners one officer and 24 soldiers.

On the 9th of March, the enemy, with a considerable number of infantry and cavalry, encountered on the road to Ortelsburg, three Cossack regiments, commanded by the Major-General Ilavoisky, and by the military Starchine Frekoff. The enemy were defeated, and obliged to retreat on Willenberg. In this affair, the enemy had 1000 belonging to the infantry, and a regiment of dragoons. From the confession of the prisoners they had killed: more than half of the dragoon officers, and they made besides 2 officers and 30 soldiers prisoners, among whom were five Polish confederates; we also took from the enemy 300 horses.

A detachment sent from the village of Outriten to reconnoitre, encountered a patrol of the enemy, attacked them, killed some men, made five prisoners, and repulsed the rest beyond the Aller.

On the 13th of March, news was. received from Dantzic, that the troops commanded by (General Stcherbatoff arrived in excellent order:—these troops were composed of two battalions, and two Cossack regiments. After the report of General Platow, .dated the 14th of March, it appears that on the 12th, he made, with the ten Cossack regiments that he had with him, a general attack on the corps of General Zayontscheck, which was posted on the banks opposite Omuleff. This attack succeeded. The corps of Zayontscheck were completely routed, and chased the distance of six miles with great slaughter. The regiment of Dombrowiki in this action was nearly annihilated; besides some officers, we took 179 soldiers. Our loss was inconsiderable; it consists of four officers killed, amongst whom is Colonel Karpoff, and seven Cossacks. We had two Ensigns and 23 Cossacks wounded. We took from the enemy a great number of horses.

As soon as we learned that the enemy, with 800 cavalry, 2,000 infantry, and 200 Polish horse had taken possession of Ortelsburg, the General Tchaplitz, with one regiment of hussars, and two pieces of horse artillery, who were stationed near to the village of Menrut, immediately moved to Ortelsburg, and supported by two Cossack regiments, attacked the enemy, drove them from their position, and notwithstanding the most obstinate resistance defeat. them, and pursued them for five miles on the road to Willenberg. The loss of the enemy must have been very considerable, as no quarter was given. Major-General Stcherbatoff transmitted from Dantzic an account, from which it appeared that the enemy had made themselves masters, on the 20th of March, of the redoubt situated on the borders of the Vistula; and that after a vigorous sortie made by the garrison, this redoubt was taken from the French by the first battalion of Russian troops, under the orders of Colonel Damarhoff, supported by some Prussian battalions.

Two important posts were taken, in this instance, and burnt. The loss of the enemy was very great. The country through which the Russians passed was covered with dead. The Cossacks made prisoners, one Etat-Major, and 22 soldiers; we had one subaltern officer, and 14 soldiers killed, and one officer, two non-commissioned officers, and 49 soldiers wounded. The Cossacks had three killed, and nine wounded. The loss of the Prussians was not more considerable than ours.

On the 22nd of March the Colonel of Cossacks (Tchemozuboff), at the head of his regiment, encountered the enemy close to the village of Rutzen, attacked them with the spear, and killed 35 men, and making 41 soldiers prisoners.

On the 1st of April the enemy, with a considerable number of infantry, and three pieces of cannon, occupied the road from Willenberg to Ortelsburg, and annoyed considerably our advanced posts; meantime a much larger detachment, commanded by General Krantzky, passed by the village of Wappliz, to repair to Passenheim. The enemy were already masters of Ortelsburg, but Major-General Ilavoisky having been joined by the troops sent to his succour, attacked them upon two points, and drove them from Ortelsburg. The enemy were obliged to retake their way to Willenberg, after having near 100 men killed; we had one Cossack killed, and two wounded. Colonel Inaeff and Lieutenant-Colonel Ilavoisky having stopped the progress of the enemy, at the distance of five miles from Passenheim, continued constantly skirmishing until the arrival of the regiment of the Attaman. After the arrival of this regiment, the enemy's cavalry were attacked and defeated, with the loss of one Major, some officers, and more than 100 men killed; and of one officer, one subaltern officer, and one soldier made prisoners; we had but three Cossacks wounded. After this affair the enemy retreated on the village of Rutzen.

On the 5th of April, the troops of the second division, under the orders of the Grand Duke Constantine, (with the exception of a small party) arrived in the environs of Schippenbeil, and returned to their cantonments.

From the 3rd to the 14th of April 43 French-deserted and joined our army.

GENERAL BENNIGSEN'S REPORTS TO THE EMPEROR OF THE OPERATIONS WHICH TOOK PLACE FROM 5TH TO 10TH JUNE 1807

Güttstadt, 5th June, 1807
General Ney's corps is defeated, and General Roger, several officers, with about 2,000 rank and file, have been taken prisoners; the enemy's loss in killed amounts to 2,000; on our side it is not very considerable. During the action which took place on the left bank of the Aller, Lieutenant-General Prince Gurtchakoff rendered himself master of Güttstadt, and took a considerable magazine. The enemy was pursued four German miles.

Between Deppen and Heiligenthal, 6th June, 1807
General Ney's corps, which, on its retreat took a strong position near Arensdorf was this day attacked at three o'clock in the morning, routed on all points, and forced to fall back to the Parsarge. The enemy's loss is very considerable, and amounts merely in prisoners taken in the course of these two days to 60 field and other officers, and at least to 1500 rank and file. The regiment of chasseurs of the guards, commanded by the Grand Duke Constantine, fought with a gallantry which became the admiration of the whole army. The regiments of Count Strogonow and the Attaman's Cossacks, also greatly distinguished themselves. The latter swam across the Aller, attacked the enemy at the most critical moment of the action, killed at least 1000 men, and took four field officers, 21 officers, and 350 rank and file prisoners.

Heilsberg, 10th June, 1807

This day at noon Buonaparte attacked the Russian army in the position on the left banks of the Aller, with his whole force. A short time before the attack, Prince Bagration was detached to Launau, where he was attacked by a force greatly superior; and was obliged to fall back. A considerable number of troops then received orders to advance from every quarter, while others formed the reserve. The firing began on all points, and the enemy was forced to leave the field of battle to the Russian troops, who acquired new glory on that day. The loss cannot yet be ascertained, but it is very considerable on both sides; and amounts on the part of the French, at least to 12,000 men in killed and wounded. The enemy were pursued a German mile from the field of battle; the action lasted from 11 o'clock in the morning till 11 o'clock at night. The prisoners state, that the enemy's whole reserve, consisting of 20 battalions, with the guards, were engaged, and driven back with the rest of the troops.

Extract of a Dispatch from General Bennigsen to the Emperor Alexander

Heilsberg, 30th May (11th June), 1807

The enemy having surrounded the whole of my right wing, and the corps commanded by Marshal Davoust being already at Grossendorff, and near Konegen, I have given him battle, which lasted four hours, and which, however, he would not renew the next day. But finding that the enemy might cut off all provisions from my army in its present position, and detach a corps to Koenigsberg, I humbly beg leave to state to your Royal Majesty, my determination to quit this place to night, and march to another position near Schippenbeil, in order to be able to protect those behind the Aller, the transport of provisions, &c.; and in case the enemy marches to Koenigsberg, to follow him immediately.

The corps d'Armée, commanded by General Kaminskoy, has already marched towards Bartenstein and Mulhausen, with a view to rejoin General Lestocq, and to protect Koenigsberg.

(Signed) *Bennigsen*

Headquarters at Wehlau, 15th June, 1807

The enemy having immediately directed the whole of his force from Heilsberg towards Friedland and Wehlau, with an intention to cut off my army from the Pregel, I humbly beg leave to inform your Royal Majesty, that I could not take up any position at Schippenbeil, but made a forced march to Friedland on the 13th instant.

The advanced detachment, which I sent forward to occupy that town, found the place at three p.m. in possession of four squadrons of the enemy, which were, however, driven out immediately.

In order to keep possession of the town, that my troops might rest from their fatigue, I sent some infantry to the left bank of the Aller during the night. But in the morning at break of day, the enemy attacked my advanced posts, and at half after five the cannonade commenced. I therefore sent another division of my army across the river, to support the other troops, as I had reason to suppose that the enemy's van only had come up. The enemy were repulsed at every point, and the Russian troops, who fought for fourteen hours together with the greatest bravery, proved always victorious. General Oudinot, whose division formed the right wing of the enemy, attempted to make an attack with the bayonet; but my left wing eagerly advanced upon him, and destroyed an entire column. Another column was routed. The cavalry of my right wing, also made an impetuous and successful attack upon the enemy's cuirassiers, pursuing them as far as Heinricksdorf, which village supported the left wing of the enemy. At three in the afternoon, Buonaparte arrived in person, with the rest of his army, and sheltered by a wood, he reinforced his right wing in such a degree, that at six, when he commenced a fresh attack, and opened upon my left wing a masked battery of forty pieces of cannon, I was under the necessity of resolving to commence my retreat, which was effected in the best order, and my rear stopped the whole force of the enemy, until all my troops had crossed the Aller. Although my loss, during a battle which lasted 16 hours, and from my army's being obliged to file off over a bridge, which was exposed to the enemy's artillery, cannot be inconsiderable, the enemy must have lost an equal number at least, from the attack with the bayonet, and of the cavalry charges; in the former of which we took from him the eagle of the 15th regiment of the line. Nor has the enemy taken any other prisoners but such as were wounded dangerously, and which could not be removed from the town, and only some dismounted pieces of cannon belonging to the regiments, with a few which could not be removed, because the horse attached to them had been shot. On the other hand all our pieces of train artillery were got off safe. I am now taking with my army a position behind the Pregel, near Wehlau, causing all the passes of that river, as far as Koenigsberg and Insterburg, to be occupied by my troops, in consequence whereof I have reopened a communication with General Lestocq. If the enemy should venture to cross the Pregel, I shall attack him immediately, and the reinforcements which already are on their march, will soon repair my loss, and enable me once more to contest with the enemy.

(Signed) *Bennigsen.*

ANOTHER DISPATCH

Camp at Polpitten, 17th June, 1807

After the surrender of Koenigsberg, my position at Wehlau was no longer tenable, and having informed General Lestocq that I should make my retreat on the road of Tilsitz, I requested him to follow me; I commenced the retreat yesterday, arid I am happy most humbly to inform your Royal Majesty, that I have this day formed a junction with that General; and that my army, besides, has this day received a reinforcement of 3600 men. Moreover, the division from Moscow will pass the frontier to-morrow, consequently my loss will not only be replaced in a very short time, but I shall even be stronger than I was before the battle of Friedland. Thus of all the results of that lost battle, the surrender of Koenigsberg proves the worst; for if the enemy do not pursue me with too great a superiority of numbers, and allow me sufficient time to draw towards me my reinforcements, I shall directly advance, and I hope to recover from the enemy the advantages which he has obtained.

(Signed) *Bennigsen*

Report of Major Von Gneisenau,
Commandant of the Fortress of Colberg,
to his Majesty, the King of Sweden

18th June, 1807

I herewith have the honour humbly to report to your Majesty the operations which have lately taken place near this fortress, for the particulars of which I respectfully refer to my report to Lieutenant-General Von Blucher.

Of materials, which were but very indifferent, I had in haste raised a small field fortification on the Wolfsberg, situated about 2000 paces from the fortress, which the enemy had already twice attacked, and twice been repulsed with considerable loss. He then began to lay a regular siege to it, completed the first and second parallels, and made mines under the protection of ten redoubts. More than 7000 shot had already been fired, when on the 11th of June, the enemy's batteries began to play on the above fortification, and made a breach; your Majesty's frigate *Chapman* came to anchor and fired on the enemy with great effect having filled his trenches with troops, he summoned the Wolfsberg, which was half destroyed! and effected a kind of capitulation, which was accepted. All the artillery was removed, thus the enemy obtained possession of that small fortification after ten days siege.

Since that time we have made two vigorous sorties, in one of which we retook the Wolfsberg in a few minutes, which had cost the enemy a regular siege. In these two sallies the enemy had upwards of 2000 men killed and wounded, one howitzer was taken, six pieces of cannon spiked, and nearly a whole battalion made prisoners, among whom were one Colonel one Lieutenant-Colonel, two Captains, and six Lieutenants.

I cannot close this report without making the most honourable mention of Baron Gedder, Lieutenant of your Majesty's frigate *Chapman,* a young man whose gallantry and zeal deserve in every point of view your Majesty's most gracious attention.

Prussian Documents

ACCOUNT OF OPERATIONS FROM THE VISTULA TO THE BATTLE OF EYLAU, PRUSSIAN OPERATIONS

First Epoch

In the middle of November, 1806, General Lestocq, with near 6,000 men, took a position on the banks of the Vistula, and established his head-quarters at Thorn. His right extended to Ostrometzko, and his left was thrown upon Wraelaweck, where the right wing of the Russians communicated.

On the 4th of December, General Bennigsen ordered the retreat from the Vistula, when General Lestocq removed his headquarters to Gollup, where, in a few days, he received instructions to retake Thorn, for which purpose his corps advanced towards Kowalewo; but, before the attack on Thorn had commenced, a retreat was again ordered.

General Lestocq then retired to Strasburg, and took a position on the river Drewentz, where he remained ten days. Several skirmishes here occurred between the out-posts, and a small magazine was taken by the enemy at Rypin.

On the 18th of December General Lestocq retired to Lautenburg, and the strong pass near Gurzno was defended by light infantry commanded by Colonel Bülow. In that position the corps remained until the 23d of December, when General Lestocq changed his headquarters to Soldan, and detached General Kall and Dieireke with the first battalion of infantry and 15 squadrons of cavalry with two battalions of horse artillery to reconnoitre the enemy at Mlawa and Biézun; but the enemy resuming the offensive, attacked the Prussian cantonments on all points, and took Soldan by storm on the 26th of December, while General Lestocq was reviewing the out-posts at Great Lentzke. When the General rejoined his main body, he ordered Soldan to be re-taken. Three hundred volunteers were directed to storm the northern gate, but their attempt was ineffectual, and the greater part were killed.

General Lestocq then retreated towards Gilginburg in the night of the 26th of December, when the inclemency of the weather was so severe, that the enemy did not attempt to pursue; but as General Lestocq, from some information received during the march, changed the route to Neidenburg, considerable distress and confusion ensued, and the corps did not re-assemble at Neidenburg for several days, and one half battery of horse artillery was moving for fourteen days through the woods in circuitous marches to avoid the enemy, who were in pursuit of it; but this half battery at length reached Rastenburg, where General Lestocq, on the 7th of January, 1807, established his headquarters, having retired from Neidenburg to Ortelsburg, thence to Great Shienen, where there was a partial action, and from thence by Sensburg to Rastenburg. On the 10th of January the corps marched to Angerburg, as the Russians were then near Arys and Rhein.

On the 11th of January General Lestocq went to Drengfurth, and, on the 16th, placed his headquarters at Barthen, and occupied Lauenburg with his right wing. Meanwhile the enemy took Shippenbeil, and then attacked and carried Lauenburg.

General Lestocq then retired to Gerdauen and Friedland, where he formed an expedition for the surprise of Shippenbeil, but not being assisted by the Russians as he expected, the enter-prize was abandoned, and Shippenbeil remained in the hands of the enemy until they voluntarily abandoned it.

Second Epoch

On the 20th of January General Lestocq marched from Friedland to Domnau; on the 21st to Landsberg; on the 22nd to Schlodien; on the 24th to Preuss Holland; and on the same night proceeded to Shierstein. On the 25th he marched to Saalfeld, which place had been carried by an assault of the Russians. On the 27th General Lestocq marched to Reisenburg; on the 28th to Rosenburg; on the 30th to Freystadt, where an order was given for the corps to proceed on the 1st of February to Graudentz; but, in the night of the 31st of January, General Lestocq received directions to march to Deutsch Eylau; on the 2nd of February to Osterode; on the 3rd to Mohrungen; on the 4th to Liebstadt, where the advanced guard was engaged with the enemy; on the 5th to Schlodien; on the 6th to Engelswalde; on the 7th to Hussehnen.

Prussian Narrative of the Battle of Eylau

Lieutenant-General von Lestocq received notice at 2 o'clock, a.m. in the morning of February the 8th last, from the Imperial Russian Commander-in-Chief, to march with his corps towards Prussian Eylau, and station it by Althoff on the right wing of the Russian army, as he was determined to accept of a battle on that day. The corps of General Lestocq was quartered, when this order arrived, by the village of Hussehnen and its environs. Several corps of the division of reserve, under the command of Lieutenant-General Von Lestocq, who had been formed in separate columns on the 7th of February, did not reach their quarters until 6 o'clock in the morning of the 8th, having performed a march of 4 leagues and a half, and having been obliged to make a practical road for the artillery. It was, therefore, out of their power to break up at half past seven o'clock in the morning of the 8th of February from the rendezvous of Hussehnen, with the troops under the command of Lieutenant-General Von Lestocq, who had reached their quarters at seven o'clock in the evening of the 7th. Men and horses wanted some repose to complete their march of two leagues and a half to the field of battle. Lieutenant-General Von Ploctz received therefore orders to follow with his division as soon as possible the main body of the column to Althoff, to which place Lieutenant General Von Lestocq hastened, to obey the orders received from the Commander-in-Chief, and to take as much in his power a share in the great events of that day. This column marched to the left in the following order:

50 Horse Towarzasy's Regiment, and 80 of Auer's Regiment of Dragoons.

SUPPORT OF THE VAN GUARD

10 Squadrons of Auer's Regiment of Dragoons.
Captain Von Breda's Horse Battery.

THE MAIN ARMY

3rd Division
Major-General Von Auer's 10 Squadrons of Towarzasy's Regiment.
Lieutenant Decker's Half Horse Battery.
Three Battalions of Wyburg's Imperial Battalion Regiment of Infantry.

2nd Division—Major General Shembow
2nd Battalion of Schoening's Regiment of Infantry.
1st Battalion of Von Schliessen's Grenadiers.

1st Division—Major General Von Diericke
1st Battalion of Von Fabecker's Grenadiers.
2nd Battalion of Von Ruchel's Regiment of Infantry.
Five Squadrons of Von Bacyno's Regiment of Dragoons.
Five Squadrons of Von Weizenfeld's Regiment of Cuirassiers.
Half Battalion, Lieutenant Von Renzal.

Rear of the Army—Major General Von Prittwitz
1st Battalion Von Stutterheim's Fusiliers.
Five Squadrons of Von Prittwitz's 1st Battalion.
Half a Battalion Lieutenant Von Iowinski.

Several detachments observed the enemy advancing towards the right of the column.

The march from the rendezvous was made through the village Miekern. From hence they were directed to march through the point of the Forest of Schlautienen, through Goercken, and so straight to Althoff; but, as soon as the head of the column came out of the forest, the enemy, coming from Bornehnes, advanced against the right flank of the column. Lieutenant General Von Lestocq ordered the 1st battalion of Retner's regiment to march against the enemy's van, during which time the 2nd battalion of the same regiment, the regiment of Towarzasy, and Von Bredries horse battalion were ordered to pass quickly by the village of Schlautiezon, on the heights of which the battery had been placed to cover the retreat of the van guard, and to stop the van guard of the enemy. The infantry and the rest of the cavalry received orders, during this time, not to follow the van to Schlautienen, but to march from Wackern by the left to Pompickern, where the cavalry from Schlautienen and the horse battery joined the column again and continued their march.

The enemy, who had, in the mean time, advanced still more, had his horse artillery also placed on the heights by Schlautienen, and by Wackern, and a brisk cannonade commenced oil both sides.

To prevent the enemy from impeding the march, two companies of infantry of Von Schoening, and three companies of the Russian regiment Von Wyburg, serving as marksmen, were posted in the forest by Wackern. The effect of their fire, together with that of the battalion Von Breda, and the position of the five squadrons Von Retner, attained the object, and the column from Pompickern was enabled to continue its march.

Lieutenant-General Von Lestocq ordered therefore the said five squadrons and the battery to rejoin his column.

The five companies, acting as marksmen, did not retreat until the enemy advanced with far superior force by Wackern, and our main column had passed the forest by the village, a the rear, under the command of General Von Prittwitz, had almost reached it.

The last named General saw at this time the van of a second column of the enemy in full march against him. Captain Von Krauzeneck, of Von Stutterheim's regiment of fusiliers begged permission to march with his company against this column, to prevent them front harassing the rear of our column. This brave officer fired upon the van of the enemy with such vigour and effect, that he could advance but slowly. The regiment of Von Bacyno's dragoons, and four squadrons, Von Wagerfeld's regiment of cuirassiers, passed in the mean time, being the rear of the main column, the village Wackern, and Captain Von Krauzeneck followed these, pressed upon by an irresistible force and a continual brisk fire.

The enemy advanced on this point in great force, gained in the mean time more ground, and extended his line. General Von Prittwitz, who was at that time with the whole of the van, exclusive of Von Krauzeneck's company, between Wackern and Hussehnen, ordered the half of the horse battery to cannonade vigorously the enemy, that they might be hindered from; taking possession of the village of Wackern for the sake of passing it; but it was impossible for this General to obtain entirely his object, the enemy being of such superior force. Part of the enemy's infantry threw themselves into the village; but Colonel Von Stutterheim attacked them with a company of his battalion with charged bayonets at quick step, forced them out of the village, and joined Captain Von Krauzeneck. The other half of the battalion of fusiliers, the five squadrons of the hussars, and the half battery, could not follow quickly enough, as the enemy advanced on the right and left of the village at that time, and took possession of it again with a strong force.

The eminent bravery of Colonel Von Stutterheim and Captain Von Krauzeneck, prevented the advancing enemy from engaging the rear of the main column in a battle, and retarded their progress; yet they succeeded in cutting off, as has been mentioned before, General Von Prittwitz with two corps and five squadrons, by which this General was forced to turn to the left towards Creutzburg. The enemy pursued him with a superior force, particularly with infantry. This General knew, however, to make such good and judicious use of any small number of troops, that the enemy could advance but slowly, and do him little injury. In this affair Lieutenant Von Sowinski, of the horse artillery, again distinguished himself.

Meanwhile, the enemy acted with his two columns, directed towards Wackern and Schlautienen, against the right flank of Lestocq's corps ; he advanced with a third column against Pompickern, which, however, arrived later than the other two. Lieutenant-General Von Lestocq ordered the entrance of the village to be taken possession of by the battalion of Von Fabacci's grenadiers, and to mount on two heights near it the horse battery, covered by Von Wagerfeld's regiment. The enemy attacked the village with infantry and artillery, but were repulsed, and, by the incessant fire of the batteries, prevented from any further endeavours to force it.

These attacks of the enemy on Wackern, Schlautienen, and Pompickern, were made in the space of half a mile, and attempted almost at the same time by the whole of Marshal Ney's corps. Lieutenant-General Von Lestocq avoided a general action with

Marshal Ney, (which was evidently sought by him, to prevent the junction of the corps with the Russian army,) only by abandoning his proposed march through Goercken to Althoff, by opposing the enemy with the van advanced to Schlautienen, by occupying, with five companies, the Forest of Wackern, and by marching, in the mean time, the column behind these troops towards Leissen and Grawentien, which column would not have been able to attain its aim, had it not been for the great bravery of the troops who fought by Wackern and Pompickern, as well as the column itself, which surmounted, with the greatest exertions and alacrity, all obstacles opposed to them in the road, and although pressed and pursued, hastened to the great object.

Lieutenant-General Von Lestocq had the fortune to engage Ney's corps, far superior to his, to keep it in awe, to continue his march, and, in spite of the circuitous route, to arrive at the field of battle at one o'clock at noon, and to take a decided part in the ever memorable battle. The actions by Wackern and Pompickern were very sharp. The troops fought in small separated divisions, yet with the greatest bravery. The five companies of Von Schoening's and Wyburg distinguished themselves particularly. They, as marksmen, drove back the enemy far superior to them, maintained their post until they were outflanked on both sides, and retreated in order and steadiness from the forest to the column. The two companies of fusiliers, commanded by Colonel Von Sutterheim, the battalion of grenadiers, commanded by Major Von Fabeck, the 1st battalion of Retner's regiment, commanded by Colonel Von Larista, Von Wagerfeld's regiment, commanded by Major Von Figler, showed in this battle an equal bravery and steadiness, and the troops, under the command of General Von Prittwitz, acted no less meritoriously; and the Prussian, as well as the Russian infantry, proved here to be equal to the so much boasted marksmen .of the enemy, with respect to activity, and superior with respect to bravery and resolution.

Besides the columns of the enemy engaged by Wackern, Schlautienen, and Pompickern, Lieutenant-General Von Lestocq was followed from Pompickern to Althoff by a fourth column of the enemy, and threatened with a general attack, which was frustrated by Lieutenant General Von Lestocq continuing his march through Leissen to Grawentien and Althoff on an advantageous height, and thereby getting between him and the enemy, the rivers running to Grawentien and Althoff, and by partial actions of infantry and cavalry keeping the enemy so far off from the main column, that it could continue its march without being engaged in general action.

When the corps had reached Althoff, Lieutenant-General Von Lestocq ordered the battalion of Von Schliessen's grenadiers, commanded by Captain Von Keworasky, to occupy that village and the bridge by Grauantien, and to cover thereby the march of the corps on the other side of the village to the right wing of the Russian army, which was also accomplished Scarce was the corps here formed, when Lieutenant-General Von Lestocq received orders to march to the left wing of the Russian army to rescue from the enemy those advantages they had gained by a superior force, He marched, therefore, to the left with all possible speed in the direction towards Schloditten, and behind the right of the Russian army; and when he found here that the enemy had not flanked the Russians, and taken already possession of the village Kutschitten, the heads of the three columns, with which formation the corps marched for facility sake, were directed upon it.

Lieutenant-General Von Lestocq not having received any further special order with respect to the operations of his corps, he determined first of all to retake the village Kutschitten, as he foresaw, that by taking this village, the enemy would be hindered by further advancing, and be himself outflanked.

The attack on the village was executed by two columns of infantry. The Russian regiment of Wyburg formed the right column, and Ruchel's regiment, with sharp-shooters at their head, formed the left column. Von Fabecke's battalion of grenadiers formed themselves into line and followed to support the two attacking columns. Von Schoening's regiment marched on, leaving the village to the left, against a body of the enemy's infantry drawn up in a line, and cannonaded it with a destructive fire of artillery, so that the enemy were obliged to retire in the forest of birch trees.

Towarzasy's regiment, led on by Major-General Von Kall, to which 200 Cossacks had re-united, marched to the left round the village, dislodged the cavalry of the enemy's right wing posted there, and made prisoners, in junction with the Cossacks, of the wreck of the enemy's infantry flying from the village into the forest, or cut them down.

The dragoons and cuirassiers, together with the horse artillery, followed in column Von Fabeck's battalion of grenadiers, and marched, when the village was taken on the other side of it, into a second line behind the infantry.

When the two attacking columns approached the village, the enemy met them on the extremity of it, but was almost instantaneously broken, and, in spite of an obstinate resistance in the village where he rallied, he was pressed through with charged bayonets, notwithstanding he set it on fire to stop the advance of our infantry. The enemy took again position close behind the village; but here also he was attacked so impetuously, that by far the greatest part were killed on the spot; the rest, totally broken, endeavoured to gain the forest, but were, at a little distance from the village, surrounded by the Cossacks and Towarzasy's regiment, and, as has been stated, the whole killed or taken. Not a man of the whole 800 who had originally occupied the village escaping.

The Russian regiment Von Wyburg recovered the three cannons which had been abandoned by the Russian left wing when previously retiring, and Towarzasy's regiment took an eagle from the enemy.

After the village of Kutschitten had thus been taken, Lieutenant-General Von Lestocq ordered the infantry to march in line, in the direction of the birch trees, between Anklappen and Lampasch, and with the rear towards the village of Kutschitten. Thus making a wheel to the right.

Von Schoening's regiment formed the right wing of the line on its left, Fabecke's battalion of grenadiers, the Russian regiment Wyburg, and Von Ruchel's regiment formed the left wing. Von Wagerfeld's regiment of cuirassiers, and Von Auer's regiment of dragoons, formed in the 2nd line behind the right wing, and Von Bucyho's regiment behind Von Ruchel's. Towarzasy's regiment marched to extend the left wing of the infantry, and keep in awe the enemy's cavalry posted by little Sausgarten.

The infantry advanced now with drums beating, and with such order and resolution, as to leave nothing more to be wished; and, without firing a shot, directed itself straight towards the forest, and upon a column of the enemy at least three times their number, until within 50 paces at the utmost. Von Ruchel's regiment, originally led on by Major-General Von Diericke, inclined to the left, leaving the forest close upon its right, and took post in a diagonal line with the enemy's right flank. Lieutenant Decker's half horse battery took post at the same time on an height somewhat more to the left, from whence he cannonaded not only a 10 gun battery of the enemy's, but also a body of troops posted behind Sausgarten and the forest.

A brisk and murderous fire now commenced upon the enemy from the artillery and small arms. The Prussian artillery fire was visibly superior to that of the enemy, and the musketry of our infantry, posted in a little valley, caused prodigious destruction amongst the mass body of the enemy, whilst most of his shot flew too high, so that our infantry, in comparison, sustained but little loss. After this tremendous fire had continued for about half an hour, by which the enemy lost, according to his own confession, 4,000 men in killed and wounded, he began to retreat again, and our infantry, till now unbroken, fell upon the enemy with charged bayonets, drove him through the forest to the heights by Little Sausgarten, and obliged him to abandon the farm of Anklappen, which he set on fire, and behind which he took post.

The setting in of the night, and the fatigue of the troops, having marched and fought incessantly since 3 o'clock in the morning, made it impossible to pursue our victory further, and to attack the enemy, yet strongly posted in the neighbourhood of Sausgarten, which would have been, no doubt, the cause of the total defeat of his right wing. The General, therefore, having advanced above 2,000 paces, ordered his infantry to mount the guards in the forest, and the main body remained in the field of battle, *animated with the sweet hopes of effecting the total defeat of the enemy on the next morning, in case he did not retire during the night, and which was the general belief of the Russians.*

The battalion of Von Schliessen's grenadiers, left behind at Althoff, could not, before 4 o'clock in the evening, effect a junction with the corps. They had been attacked in this village by the enemy on all sides, of far superior force, but made good their march to the army under the command of the brave Captain Von Kurowsky, who formed a square between Schloditten and Schmoditten when surrounded and pursued by the enemy.

Thus ended the day so glorious to the Russians and the corps of Lieutenant-General Von Lestocq. The infantry and cavalry not only signalized themselves in the actions by Wackern, Schlautienen, and Pompickern, but also in the battle itself, and they have once more established the old fame of Prussian bravery, resolute courage, and skilfulness in manoeuvring with celerity and precision.

The attack upon Kutschitten, and the forest by Anklappen, were undertaken and executed in die best order, and with the greatest bravery, by Von Ruchel's and Von Schoening's regiment, and Von Fabecke's battalion of grenadiers, and also by the Russian regiment Wyburg under command of General Von Diericke and Von Renbow Colonel Von Hamilton, and Von Piller; Lieutenant-Colonel Von Below, and Major Von Fabeck; the regiment of Towarzasy, commanded by Major-General Von Kall, and the 200 Cossacks united to them, by moving quickly round the village, forced the enemy's cavalry to forsake the infantry, and, completed their destruction.

The remaining cavalry, namely, Von Auer's regiment, under command of Major-General Von Auer, Von Bacyno's, and Von Wagerfeld's four squadrons, under Major Zieglu, showed not only by Schlautienen and Pompickern, the greatest bravery, but also supported with vigour, as far as the ground would permit, the attack of the infantry, but the greatest coolness, and order during the fire of the enemy's artillery, to which Von Bacyno's regiment by Wackern, and Towarzasy's regiment between Kutschitten and Lampasch, were so much exposed. The horse artillery, by its activity and effect, greatly contributed to the success in all the affairs, all well as in the battle of Eylau.

The commandant-general feels the greatest satisfaction in laying this account before the,' public, and in declaring, that the officers, the *aides-de-camp*, and the staff, have merited his, highest approbation, having executed their orders with much penetration and courage. It if also gratifying and pleasing to the General to know that he has no reason to be discontented with any commander or regiment on that glorious day. All ranks burnt with desire to do every thing for his chief and country, on this decisive moment, that emulous exertion could do, and to seal their efforts willingly with death.

When the army perceived the Russian army fighting, they were so eager to support their brethren in arms, that they wished to advance before their cannon, and with the greatest difficulty could be persuaded to take them on with them. The sight of the Russian army, who had with such obstinate courage at many times withstood daringly the repeated furious attacks of a far superior enemy, and kept the most perfect order, inspired every Prussian with esteem and confidence.

Though the Commandant-General was convinced that the part of his corps, which ho posted at Althoff, was of great and decisive use, by engaging and preventing further operations of Marshal Ney's corps, yet in the field of battle by Kutschitten he felt its absence, as the strength of his corps there, including the Russian regiment of Wyburg, consisted only of nine battalions and 29 squadrons, making an effective force of 5584 men.

Lieutenant-General Von Lestocq received orders at 10 o'clock at night, to leave, before day-break, the field of battle, and to march towards, the Aller, as the Russian army would move in the direction of Koenigsberg.

The corps marched at 2 o'clock without any guide (as the inhabitants had abandoned all the villages) on Domnau, selecting this road for the purpose of keeping up the communication with the Russian army, and with the Russian frontier, and to secure (what was very unlikely) a further retreat. At Domnau he left his van, and establishing his head-quarters at Friedland put his troops for repose into quarters.

ACCOUNT OF OPERATIONS FROM THE BATTLE OF EYLAU
UNTIL THE RETURN TO KOENIGSBERG

Third Epoch

On the 10th of February Lieutenant General Lestocq established his head-quarters at Allenberg, and, on the 12th, at Tapian. On the 19th of February, being reinforced, and his corps being about 10,000 strong, he advanced from Tapian, over Allenberg, Domnau, Bartenstein, Heilsberg, (from which place the enemy were driven,) Wormditt, Muhlsack, Peterswalde, to Heiligenbeil. On the 10th of March, the enemy having driven General Plotz from Braunsberg, General Lestocq was posted from the Haff, with the Parsarge in his front, to Muhlsack, and the Russians from Muhlsack to Heilsberg, &c. and a Prussian corps drove the enemy out of Bishoffsburgh.

Both armies remained in their position near two months and a half, during which period Dantzic was taken, after General Kaminskoy's ineffectual attempt to relieve it, and also General Bülow's who, with 2000 Prussians, had attempted to penetrate by the Nehrung.

On the 4th of June, when the Russians moved upon the Parsarge across the Aller, General Lestocq engaged the enemy in his front, to prevent the succour of Marshal Ney.

When Buonaparte with his army re-advanced, a French corps was pushed to Muhlsack, which interrupted the direct communication with the Russian army and the Prussian corps General Lestocq then fell back upon Linthen, where, receiving advice of General Bennigsen's retrograde movement on the Pregel, and having previously captured a courier with orders to Marshal Victor, he retired upon Koenigsberg, being joined by General Kaminskoy, the Prussian cavalry, and 9000 Russians, which additional strength enabled him to effect his movement upon the city with safety and honour, and only the loss of a brigade which had been posted upon the right to watch Braunsberg, and which was cut off by Marshal Soult after a gallant attempt to effect a passage.

APPENDIX 5

Miscellaneous Papers

ARMISTICE BETWEEN FRANCE AND RUSSIA

As his Majesty the Emperor of the French, and his Majesty the Emperor of Russia, are anxious to put an end to the war which has so long divided the two nations, they have in the mean time resolved to conclude an Armistice; their Majesties have named and empowered the following Plenipotentiaries, viz. on the one part the Prince of Neufchatel, Marshal of the Empire, Major-General in the Grand Army; and on the other part, Lieutenant-General Prince Labanoff Von Rostrow, Knight of the Order of St. Anne, Grand Cross; who have agreed upon the following Preliminaries:

1. An armistice shall take place between the French and Russian armies, in order that, in the mean time, a peace may be negotiated, concluded and signed, to put an end to that bloodshed which is so contrary to humanity.
2. If either of the two contracting parties shall incline to break this armistice, which God forbid! the party so inclining shall be bound to signify this at the head-quarters of the other army, and hostilities shall not again commence until one month after the above notification.
3. The French and Prussian armies shall conclude a separate armistice, and Officers shall be appointed for that purpose. During the four or five days requisite for the conclusion of this armistice, the French army shall undertake no hostilities against the Prussians.
4. The limits of the French and Russian armies, during the armistice, shall be from the Churisch Haff, the Thalweg of the Niemen, and up the left bank of that river to the mouth of the Arama at Stakin, and pursuing the course of that river to the mouth of the Bobra, following this rivulet through Rozano, Lipsk, Habin, Dolitawo, Gomadz, and Wyna, up to the mouth of the Bobra in the Narew, and from thence ascending the left

bank of the Narew by Tylyoczyui, Suratz, Narew, to the frontiers of Prussia and Russia. On the Curisch Nehrung the limits shall be at Nidden.

5. His Majesty the Emperor of the French, and his Majesty the Emperor of Russia, shall name Plenipotentiaries within the shortest time possible, who are to be provided with the necessary powers for negotiating, concluding, and signing a definitive Peace between these two great and powerful nations.

6. Commissaries shall be named on both sides, in order to proceed immediately to the exchange of prisoners, which exchange shall take place by rank for rank,and man for man.

7. The exchange of the ratifications of the present armistice, shall take place within 48 hours, or sooner, if possible, at the head-quarters of the Russian army.

Done at Tilsit, this 21st of June, 1807

(Signed) *The Prince of Neufchatel Marshal Alexander Berthier Prince Labanoff Von Rostrow*

Approved of, Tilsit, 22nd June, 1807 (Signed) *Napoleon*

Undersigned by the Emperor, the Minister and Secretary of State, H. B. Maret.

I hereby ratify the whole contents of the armistice concluded between the Marshal Prince of Neufchatel, and Lieutenant-General Prince Labanoff Von Rostrow.

Teurogen, 11th-23rd June, 1807

Alexander

In testimony of his approbation.

Undersigned the Major-General Marshal Alexander Berthier, Prince of Neufchatel.

Treaty of peace between His Majesty the Emperor of the French and King of Italy, and His Majesty the Emperor of all the Russias
Done at Tilsit, 7th July (25th June), 1807

His Majesty, the Emperor of France, King of Italy, Protector of the Confederation of the Rhine, and his Majesty the Emperor of Russia, animated with the same interest in putting an end to the devastations of war, have, for this purpose, nominated and furnished with full power on the part of His Majesty the Emperor of France and King of Italy, Charles Maurice Talleyrand, Prince of Benevento, his Great Chamberlain, and Minister of Foreign Affairs, Grand

Cross of the Legion of Honour, Knight of the Prussian Order of the Black and of the Red Eagle, of the Order of St. Hubert. His Majesty, the Emperor of all the Russias, has, on his part, appointed Prince Kurakin, his actual Privy Counsellor; Member of the Council of State, and of the Senate; Chancellor of all the Orders in the Empire; Ambassador Extraordinary, and Plenipotentiary of His Majesty of all the Russias to His Majesty the Emperor of Austria: Knight of the Russian Order of St. Andrew; of St. Alexander; of St. Aube; of the first class of the Order of St. Wolodimir, and of the second class of the Prussian Orders of the Black and Red Eagle; of the Bavarian Order of St. Hubert; of the Danish Order of Dannebrog, and the Perfect Union, and Bailiff and Grand Cross of the Sovereign Order of St. John of Jerusalem; and Prince Demety Labanoff Van Rostoff, Lieutenant-General of the Armies of His Majesty the Emperor of all the Russias; Knight of the first class of the Order of St. Anne, of the Military Order of St. Joris, and of the third class of the Order of Wolodimir. The above mentioned, after exchanging their full, powers, have agreed upon the following Articles:

1. From the day of exchanging the ratification of the present treaties, there shall be perfect peace and amity between His Majesty the Emperor of the French and King of Italy, and His Majesty the Emperor of all the Russias.

2.. Hostilities shall immediately cease at all points by sea or land, as soon as the intelligence of the present treaty shall be officially received. In the mean while, the high contracting parties shall dispatch couriers extraordinary to their respective generals and commanders.

3. All ships of war or other vessels, belonging to the high contracting parties or their subjects, which may be captured after the signing of this treaty, shall be restored. In case of these vessels being sold, the value shall be returned.

4. Out of esteem for His Majesty the Emperor of all the Russias, and to afford to him a proof of his sincere desire to unite both nations in the bands of immutable confidence and friendship, the Emperor Napoleon wishes that all the countries, towns, and territory, conquered from the King of Prussia, the ally of His Majesty the Emperor of all the Russias, should be restored, namely, that part of the Duchy of Magdeburg, situated on the

right bank of the Rhine, the Mark of Prignitz; the Uker Mark; the Middle and New Mark of Brandenburg, with the exception of the Circle of Kotbuss, in Lower Alsace; the Duchy of Pomerania; Upper, Lower, and New Silesia, and the County of Glatz; that part of the District of the Netze, which is situated to the northward of the road of Driesen and Schneidemuhl, and to the northward of a line drawn from Schneidemuhl through Waldau to the Vistula, and extending along the frontier of the circle of Bromberg, and the navigation of the river Netze and of the canal of Bromberg, from Driesen to the Vistula and back, must remain open and free of all tolls; Pomerelia; the island of Nogat; the country on the right bank of the Vistula and of the Nogat, to the West of Old Prussia, and to the northward of the circle of Calm; Ermeland. Lastly, the kingdom of Prussia, as it was on the 1st of January, 1772, together with the fortresses of Spandau, Stettin, Custrin, Glogau, Breslau, Schweidnitz, Neisse, Brieg, Kosel, and Glatz, and in general all fortresses, citadels, castles, and strong holds of the countries above-named, in the same condition in which those fortresses, citadels, castles, and strong holds may be at present; also, in addition to the above, the city and citadel of Graudentz.

5. Those provinces which, on the 1st of January, 1772, formed a part of the kingdom of Poland, and have since, at different times, been subjected to Prussia, (with the exception o the countries named or alluded to in the preceding article, and of those which are describe below the 9th article,) shall become the possession of His Majesty the King of Saxony with power of possession and sovereignty, under the title of the Duchy of Warsaw, and shall be governed according to a regulation, which will insure the liberties and privileges of the people of the said Duchy, and be consistent with the security of the neighbouring states.

6. The city of Dantzic, with a territory of two leagues round the same, is restored t her former independence, under the protection of His Majesty the King of Prussia, and Hi Majesty the King of Saxony; to be governed according to the laws by which she was governed at the time when she ceased to be her own mistress.

7. For a communication betwixt the kingdom of Saxony and the Duchy of Warsaw, His Majesty the King of Saxony is to have the free use of a military road through the states of His Majesty the King of Prussia. This road, the number of troops

which are allowed to pass at once, and the resting places, shall be fixed by a particular agreement between the two sovereigns, under the mediation of France.

8. Neither His Majesty the King of Prussia, His Majesty the King of Saxony, nor the city of Dantzic, shall oppose any obstacles whatever to the free navigation of the Vistula under the name of tolls, rights, or duties.

9. In order as far as possible to establish a natural boundary between Russia and the Duchy of Warsaw, the territory between the present confines of Russia, from the Bug to the mouth of the Lassona, shall extend in a line from the mouth of the Lassona along the towing path of the said river; and that of the Bobra, up to its mouth; that of the Narew from the mouth of that river as far as Suradiz; from Lissa to its source near the village of Mien; from this village to Nutzeck, and from Nutzeck to the mouth of that river beyond Nurr; and finally, along the towing path of the Bug upwards, to extend as far as the present frontiers of Russia. This territory is for ever united to the Empire of Russia.

10. No person of any rank or quality whatever, whose residence or property may be within the limits stated in the abovementioned article, nor any inhabitant in those provinces of the ancient kingdom of Poland, which may be given up to His Majesty the King of Prussia, or any person possessing estates, revenues, pensions, or any other kind of income, shall be molested in his person, or in any way whatever, on account of his rank, quality, estates, revenues, pensions, income, or otherwise, or in consequence of any part, political or military, which he may have taken in the events of the present war.

11. All contracts and engagements between his Majesty the King of Prussia, and the ancient possessors, relative to the general imposts, the ecclesiastical, the military or civil benefices, of the creditors or pensioners of the old Prussian government, are to be settled between the Emperor of all the Russias, and His Majesty the King of Saxony; and to be regulated by their said Majesties, in proportion to their acquisitions, according to articles 5. and 9.

12. Their Royal Highnesses the Dukes of Saxe Cobourg, Oldenburg, and Mecklenburg Schwerin, shall each of them he restored to the complete and quiet possession of their estates; but

the ports in the Duchies of Oldenburg and Mecklenburgh shall remain in the possession of French garrisons till the definitive treaty shall be signed between France and England.

13. His Majesty the Emperor Napoleon accepts of the mediation of the Emperor of all the Russias, in order to negotiate and conclude a definitive treaty of peace between France and England; however, only upon condition that this mediation shall be accepted by England in one month after the exchange of the ratification of the present treaty.

14. His Majesty the Emperor of all the Russias being desirous on his part to manifest how ardently he desires to establish the most intimate and lasting relations between the two Emperors, acknowledges His Majesty Joseph Napoleon, King of Naples, and His Majesty Louis Napoleon, King of Holland.

15. His Majesty the Emperor of all the Russias acknowledges the Confederation of the Rhine, the present state of the possessions of the princes belonging to it, and the titles of those which were conferred upon them by the act of confederation, or by the subsequent treaties of accession. His said Majesty also promises, information being communicated to him on the part of the Emperor Napoleon, to acknowledge those sovereigns who may hereafter become members of the Confederation, according to their rank specified in the act of Confederation.

16. His Majesty the Emperor of all the Russias cedes all his property in the right of sovereignty to the Lordship of Jevor, in East Friesland, to his Majesty the King of Holland.

17. The present treaty of peace shall be mutually binding, and in force for His Majesty the King of Naples, Joseph Napoleon, His Majesty Louis Napoleon, King of Holland, and the Sovereigns of the Confederation of the Rhine, in alliance with the Emperor Napoleon.

18. His Majesty the Emperor of all the Russias also acknowledges His Imperial Highness Prince Jerome Napoleon, as King of Westphalia.

19. The Kingdom of Westphalia shall consist of the provinces ceded by the King of Prussia on the left bank of the Elbe, and other states at present in the possession of His Majesty the Emperor Napoleon.

20. His Majesty the Emperor of all the Russias engages to recognize the limits which shall be determined by his Majesty the

Emperor Napoleon, in pursuance of the foregoing 19th article, and the cessions of His Majesty the King of Prussia, (which shall be notified to His Majesty the Emperor of all the Russias,) together with the state of possession resulting therefrom to the sovereigns for whose behalf they shall have been established.

21. All hostilities shall immediately cease between the troops of His Majesty the Emperor of all the Russias and those of the Grand Seignior, at all points, wherever official intelligence shall arrive of the signing of the present treaty. The high contracting parties shall, without delay, dispatch couriers extraordinary to convey the intelligence, with the utmost possible expedition, to the respective generals and commanders.

22. The Prussian troops shall be withdrawn from the Provinces of Moldavia, but the said provinces may not be occupied by the troops of the Grand Seignior, till after the exchange of the ratifications of the future definitive treaty of peace between Russia and the Ottoman Porte.

23. His Majesty the Emperor of all the Russias accepts the mediation of His Majesty the Emperor of France and King of Italy, for the purpose of negotiating a peace advantageous and honourable to the two powers, and of concluding the same. The respective Plenipotentiaries shall repair to that place which will be agreed upon by the two powers concerned, thereto open the negotiations, and to proceed therewith.

24. The periods within which the high contracting parties shall withdraw their troops from the places which they are to evacuate, pursuant to the above stipulations, as also the manner in which the different stipulations contained in the present treaty shall be executed, will be settled by a special agreement.

25. His Majesty the Emperor of the French, King of Italy, and His Majesty the Emperor of all the Russias, mutually ensure to each other the integrity of their possessions, and of those of the powers included in this present treaty, in the state in which they are now settled, or further to be settled, pursuant to the above stipulations.

26. The prisoners made by the contracting parties, or those included in the present treaty, shall be restored in a mass, and without any cartel of exchange on both sides.

27. The commercial relations between the French Empire, the Kingdom of Italy, the Kingdoms of Naples and Holland, and the Confederated States of the Rhine on one side, and the

Empire of Russia on the other, shall be replaced on the same footing as before the war.

28. The ceremonial between the two Courts of the Thuilleries and Petersburg, with respect to each other, and also their respective ambassadors, ministers, and envoys, mutually accredited to each other, shall be placed on the footing of complete equality and reciprocity.

29. The present treaty shall be ratified by His Majesty the Emperor of the French, King of Italy, and his Majesty the Emperor of all the Russias; the ratifications shall be exchanged hi this city within the space of four days.

(Signed) *C. Maurice Talleyrand,* Prince of Benevento

Prince Alexander Kourakin

Prince Dimitry Labanoff Van Rostoff

(Signed) *A true Copy, C. M. Talleyrand, Prince of Benevento*

CONDITIONS OF PEACE BETWEEN HIS MAJESTY THE EMPEROR OF THE FRENCH AND KING OF ITALY AND HIS MAJESTY THE KING OF PRUSSIA

Done at Tilsitz, 9th July, 1807

His Majesty the Emperor of the French, King of Italy, and Protector of the Confederation of the Rhine, and his Majesty the King of Prussia, animated with the same desire of putting an end to the calamities of war, for that purpose appointed plenipotentiaries, namely; on the part of his Majesty the Emperor of France and King of Italy, Protector of the Confederation of the Rhine, M. Ch. Maurice Talleyrand, Prince of Benevento, his Great Chamberlain, and Minister for Foreign Affairs, &c. &c.; and on that of his Majesty the King of Prussia, M. Marshal Count de Kalkreuth, Knight of the Prussian Orders of the Black and Red Eagle, and Count Von Golz, his Privy Counsellor, Envoy Extraordinary, and Minister Plenipotentiary to his Majesty the Emperor of all the Russias, and Knight of the Prussian Order of the Black Eagle: who after the exchange of their several full powers, have agreed on the following articles:

1. From the day of the exchange of the ratifications of the present treaty, there shall be perfect peace and amity between the King of Prussia and the Emperor of France.

2. The part of the Duchy of Magdeburg which lies on the right bank of the Elbe; the Mark of Preignitz, the Ukermark, and the new Mark of Brandenburg, with the exception of the Circle of Collins, in Lower Lusatia ; the Duchy of Pomerania; Upper, Lower, and New Silesia, with the County of Glatz; the part of the district of Mess which lies to the road from Driesen to Schneidemuhl, and to the north of a line passing from Schneidemuhl, by Woldau, to the Vistula, and to the frontier of the Circle of Bromberg Pomerelia; the Island of Nogat, and the country on the right bank of the Vistula and the Nogat, to the west of Old Prussia; and to the Circle Culmer: finally, the kingdom of Prussia, as it was on the 1st of January, 1772, shall be restored to his Majesty the King of Prussia, with the fortresses of Spandau, Stettin, Custrin, Glogau, Breslaw, Schweidnitz, Neisse, Brieg-Cosel, and Glaz; and, in general, all the places, citadels, castles, and forts of the above mentioned, shall be restored in the state in which they at present are: the town and citadel of Graudenz, with the villages of Neudorf, Parschken, and Schwierkorzy, shall likewise be restored to his Majesty the King of Prussia.

3. His Majesty the King of Prussia acknowledges his Majesty the King of Naples, Joseph Napoleon, and his Majesty the King of Holland, Louis Napoleon.

4. His Majesty the King of Prussia in like manner acknowledges the Confederation of the Rhine, and the present state of the possessions of the sovereigns of which it is composed, and the titles which have been bestowed on them, either by the act of confederation, or by the subsequent treaties. His said Majesty likewise engages to acknowledge those sovereigns who, in future, shall become members of the said Confederation, and the titles they may receive by their treaties of accession.

5. The present Treaty of Peace and Amity shall be in common for his Majesty the King of Naples, Joseph Napoleon, for his Majesty the King of Holland, and for the Sovereigns of the Confederation of the Rhine, the allies of his Majesty the Emperor Napoleon.

6. His Majesty the King of Prussia, in like manner, acknowledges his Imperial Highness Prince Jerome Napoleon as King of Westphalia.

7. His Majesty the King of Prussia cedes, in full right of property and sovereignty to the Kings, Grand Dukes and Dukes, and

Princes, who shall be pointed out by his Majesty the Emperor of the French and King of Italy, all the Duchies, Margravates Principalities, Counties, and Lordships, and, in general, all the territories and domains, and all territorial property of whatever kind, or by whatever title possessed, by his Majesty the King of Prussia, between the Rhine and the Elbe, at the commencement of the present war.

8. The kingdom of Westphalia shall consist of the provinces ceded by his Majesty the King of Prussia, and of other states which are at present in possession of his Majesty the Emperor Napoleon.

9. The arrangements which his Majesty the Emperor Napoleon shall make in the countries alluded to in the two preceding articles, and the occupation of the same by those sovereigns in whose favour he shall make such arrangements, shall be acknowledged by his Majesty the King of Prussia in the same manner as if they were contained and stipulated in the present treaty.

10. His Majesty the King of Prussia renounces for himself, his heirs, and successors, all actual or future right which he has or may require.

1. To all territory without exception, situate between the Elbe and the Rhine, and in general to all not described in Article 7.

2. To all possessions of his Majesty the King of Saxony and of the House of Anhalt, situate on the right bank of the Elbe. On the other hand, all rights or claims of the states situate between the Rhine and the Elbe to the possessions of his Majesty the King of Prussia, as they are defined by the present Treaty, shall be for ever extinguished and annulled.

11. All negotiations, conventions, or treaties of alliance, that may have been publicly or privately concluded between Prussia and any States on the left bank of the Elbe, and which have not been broken by the present war, shall remain without effect, and be considered as null and not concluded.

12. His Majesty the King of Prussia cedes the Circle of Colbus, in Lower Lusatia, to his Majesty the King of Saxony, with full light of proprietorship and sovereignty.

13. His Majesty the King of Prussia renounces for ever possession to all the provinces which formerly constituted parts of the kingdom of Poland, have at different periods come under the dominion of Prussia, excepting Ermeland, and the country

to the west of Ancient Prussia, to the east of Pomerania and the Newark, to the north of the Circle of Halm, and a line which passes from the Vistula by Waldau to Schneidemuhl, and passes along the boundaries of Bromberg and the road from the Schneidemuhl to Driesen, which provinces, with the town and citadel of Graudentz, and the villages of Neudorf, Parschken, and Swiethorzy, shall in future be possessed, with all rights of proprietorship and sovereignty, by his Majesty the King of Prussia.

14. His Majesty the King of Prussia renounces in like manner, for ever, possession of the city of Dantzic.

15. The provinces which his Majesty the King of Prussia renounces in the 13th article, with exception of the territories mentioned in the 18th article, shall be possessed with right of property and sovereignty by his Majesty the King of Saxony, under the title of a Dukedom of Warsaw, and governed according to a constitution which shall secure the liberties and privileges of the people of that duchy, and be conformable to the tranquillity of the neighbouring states.

16. To secure a connection and communication between the kingdom of Saxony and the duchy of Warsaw, the free use of a military road shall be granted to the King of Saxony through the states of his Majesty the King of Prussia. This road, the number of troops which shall pass through it at one time, and the places at which they shall halt, shall be settled by a particular agreement between the two sovereigns, under the mediation of France.

17. The navigation of the river Ness, and the canal of Bromberg, from Driesen to the Vistula and back, shall remain free from any toll.

18. In order to establish, as much as possible, natural boundaries between Russia and the duchy of Warsaw, the territory between the present boundaries of Russia, from the Berg, to the mouth of the Lassosna, and a line which passes from the said mouth, and along the channel of that river, the channel of the Bobro to its mouth, the channel of the Narew from its mouth to Suradz, the channel of the Lisa to its source near the village of Mien, and of the two neighbouring arms of the Nurzuck, riling near that village, and the channel of the Nurzuck itself to its mouth; and lastly, along the channel of the Bug, up the stream to the present boundaries of Russia, shall for ever be incorporated with the Russian empire

19. The city of Dantzic, with a territory of two miles circumference, shall be restored to its former independence, under the protection of his Majesty the King of Prussia and the King of Saxony, and be governed by the rules by which it was governed when it ceased to be its own mistress.

20. Neither his Majesty the King of Prussia, nor his Majesty the King of Saxony, shall obstruct the navigation of the Vistula by any prohibition, nor by any customs, duty, or imports whatsoever.

21. The city, port, and territory of Dantzic, shall be shut up during the present maritime war against the trade and navigation of Great Britain.

22. No individual of any rank or description whatsoever, whose property and abode are situated in such provinces as formerly belonged to the kingdom of Poland, or which the King of Prussia is henceforth to possess; and no individual of the duchy of Warsaw, or residing within the territory incorporated with Russia, or possessing any landed property, rents, annuities, or any income whatsoever, shall either with regard to his person, his estates, rents, annuities, and income, nor with respect to his rank and dignities, be prosecuted on account of any part which he may have taken, either in a political or military point of view, in the event of the present war.

23. In the same manner, no individual residing or possessing landed property in the countries which belong to the King of Prussia, prior to the 1st of January, 1772, and which are restored to him by virtue of the preceding second article; and in particular, no individual of the Berlin civic guard or of the gens d'armes, who have taken up arms in order to main in tranquillity, shall be prosecuted in his person, his estates, rents, annuities, or any income whatsoever, or in his rank or dignity, nor in any manner whatsoever, on account of any part which he may have taken in the events of the present war, or be subjected to any inquiry.

24. The engagements, debts, or obligations of any nature whatsoever, which his Majesty the King of Prussia may have contracted or concluded, prior to the present war, as possessor of the countries, dominions, and revenues, which his Majesty cedes and renounces in the present treaty, shall be performed and satisfied by the new possessors, without any exception or reservation whatsoever.

25. The funds and capitals which belong to private persons, or public religion, civil, or military associations, countries which his Majesty the King of Prussia, or, which he renounces by the private treaty, whether the said capitals be vested in the Bank of Berlin, in the chest of the territory of Noviltrade, or in any other manner, in the dominions of the King of Prussia, shall neither be confiscated nor attached by the proprietors of the funds or capitals, shall be at liberty to dispose of the same, and they are to continue to enjoy the interest thereof, whether such interest be already due, or may yet become due at the periods stipulated in the conventions or bonds; the same shall, on the other side, be observed with regard to all funds and capitals which are vested by private individuals, or public institutions whatsoever, in such countries which are ceded or renounced by his Prussian Majesty by virtue of the present treaty.

26. The archives which contain the titles of property, documents, and in general all the papers which relate to the countries, territories, dominions, as well as the maps and plans of the strong places, citadels, castles, and forts seated in the above-mentioned countries, are to be delivered up by commissioners of his said Majesty, within the time of three months next ensuing the exchange of the ratification of this treaty, to commissioners of his Majesty the Emperor Napoleon, with regard to the countries seated on the left bank of the Rhine; and to commissioners of his Majesty the Emperor of Russia, of the King of Saxony, and of the city of Dantzic, with regard to all the countries which their said Majesties and the city of Dantzic are in future to possess, by virtue of the present compact.

27. Until the day of the ratification of the future definitive treaty of peace between France and England, all the countries under the dominion of his Majesty the King of Prussia, without any exception whatsoever, shall be shut against the trade and navigation of the English. No shipment to be made from any Prussian port for the British Isles or British Colonies; nor shall any ship which sailed from England, or her colonies, be admitted in any Prussian port.

28. The necessary arrangements shall immediately be made to settle every point which relates to the manner and period of the surrender of the places which are to be restored to his

Majesty the King of Prussia, and to the civil and military administration of the said countries.

29. The prisoners of war taken on both sides are to be returned without any exchange and in mass, as soon as circumstances shall admit.

30. The present treaty is to be ratified by his Majesty the Emperor of the French, and by his Majesty the King of Prussia, and the ratifications shall he exchanged at Koenigsberg by the undersigned, within the time of six days next ensuing the signing of the treaty.

(Signed) *C. M. Talleyrand*, Prince of Benevento
Count Kalkreuth, Field-Marshal
Augustus Count Goltz

The ratifications of this treaty were exchanged at Koenigsberg, on the 12th July, 1807.

Maps

Explanation of the Plan
of the Battle of Pultusk

Between the Corps of the Imperial Russian Troops commanded by Baron Bennigsen, the General of Cavalry, and the French Army under the Command of Bonaparte, 14th December, 1806.

A. The position of the Russian infantry, covering the high road to Ostrolenka, and the bridges of communication, with the corps of Count Buxhowden, the General of infantry, who was within twelve English miles of the field of battle. *B.* The advanced guard commanded by Major-General Barclay de Tolly: three regiments of sharpshooters occupied the heath, two battalions of infantry were posted in reserve, whilst a third battalion covered the battery placed at *C*, to defend the high road from Novo. A detachment under Major-General Baggavout was posted at *D*, to cover the bridge, (whereat, on the opposite side of the river. Narew, was stationed at *E*, a battalion of the 14th division) in order to prevent the enemy from advancing upon the rear of the Russian corps, by Pultusk. The cavalry posted at *F*, supported the Cossacks G, who, on the approach of the enemy, immediately engaged the chasseurs à cheval, which had formed line in front of several French columns at *H*. In order that a line might likewise be formed on the Russian side, with the advanced guard, and the detachment of Major-General Baggavout, a detachment of cavalry was removed towards *I*. The enemy's corps under Marshal Davoust made its first attack on the detachment of Major-General Baggavout: the horse at *K*, posted in its front, repeatedly overturned the enemy's cavalry, and slowly retreated towards *L;* after which General Baggavout, on observing, that the enemy was advancing upon him with six columns, under the protection of a line of chasseurs a cheval, which were rushing in three columns on each of his flanks, ordered the fourth regiment of sharpshooters to disperse at *N*, in the front of his foot; mean while Lieutenant-General Count Osterman ran up to reinforce him, with four battalions of infantry (vide. No. 2,), which formed in order of battle at *0*.

P. A sharp charge with the bayonet by one of the battalions of sharpshooters, which was ordered afterwards to assemble at *Q*. At the same time seven squadrons of cavalry, under the command of Major-General Kojin, likewise retired towards *R*. The enemy shouting, made a charge upon the sharpshooters, but was received with a heavy fire of musketry and pieces of cannon : but as his progress was not yet checked by that reception, Major-General Kojin, with the cavalry, penetrated into the flank of the enemy's column *S*, while a battalion of sharpshooters, and one of the grenadiers of the regiment of Staroskel, rushed on with the bayonet, and destroyed the whole of the column on the spot; after which, the horse took post at *T*, and the foot at *U*. On the other side, the two remaining battalions of sharpshooters, the regiment of horse Tartars, with two squadrons of the Kioff dragoons, attacked and checked the enemy's columns *V*, which having received a reinforcement, made a rapid charge again;— the sharpshooters, however, having formed a strong front *W*, rushed on with the bayonet, while the cavalry penetrated into the columns, which were thus completely overturned. At the same time Major-General Doctoroff, with the regiment of the Izum hussars, making a feigned retreat towards *X*, but suddenly taking to the left *Y*, brought the enemy's columns under the batteries *Z*.

The rest of the Russian cavalry having made some partial attacks, retired towards *a;* then after having passed through the front of the infantry, took post in its rear at *b*. A fire was at that time opened from all the batteries upon the enemy's columns, which were by a successful execution of the artillery checked and overturned.

Meanwhile the advanced guard of Major-General Barclay de Tolly was equally attacked on different points by six columns of the enemy, under the command of Marshal Lannes, two of which, under the protection of chasseurs a cheval, having charged the chasseurs *c*, obliged both them and the two regiments of sharpshooters to retire towards *d*, and had like to have got possession of the battery *e*, but the regiment of Tinghin, together with the sharpshooters who had concentrated themselves in front, having rushed on with the bayonet, overturned the enemy, and regained their cannon. At the same time the Polish regiment of horse, after having repeatedly charged the enemy's columns *f*, routed them and then retreated towards *g*. The Cossacks made then a rapid charge *h*, during which the Commander-in-Chief changed the front, and brought the whole of the right wing to fall back towards *i*, in order to secure it from being surrounded on the flank; on which he had sent, for protecting the retreat of the advanced guard *k*, first, the regiment of the musketeers of Tchernigow *l*, and sub-sequently that of Litver, with twenty squadrons of cavalry *m* (vid. No. 3,). On firing several rounds with the enemy, the regiments of Tchernigow and Tinghin, together with the sharpshooters, having rushed on with the bayonet *n*, overturned the enemy, while the battery *o*, pushed on towards his front, disconcerted it by successful discharges of cannon, and thereby contributed to a complete rout of the French. Notwithstanding the overthrow he had sustained three times, the enemy having received a considerable reinforce-ment upon the left wing of the Russians, renewed a charge on the detachment of General Baggavout on all points, and obliged him to retreat towards the ditch *p*, with loss of his cannon; but he was in the mean time reinforced again with five battalions *q*, and pro-tected by the batteries *r*, placed on the heights by Lieutenant-Gen-eral Osterman; where by the progress of the enemy was checked, while the detachment of General Baggevout, with renewed cour-age, made a charge on the enemy's columns, and having thrown them into disorder, regained its guns. After similar attacks had been repeated several times, Major-General Somoff, with the regiment of Touler, at last made a charge with the bayonet, and completed the final overthrow of the enemy, who were pursued till night.

The battle terminated nearly at the same time on both flanks. The number of the French troops amounted to 60,000 men, and that of the Russians to 45,000. The army lost 40,000 men in killed and dangerously wounded, and about 700 taken prisoners. The Russians had near 3000 men killed.

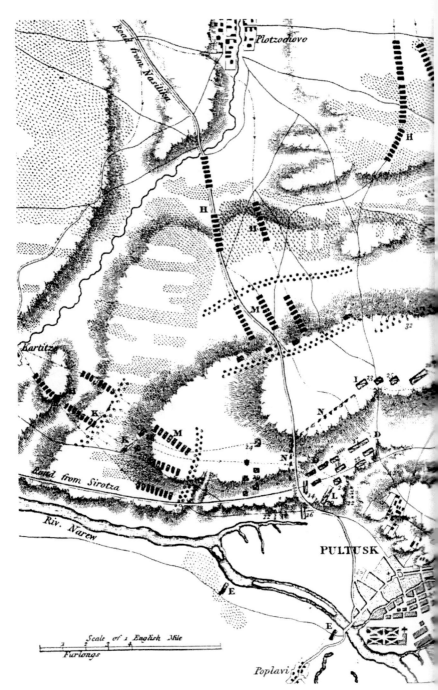

PLAN OF THE BATTLE OF PULTUSK

285

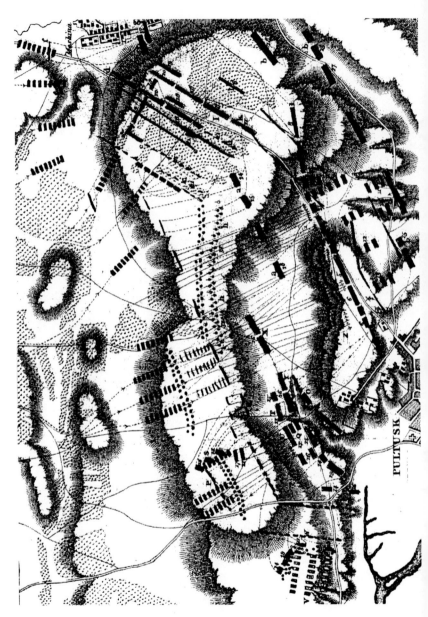

BATTLE OF PULTUSK

286

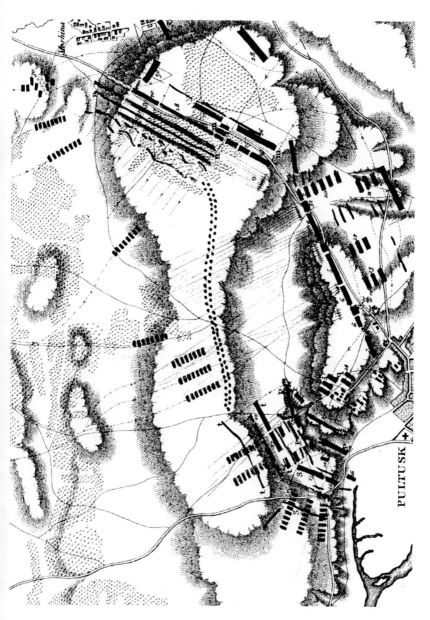

BATTLE OF PULTUSK

SKETCH OF THE POSITION OF EYLAU

288

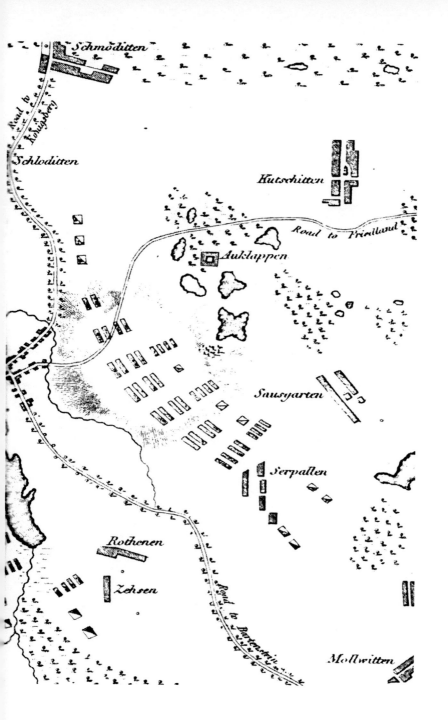

Schmödittén

Road to Königsberg

Schloditten

Kutschitten

Road to Friedland

Auklappen

Sausgarten

Serpallen

Rothenen

Zehsen

Road to Bartenstein

Mollwitten

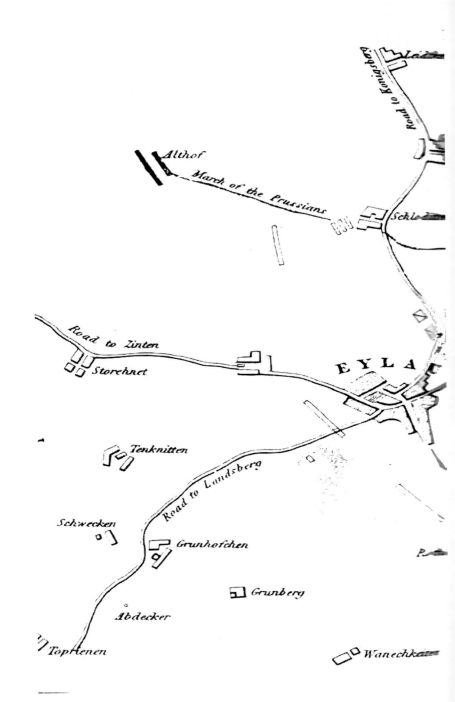

POSITION OF COMBINED ARMY O NIGHT OF 8TH FEBRUARY AFTER

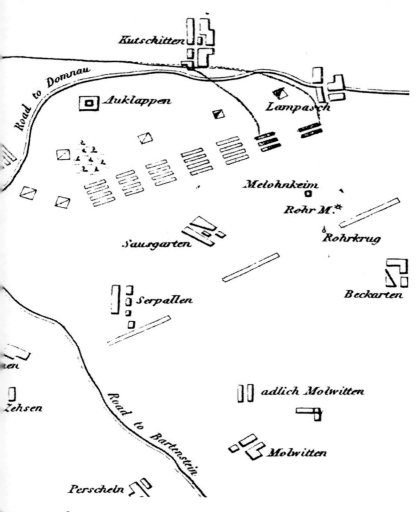

Sollseyn

oditten

Kutschitten

Road to Domnau

Auklappen

Lampasch

Melohnkeim

Rohr M.*

Rohrkrug

Saurgarten

Beckarten

Serpallen

en

Zehsen

Road to Bartenstein

adlich Molwitten

Molwitten

Perscheln

HE BATTLE & THE POINTS TO WHICH THE ENEMY WERE REPELLED

Track by with the French turned the Russians Right

Grossendorf

Road to Eylau or Königsberg

Road to Mehlsack

HEILSBERG

Worrmdit

Road to

Amt Heilsberg

Road to Guttstadt

Road to Wonter

SKETCH OF THE POSITION OF HEILSBERG

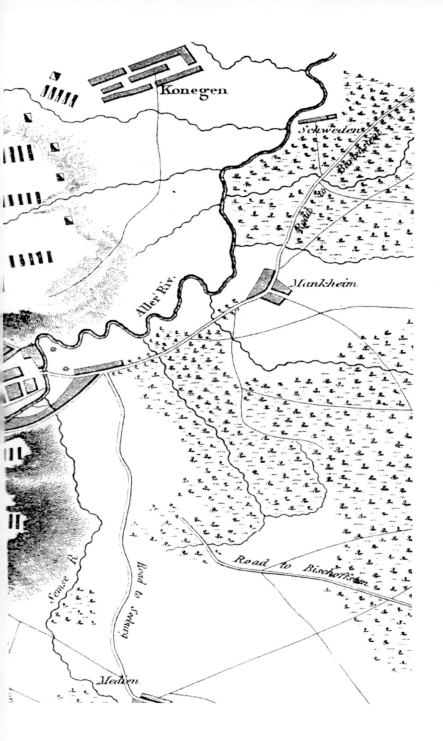

Konegen

Schweden

Road to Barkelau

Mankheim

Aller Riv.

Road to Bischoffen

Road to Selzing

Fence R.

Medien

293

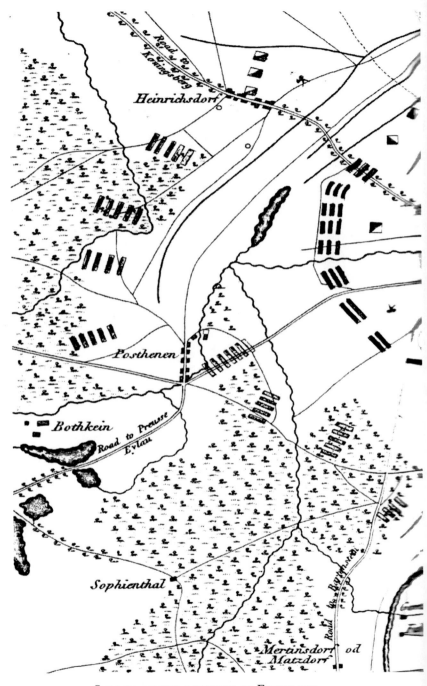

SKETCH OF THE POSITION OF FRIEDLAND

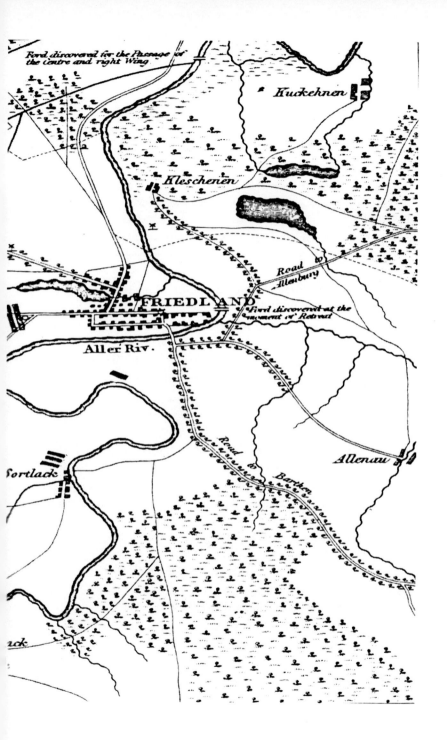

Ford discovered for the Passage of
the Centre and right Wing

Kuckehnen

Kleschenen

Road to
Allenburg

FRIEDLAND

Ford discovered at the
moment of Retreat

Aller Riv.

Road to Barten

Sortlack

Allenau

 uck

LEONAUR

ALSO FROM LEONAUR
AVAILABLE IN SOFTCOVER OR HARDCOVER WITH DUST JACKET

THE JENA CAMPAIGN: 1806 *by F. N. Maude*—The Twin Battles of Jena & Auerstadt Between Napoleon's French and the Prussian Army.

PRIVATE O'NEIL *by Charles O'Neil*—The recollections of an Irish Rogue of H. M. 28th Regt.—The Slashers— during the Peninsula & Waterloo campaigns of the Napoleonic wars.

ROYAL HIGHLANDER *by James Anton*—A soldier of H.M 42nd (Royal) Highlanders during the Peninsular, South of France & Waterloo Campaigns of the Napoleonic Wars.

CAPTAIN BLAZE *by Elzéar Blaze*—Elzéar Blaze recounts his life and experiences in Napoleon's army in a well written, articulate and companionable style.

LEJEUNE VOLUME 1 *by Louis-François Lejeune*—The Napoleonic Wars through the Experiences of an Officer on Berthier's Staff.

LEJEUNE VOLUME 2 *by Louis-François Lejeune*—The Napoleonic Wars through the Experiences of an Officer on Berthier's Staff.

FUSILIER COOPER *by John S. Cooper*—Experiences in the 7th (Royal) Fusiliers During the Peninsular Campaign of the Napoleonic Wars and the American Campaign to New Orleans.

CAPTAIN COIGNET *by Jean-Roch Coignet*—A Soldier of Napoleon's Imperial Guard from the Italian Campaign to Russia and Waterloo.

FIGHTING NAPOLEON'S EMPIRE *by Joseph Anderson*—The Campaigns of a British Infantryman in Italy, Egypt, the Peninsular & the West Indies During the Napoleonic Wars.

CHASSEUR BARRES *by Jean-Baptiste Barres*—The experiences of a French Infantryman of the Imperial Guard at Austerlitz, Jena, Eylau, Friedland, in the Peninsular, Lutzen, Bautzen, Zinnwald and Hanau during the Napoleonic Wars.

MARINES TO 95TH (RIFLES) *by Thomas Fernyhough*—The military experiences of Robert Fernyhough during the Napoleonic Wars.

HUSSAR ROCCA *by Albert Jean Michel de Rocca*—A French cavalry officer's experiences of the Napoleonic Wars and his views on the Peninsular Campaigns against the Spanish, British And Guerilla Armies.

SERGEANT BOURGOGNE *by Adrien Bourgogne*—With Napoleon's Imperial Guard in the Russian Campaign and on the Retreat from Moscow 1812 - 13.

LEONAUR

ALSO FROM LEONAUR

AVAILABLE IN SOFTCOVER OR HARDCOVER WITH DUST JACKET

WELLINGTON AND THE PYRENEES CAMPAIGN VOLUME I: FROM VITORIA TO THE BIDASSOA *by F. C. Beatson*—The final phase of the campaign in the Iberian Peninsula.

WELLINGTON AND THE INVASION OF FRANCE VOLUME II: THE BIDASSOA TO THE BATTLE OF THE NIVELLE *by F. C. Beatson*—The second of Beatson's series on the fall of Revolutionary France published by Leonaur, the reader is once again taken into the centre of Wellington's strategic and tactical genius.

WELLINGTON AND THE FALL OF FRANCE VOLUME III: THE GAVES AND THE BATTLE OF ORTHEZ *by F. C. Beatson*—This final chapter of F. C. Beatson's brilliant trilogy shows the 'captain of the age' at his most inspired and makes all three books essential additions to any Peninsular War library.

NAVAL BATTLES OF THE NAPOLEONIC WARS *by W. H. Fitchett*—Cape St.Vincent, the Nile, Cadiz, Copenhagen, Trafalgar & Others

SERGEANT GUILLEMARD: THE MAN WHO SHOT NELSON? *by Robert Guillemard*—A Soldier of the Infantry of the French Army of Napoleon on Campaign Throughout Europe

WITH THE GUARDS ACROSS THE PYRENEES *by Robert Batty*—The Experiences of a British Officer of Wellington's Army During the Battles for the Fall of Napoleonic France, 1813.

A STAFF OFFICER IN THE PENINSULA *by E. W. Buckham*—An Officer of the British Staff Corps Cavalry During the Peninsula Campaign of the Napoleonic Wars

THE LEIPZIG CAMPAIGN: 1813—NAPOLEON AND THE "BATTLE OF THE NATIONS" *by F. N. Maude*—Colonel Maude's analysis of Napoleon's campaign of 1813.

BUGEAUD: A PACK WITH A BATON *by Thomas Robert Bugeaud*—The Early Campaigns of a Soldier of Napoleon's Army Who Would Become a Marshal of France.

TWO LEONAUR ORIGINALS

SERGEANT NICOL *by Daniel Nicol*—The Experiences of a Gordon Highlander During the Napoleonic Wars in Egypt, the Peninsula and France.

WATERLOO RECOLLECTIONS *by Frederick Llewellyn*—Rare First Hand Accounts, Letters, Reports and Retellings from the Campaign of 1815.

LEONAUR

ALSO FROM LEONAUR

AVAILABLE IN SOFTCOVER OR HARDCOVER WITH DUST JACKET

CAPTAIN OF THE 95th (Rifles) *by Jonathan Leach*—An officer of Wellington's Sharpshooters during the Peninsular, South of France and Waterloo Campaigns of the Napoleonic Wars.

BUGLER AND OFFICER OF THE RIFLES *by William Green & Harry Smith* With the 95th (Rifles) during the Peninsular & Waterloo Campaigns of the Napoleonic Wars

BAYONETS, BUGLES AND BONNETS *by James 'Thomas' Todd*—Experiences of hard soldiering with the 71st Foot - the Highland Light Infantry - through many battles of the Napoleonic wars including the Peninsular & Waterloo Campaigns

THE ADVENTURES OF A LIGHT DRAGOON *by George Farmer & G.R. Gleig*—A cavalryman during the Peninsular & Waterloo Campaigns, in captivity & at the siege of Bhurtpore, India

THE COMPLEAT RIFLEMAN HARRIS *by Benjamin Harris as told to & transcribed by Captain Henry Curling*—The adventures of a soldier of the 95th (Rifles) during the Peninsular Campaign of the Napoleonic Wars

WITH WELLINGTON'S LIGHT CAVALRY *by William Tomkinson*—The Experiences of an officer of the 16th Light Dragoons in the Peninsular and Waterloo campaigns of the Napoleonic Wars.

SURTEES OF THE RIFLES *by William Surtees*—A Soldier of the 95th (Rifles) in the Peninsular campaign of the Napoleonic Wars.

ENSIGN BELL IN THE PENINSULAR WAR *by George Bell*—The Experiences of a young British Soldier of the 34th Regiment 'The Cumberland Gentlemen' in the Napoleonic wars.

WITH THE LIGHT DIVISION *by John H. Cooke*—The Experiences of an Officer of the 43rd Light Infantry in the Peninsula and South of France During the Napoleonic Wars

NAPOLEON'S IMPERIAL GUARD: FROM MARENGO TO WATERLOO by *J. T. Headley*—This is the story of Napoleon's Imperial Guard from the bearskin caps of the grenadiers to the flamboyance of their mounted chasseurs, their principal characters and the men who commanded them.

BATTLES & SIEGES OF THE PENINSULAR WAR by *W. H. Fitchett*—Corunna, Busaco, Albuera, Ciudad Rodrigo, Badajos, Salamanca, San Sebastian & Others

Lightning Source UK Ltd.
Milton Keynes UK
UKOW051245031111

181426UK00001B/46/P